Deportation, Anxiety, Justice

This book provides new ethnographic perspectives on the intersections between deportation, anxiety, and justice. As an instrument for controlling international migration, deportation policies may be justified by public authorities as measures responding to anxieties over (unregulated) migration. At the same time, they also bring out uncertainty and unrest to deportable and deported migrants as well as to their social and institutional environments, in which this act of the state may appear deeply unjust.

Providing new and complementary insights into what 'deportation' as a legal and policy measure actually embraces in social reality, this book argues for an understanding of deportation as a process that begins long before (and carries on long after) the removal from one country to another has taken place. It provides a transnational perspective over the 'deportation corridor', covering different places, sites, actors, and institutions. Most importantly, it reasserts the emotional and normative elements inherent to contemporary deportation policies and practices, emphasising the interplay between deportation, perceptions of justice, and national, institutional, and personal anxieties.

Written by leading experts in the field, the contributions cover a broad spectrum of geographical sites, deportation practices and perspectives, bringing together a long overdue addition to the current scholarship on deportation studies.

This book was originally published as a special issue of the *Journal of Ethnic and Migration Studies*.

Heike Drotbohm is Professor for Social and Cultural Anthropology in the Department of Anthropology and African Studies at the University of Mainz, Germany.

Ines Hasselberg is a Postdoctoral Research Fellow at the Centre for Criminology, University of Oxford, UK. She is the author of *Enduring Uncertainty. Deportation, Punishment and Everyday Life* (2016).

Research in Ethnic and Migration Studies
Series editor: Paul Statham
Director, Sussex Centre for Migration Research (SCMR), University of Sussex, UK

The *Research in Ethnic and Migration Studies* series publishes the results of high-quality, cutting-edge research that addresses key questions relating to ethnic relations, diversity and migration. The series is open to a range of disciplines and brings together research collaborations on specific defined topics on all aspects of migration and its consequences, including migration processes, migrants and their experiences, ethnic relations, discrimination, integration, racism, transnationalism, citizenship, identity and cultural diversity. Contributions are especially welcome when they are the result of comparative research, either across countries, cities or groups. All articles have previously been published in the *Journal of Ethnic and Migration Studies* (*JEMS*), which has a rigorous peer review system. Collective volumes in this series are either the product of Special Issues published in the journal or published articles that the Editor has selected from individual submissions.

Titles in the series:

International Organisations and the Politics of Migration
Edited by Martin Geiger and Antoine Pécoud

Regulation of Speech in Multicultural Societies
Edited by Marcel Maussen and Ralph Grillo

Deportation, Anxiety, Justice
New ethnographic perspectives
Edited by Heike Drotbohm and Ines Hasselberg

Deportation, Anxiety, Justice
New ethnographic perspectives

Edited by
Heike Drotbohm and Ines Hasselberg

LONDON AND NEW YORK

First published 2017
by Routledge
2 Park Square, Milton Park, Abingdon, Oxon, OX14 4RN, UK

and by Routledge
711 Third Avenue, New York, NY 10017, USA

Routledge is an imprint of the Taylor & Francis Group, an informa business

© 2017 Taylor & Francis

All rights reserved. No part of this book may be reprinted or reproduced or utilised in any form or by any electronic, mechanical, or other means, now known or hereafter invented, including photocopying and recording, or in any information storage or retrieval system, without permission in writing from the publishers.

Trademark notice: Product or corporate names may be trademarks or registered trademarks, and are used only for identification and explanation without intent to infringe.

British Library Cataloguing in Publication Data
A catalogue record for this book is available from the British Library

ISBN 13: 978-1-138-22273-1

Typeset in Minion
by RefineCatch Limited, Bungay, Suffolk

Publisher's Note
The publisher accepts responsibility for any inconsistencies that may have arisen during the conversion of this book from journal articles to book chapters, namely the possible inclusion of journal terminology.

Disclaimer
Every effort has been made to contact copyright holders for their permission to reprint material in this book. The publishers would be grateful to hear from any copyright holder who is not here acknowledged and will undertake to rectify any errors or omissions in future editions of this book.

Contents

Citation Information   vii

1. Introduction – Deportation, Anxiety, Justice: New Ethnographic Perspectives   1
   Heike Drotbohm and Ines Hasselberg

2. Balancing Legitimacy, Exceptionality and Accountability: On Foreign-national Offenders' Reluctance to Engage in Anti-deportation Campaigns in the UK   13
   Ines Hasselberg

3. The Jewish State of Anxiety: Between Moral Obligation and Fearism in the Treatment of African Asylum Seekers in Israel   30
   Barak Kalir

4. The Management of Anxiety. An Ethnographical Outlook on Self-mutilations in a French Immigration Detention Centre   49
   Nicolas Fischer

5. 'We Deport Them but They Keep Coming Back': The Normalcy of Deportation in the Daily Life of 'Undocumented' Zimbabwean Migrant Workers in Botswana   67
   Treasa M. Galvin

6. Deportation Stigma and Re-migration   85
   Liza Schuster and Nassim Majidi

7. The Reversal of Migratory Family Lives: A Cape Verdean Perspective on Gender and Sociality pre- and post-deportation   103
   Heike Drotbohm

8. Deportation Studies: Origins, Themes and Directions   121
   Susan Bibler Coutin

Index   133

Citation Information

The chapters in this book were originally published in the *Journal of Ethnic and Migration Studies*, volume 41, issue 4 (April 2015). When citing this material, please use the original page numbering for each article, as follows:

Chapter 1
Introduction – Deportation, Anxiety, Justice: New Ethnographic Perspectives
Heike Drotbohm and Ines Hasselberg
Journal of Ethnic and Migration Studies, volume 41, issue 4 (April 2015), pp. 551–562

Chapter 2
Balancing Legitimacy, Exceptionality and Accountability: On Foreign-national Offenders' Reluctance to Engage in Anti-deportation Campaigns in the UK
Ines Hasselberg
Journal of Ethnic and Migration Studies, volume 41, issue 4 (April 2015), pp. 563–579

Chapter 3
The Jewish State of Anxiety: Between Moral Obligation and Fearism in the Treatment of African Asylum Seekers in Israel
Barak Kalir
Journal of Ethnic and Migration Studies, volume 41, issue 4 (April 2015), pp. 580–598

Chapter 4
The Management of Anxiety. An Ethnographical Outlook on Self-mutilations in a French Immigration Detention Centre
Nicolas Fischer
Journal of Ethnic and Migration Studies, volume 41, issue 4 (April 2015), pp. 599–616

Chapter 5
'We Deport Them but They Keep Coming Back': The Normalcy of Deportation in the Daily Life of 'Undocumented' Zimbabwean Migrant Workers in Botswana
Treasa M. Galvin
Journal of Ethnic and Migration Studies, volume 41, issue 4 (April 2015), pp. 617–634

CITATION INFORMATION

Chapter 6

Deportation Stigma and Re-migration
Liza Schuster and Nassim Majidi
Journal of Ethnic and Migration Studies, volume 41, issue 4 (April 2015), pp. 635–652

Chapter 7

The Reversal of Migratory Family Lives: A Cape Verdean Perspective on Gender and Sociality pre- and post-deportation
Heike Drotbohm
Journal of Ethnic and Migration Studies, volume 41, issue 4 (April 2015), pp. 653–670

Chapter 8

Deportation Studies: Origins, Themes and Directions
Susan Bibler Coutin
Journal of Ethnic and Migration Studies, volume 41, issue 4 (April 2015), pp. 671–681

For any permission-related enquiries please visit:
http://www.tandfonline.com/page/help/permissions

Introduction
Deportation, Anxiety, Justice: New Ethnographic Perspectives

Heike Drotbohm and Ines Hasselberg

This paper introduces a collection of articles that share ethnographic perspectives on the intersections between deportation, anxiety and justice. As a form of expulsion regulating human mobility, deportation policies may be justified by public authorities as measures responding to anxieties over (unregulated) migration. At the same time, they also bring out uncertainty and unrest to deportable/deported migrants and their families. Providing new and complementary insights into what 'deportation' as a legal and policy measure actually embraces in social reality, this special issue argues for an understanding of deportation as a process that begins long before, and carries on long after, the removal from one country to another takes place. It provides a transnational perspective over the 'deportation corridor', covering different places, sites, actors and institutions. Furthermore, it reasserts the emotional and normative elements inherent to deportation policies and practices emphasising the interplay between deportation, perceptions of justice and national, institutional and personal anxieties. The papers cover a broad spectrum of geographical sites, deportation practices and perspectives and are a significant and long overdue contribution to the current state of the art in deportation studies.

Deportation, the forced removal of foreign nationals from a given national territory, is not a singular event. It is a process that begins long before, and carries on long after, the removal from one country to another takes place. Deportation crosses places and spaces, connects countries and nations. Most important, deportation

---

Heike Drotbohm currently works as a Guest Professor at the Institute for Social and Cultural Anthropology, University of Freiburg, Freiburg, Germany. Ines Hasselberg is a postdoctoral research fellow at the Centre for Criminology, University of Oxford, Oxford, UK.

involves more than those who are or might be deported. The experience of deportation ties together deportable and deported individuals as well as their families with the decisions and actions of state officials, bureaucrats, lawyers and judges, it brings them together with security personnel, agents of border control and prison staff, it involves political activists, rights-focused non-governmental organisations (NGOs) as well as the media (Peutz 2006; Drotbohm 2013; Hasselberg 2013).

Throughout history, deportation has served as a key means of dividing insiders from outsiders, the wanted from the unwanted, the deserving from the undeserving (Walters 2002). Like other practices of expulsion and transfer of population groups, deportation has thus been intrinsically linked to the establishment of boundaries of belonging and, ultimately, to definitions of citizenship (Anderson, Gibney, and Paoletti 2011). While the categories of people targeted by forced removal have been changing over time, in present liberal democracies the status of 'deportability' (De Genova 2002) is restricted to foreign nationals.[1] Particularly in the course of the last two decades, the territorial exclusion of unwanted foreigners, constructed as a threat to national security, has become an important tool of current policies of migration to act both as deterrent and control (De Genova 2007; De Genova & Peutz 2010). In Europe and North America, the quest for border-based national security has led to a substantial transformation in the application of immigration penalties, culminating in the 'normalisation' of the administrative entanglement of detention and forced return (Bloch and Schuster 2005; Kanstroom 2007, 2012). This development contributed to a discursive association between terrorism, security and immigration, resulting in a rising application of deportation as a tool to effect departure (Coutin 2007; De Genova 2002, 2007; Pratt 2005). The term 'deportation turn' (Gibney 2008) is now commonly used in the literature to capture this significant change in the governing of mobile and immigrant populations.

Scholarly interest in deportation has accompanied these developments and a set of excellent historically and empirically grounded work on deportation has been provided by social scientists focusing on the intersections between the acceleration of transnational labour migration, the illegalities constituted and regimented by migration law and the multiple dimensions of citizenship (De Genova 2002, 2007; Coutin 2003, 2007; Nyers 2003; Zilberg 2004; Inda 2006, 2013; Kanstroom 2007, 2012; Gibney 2008; Peutz 2006, 2007; Peutz and De Genova 2010; Willen 2007; Bosworth 2008, 2011; Ellermann 2009; Anderson, Gibney, and Paoletti 2011; Drotbohm 2011, 2012; Feldman 2011; Khosravi 2010; Aas and Bosworth 2013; Golash-Boza and Hondagneu-Sotelo 2013; Das Gupta 2014; Golash-Boza 2014). In her contribution to this special issue, Susan Bibler Coutin discusses the particularities of deportation studies in relation to both security studies and migration studies. With regard to prospects, condition, direction and outcome of migration, deportation studies question assumptions already taken for granted in migration studies. Additionally, deportation studies examine not only the human impact of closing borders and surveillance but also macro-level perspectives, governmental positions, political regimes and the societal effect of involuntary return (Coutin 2014).

This special issue is the outcome of an international workshop at the biennial conference of the European Association of Social Anthropologists, with the overall theme *Uncertainty and Disquiet*, which took place in Nanterre, France.[2] Comprising six empirical papers, and a discussion note by Susan Bibler Coutin, this collection of papers seeks to complement the present body of literature on deportation in a number of ways: first in establishing a transnational perspective over the deportation corridor, second in reasserting both the emotional and normative elements inherent to deportation policies and practices and third in presenting ethnographically grounded accounts of different elements and perspectives.

The 'deportation corridor'

Referring to the processual quality of deportation described above, we intend to establish a transnational perspective over the 'deportation corridor', which covers different places, actors and institutions. A comparable approach has been introduced by Nathalie Peutz, who argued for an 'anthropology of removal', which would include not only the different domains and sites of experience, such as imprisonment, detention, deportation, return, but also the different types of organisations and institutions involved (Peutz 2006, 218–219). Corridors are spaces of in-between-ness and movement, connecting and referring to rooms of clearer positionality, assignment and representation. In many corridors of institutional spaces, empty chairs signal the passive, waiting position to which actors have to submit themselves; corridors here host an atmosphere of clear hierarchies, governing and spatial order. In contrast to those spaces, they refer to—that appear clear, agreeable and inviting—corridors are often poorly lit, shady and suspect. They may be impersonal and affectively cold as nobody is supposed to live in them. By connecting the notion of the corridor to the enactment and the experience of deportation, we wish to highlight a spatial, institutional and affective state of transit, which appears permanent and transitory at the same time. We also pinpoint dichotomies such as inside/outside, centre/margins, inclusion/exclusion, which are produced through the process of deportation.

The papers included here trace this 'deportation corridor'. Due to the temporal (and often financial limits of ethnographic fieldwork), our individual case studies do not cover the entire process and all actors of removal.[3] Instead, we unite case studies under a corresponding perspective, each one covering different steps, stages and perspectives along the 'deportation corridor' in different parts of the world. Our ethnographies make clear that these different case studies can be understood complementary to each other. Additionally, our approach does exceed not only the boundaries of the territory but also the boundaries of state politics and hence, point to the limits of a state-centric model of sovereignty. Hence, from an empirical point of view, the situation and experiences met along a chronology of deportation are related, connected and constitutive to each other.

In this special issue, Heike Drotbohm examines the conflicts experienced within transnational families that are generated by the threat as well as the realisation of deportation. In her paper, she includes both the perspectives of family members staying behind in the country of destination and the problematic living conditions of Cape Verdean deportees after their involuntary return from the USA and their aim to reintegrate into rather hostile 'home' communities. Other papers cover the conditions and experiences of deportability as well as the fear of and protest against deportation in the migrants' destination countries. Ines Hasselberg, concentrating on the British case, reflects on the impact that migrants' perception of their own deportation process bear in their perceived entitlement to participate in open forms of political action such as demonstrations and protests, while Barak Kalir takes a closer look at the Israeli case, where the public debate on the treatment of asylum seekers carries strong references to a Jewish history of persecution.

In addition to papers examining the situation of migrants under the threat of deportation, others examine the transient phase, which involves state measures such as arrest and detention, deportation flights as well as the political collaboration between the 'country of origin' and 'country of destination'[4] that have to negotiate over the migrants' condition of return. In this special issue, Nicholas Fischer reflects on his fieldwork carried out in a detention centre located in the international airport of a French city, where he concentrated on the everyday interactions between detainees, the centre staff, lawyers and other professional groups.

Finally, two papers included here cover the situation of deportees in their alleged countries of origin. Treasa Galvin as well as Liza Schuster and Nassim Majidi elaborate on the situation of deportees returned to Zimbabwe and Afghanistan, respectively. Treasa Galvin centres on the normalisation of deportation in what has become a routine border crossing between Botswana and Zimbabwe, focusing both on the disruptive impact of deportability and actual removal, and on migrants' strategies to minimise its impact, while Liza Schuster and Nassim Majidi focus more specifically on the experience of returning empty-handed upon deportation to Afghanistan and the role that stigma has on deportees' aspirations to re-emigrate.

Additionally, we wish to expand the scope of deportation studies in terms of topographies. We do so by extending the geographical sites not only to cover Europe, Africa and Asia, but also, and most importantly, by going beyond the north–south perspective and including an examination of south–south deportation trajectories. Through contrasting examples of deportation, which occur within the so-called Global South, we are able to take into account the hierarchisation of different countries. This is an ordering undertaken not only by policy-makers and border control agents but also by migrants and their social communities who give meaning to different types of spatial mobility. Such is well evidenced in the above-mentioned contribution by Schuster and Majidi that reveals the different experiences of forced return according to the deporting region. In Afghanistan, as the authors so clearly show, not only migration but also forced return is now seen as part of a daily routine with neighbouring countries, such as Iran and Pakistan. This echoes Galvin's findings of deportation from Botswana to neighbouring Zimbabwe that point to the normalcy of deportation, despite the hardship that it provokes. Interestingly, however, Schuster and Majidi show that this perception of deportation as a side event is not applicable to those returning from further afield as Europe, the USA or Australia. In these instances, deportation is taken as a serious failure and deportees (and their families) suffer from high levels of stigmatisation.

All these insights make clear that deportation has become an often-experienced state practice, which can go along with a certain process of adaption and normalisation, while at the same time producing agency and resistance. We also consider those approaches that include the perspectives of different actors of the deportation process both in the countries of settlement and in the countries of origin. Alpes and Spire (2013), for instance, examined the decisions taken by visa officials at French consulates in Cameroon, Hall (2012) worked on the perspective of staff at a British detention centre and Vigneswaran's (2013) work relied on the work of South African immigration officials. Likewise, our special issue addresses the points of view and experiences not only of migrants themselves but also of politicians, government agencies, lawyers, civil society, agents of border control and deportees' family members. It does so by examining the perspectives and interests of different types of actors along the 'deportation corridor' such as: the production of, and response to, deportability among deportable migrants, their families as well as their ethnic communities, NGOs and political activists (Galvin 2014; Hasselberg 2014b; Kalir 2014); those involved in removal procedures and related practices, such as local government authorities, Human Rights advocates, medical staff as well as the detainees themselves (Galvin 2014; Fischer 2014); and finally, those actors coming together in the moment of arrival, when deportees have to familiarise themselves and resettle in often unknown 'home' countries, in which they are received by state authorities as well as rather unfamiliar local communities (Drotbohm 2014; Schuster and Majidi 2014).

Justice and Anxiety

A second way in which we wish to add to the present body of literature on deportation studies is by reasserting the emotional and normative elements inherent to deportation policies and practices and emphasise the interconnections between deportation, justice and anxiety. These go hand in hand with public and individual perceptions of fairness and justice that shape and influence how deportation is experienced, felt and interpreted. As the papers to the special issue show, governments, agents of border control, the media and citizens of host societies can both produce and struggle with conflicting feelings of anxiety, channelled to irregular(ised) migrants who are perceived as a diffuse threat in the pursuit of security. As migration is increasingly tied to security concerns (Inda 2006; Guild 2009; Bigo 2008), it becomes vital to look at how such concerns and anxieties are produced and operationalised both in the management of border control (Feldman 2011) and how they are digested in migrants' own daily lives (Willen 2007; Wicker 2010; Hasselberg 2014a).

Deportable migrants have become a segment of the population to be produced and understood as a threat to security and governed accordingly (Bigo 2008; Hall 2012; Hasselberg 2014a). Writing about the treatment of self-mutilations in French detention centres, Nicholas Fischer analyses the tension between repressing and protecting immigrants. His ethnography shows clearly that the anxiety felt by detainees can become an object of debate as well as of control. Detention and medical staff have to assess the emotional stage of detainees, they have to prevent or justify their suffering and their wounds. And—as Fischer shows—these interactions can also produce anxieties among those who are supposed to manage detention and deportation. A comparable struggle between humanitarian concerns and xenophobic tensions is examined in Barak Kalir's paper that looks at deportation in the context of asylum in Israel. Here, Kalir argues that a specific Jewish-Israeli ideology of 'fearism', nourished by the Israeli experience of historic persecution and need to protect a Jewish nation-state, underlie the construction of the non-Jewish immigrant Other. As in many other national contexts, these tensions are used by policy-makers for justifying the exclusion and deportation of immigrants and asylum seekers.

Migrants too and their social environment can struggle with feelings of anxiety while coping with their irregular or contested residence status. This is so whether their deportability is enacted in anticipation and translated into active invisibility and evasion strategies, as emphasised in most illegality studies (Wicker 2010; Willen 2007; Talavera, Nunez-Mchiri, and Heymen 2010; Castañeda 2010; Lucht 2012), or is experienced only once deportation proceedings against them are initiated (Achermann 2012; Hasselberg 2014a). Research on the social consequences of deportability has shown that not only those under threat of deportation but also their close social environment suffer from fears of detection (in the case of irregular residency) or denied immigration appeals (in the case of contested claims)— both cases often leading to involuntary family separation (Drotbohm 2014). Due to these constraints, some families try to avoid any contact with state officials, health care or even the school system (Hagan, Eschbach, and Rodriguez 2008; Dreby 2012) and this socio-political mode of existence (Willen 2007) works to shape migrants' 'subjective experiences of time, space, embodiment, sociality and self' (Willen 2007, 10). In this special issue, the contributions by Galvin and Kalir pay special attention to these matters, whether in relation to the importance of social networks in developing coping strategies or in public perceptions of informal or clandestine spaces of childcare, work and residence.

After the forced return, anxiety remains through family separation, the experience of 'home' communities ambivalent or even hostile, or the prospect of a life under conditions of exclusion, lack of opportunities and spatial immobility. Schuster and Majidi show that families and communities tend to stigmatise those who return involuntarily from distant countries, and that deported migrants have to respond to a notion of failure. Drotbohm also takes into account the perspective of family members who continue to live in the (former) destination country and who have to cope with the absence of their deported relative(s): within transnational family networks, anxieties are felt not only among those who remain behind and have to cope with feelings of guilt and lack of information but also among those living where deported migrants are returned to and where the particularity of their return can produce mistrust or even fear. At the same time, deportees have to find means to cope with their involuntary separation from family members remaining in the country of destination and the prospects of a life under different conditions. Deported parents, for instance, may fear that they might lose custody of their children and cannot control or influence the respective legal procedures (Drotbohm 2014). Treasa Galvin's paper offers a contrasting perspective, where in the context of migration from Zimbabwe to Botswana, anxiety arises mostly from the need to establish strategies that allow migrants to retain their work and possessions in Botswana in the very likely event of forced removal. In this context, deportation has become an intrinsic part of Zimbabwean migrants' lives—and a disquieting interruption of their lives—but has not succeeded in hindering the mobility of deported migrants who are able to return to Botswana and pursue with their livelihoods. This special issue thus points to the need to look not only to the dramatic effect of deportation but also to processes of normalisation and routinisation (see also Coutin 2014).

In a comparable vein, notions and perceptions of 'justice' are shaped by multiple state and non-state actors, who orient their normative understanding and their questions of legal and social belonging towards issues of, and access to, territory and citizenship. As mentioned above, national security concerns are evermore the rationale for the expansion of deportation. Reflecting on this ambivalent notion, Kanstroom writes that:

> 'national security' is about as elastic and potentially inflammatory a phrase as one could possibly conjure. It embeds a warm notion (security) with a malleable political theory (nationalism) as it responds implicitly to a threat from outsiders, strangers, aliens, etc. (2012, 61)

Seen through the lens of the state, deportation could be a 'just' measure, understood as a duty of surveillance that protects deserving citizens from dangerous border-crossers and potential terrorists. Others argue that deportation is a disproportionally harsh and unforgiving form of state punishment that expels individuals who have already served their sentence (Fekete and Webber 2009; Webber 2012; Hasselberg 2014a). As Drotbohm has showed in an article on the notion of citizenship, deportation produces an ambivalent quality. Citizenship proves to be powerful, as it draws deportees back to their alleged countries of origin, while at the same time it appears decomposed and weak, as the position of migrants, after their involuntary return is questioned and their exclusion is justified (Drotbohm 2011). Deportation, although never legally conceptualised as a punishment, is often experienced an archaic and deeply unjust measure: it punishes not only deportees through banishment but also those who remain behind as well as their societies of origin, which are often incapable of integrating migrants who return involuntarily and empty-handed.

Deportees and their families, lawyers as well as activists fighting deportation draw on their own perceptions of 'justice' in attempting to redefine more humane and rightful lines of social belonging in a globalised world. Yet, these are not uncontested or necessarily consistent as exemplified in several papers of this collection. In the Israeli context, Kalir shows how different actors, though all making use of history, will resort to different, and often competing, discourses on human rights, belonging and security to make their case for/against the inclusion of asylum seekers, while Hasselberg's paper reveals how migrants' own perceptions of justice related to deportation may be self-conflicting and not in line with those of other actors, including their families and migrant support groups. In Drotbohm's paper, the protection of 'the family', which is supported by international law, may conflict with the state act of deportation, which separates family members, sometimes for good. Human rights groups refer to this paradox and try to distinguish between the 'good' migrant, who deserves to remain with his family and should not be deported, and the 'bad' one who committed crimes and lost his individual eligibility to society's mercy. Generally, deportation appears as a senseless state action, bearing emotional suffering and economic costs, which need to be compensated again by actors such as states, civil societies, families or other collectivities (Drotbohm 2014). 'Justice' proves to be constantly shifting between moral lines of inclusion and exclusion, which can appear arbitrary and circumstantial. Furthermore, what constitutes an act of resistance is often dependant on positionality and intention, as well captured in Fischer's paper with regards to detainees' acts of self-mutilation.

According to our understanding, it is the diversity of emotions as well as the diversity of normative standards inherent to the 'corridor of deportation' that shed light on the complexity as well as the inconsistencies and contingencies of deportation. In her commentary to this special issue, Coutin highlights crucial legal paradoxes stemming from deportation. Protection or control, compassion or justice, individual or collective rights, humanitarianism or enforcement prove to be highly contradictive, 'doublebind' categories in the context of deportation (Coutin 2014).

Ethnographic Perspectives on Deportation

Finally, and in a manner of conclusion, this collection of papers adds to the present literature in that the contributions presented here are all ethnographically grounded. Ethnographically sound accounts of deportation allow a better understanding of how these policies are in effect developed, understood and experienced by the different actors involved. They can, and also do emphasise how deportation goes beyond the removal of individuals from one nation to another, how it is lived continuously (Peutz 2006). Further, ethnographic methods are important in perceiving deportees and their relatives as active agents that are not only just being deported but also reacting to their removal, developing their own strategies, (re)formulating their own aspirations and carrying their own cultural understanding, agency and identity. The same is true for other actors involved, as made clear here in the contributions by Fischer and Kalir. The papers included in this special issue take forward the questions of who belongs where and on which kinds of grounds; who needs and who deserves protection from whom; and who can claim to be included albeit being an outsider?

Reflecting on significant avenues for future research, Coutin details the need to look more closely to the exceptional situation of deportability and deportation as a means of studying techniques and experiences of normalisation. In which way does an understanding of deportation shed light on experiences beyond the deportation corridor? She also struggles with the question, why deportation, albeit irrational, inhumane and ineffective, continues to persist? For understanding the 'reason' or persuasiveness of deportation, she suggests tackling the 'fantasies' deportation may feed among those not living under the threat of it. And finally, she calls for a critical analysis of the power imbalances between researcher and deportees, which often constitute the reason as well as the ground for studying deportation, and which establish 'irreconcilable incompatibilities' during ethnographic fieldwork (Coutin 2014).

Despite its dubious effectiveness both in managing migration and protecting national security, deportation has come to be regarded as the unavoidable way to deal with those foreign nationals who are deemed unwanted. Providing new and complementary insights into what 'deportation' as a legal and policy measure actually embraces in social reality, the contributions to this special issue shed light on the effects of deportation practices on the lives of the people concerned before, during and after forced removal and on migratory aspirations of future or already deported migrants. Most importantly, the articles covering different regions of the world highlight the social suffering inherent to deportation and show clearly that the deterring intention and security rationale of deporting states is hardly ever realised and thus calling into question the legitimacy of such practices.

Acknowledgements

We are thankful to all delegates of the initial EASA workshop who shared their thoughts and contributed to the discussion that gave rise to this publication—special thanks go to Christin Achermann who convened the workshop with us, and on whose input and contributions we heavily draw upon here. We also thank all the anonymous peer-reviewers who commented on the different papers and contributed to the enhancement of this issue. We are very grateful to Susan Bibler Coutin, not only for her contribution to the special issue but also for the support and encouragement she provided with regards to this venture. Finally, many thanks go to the editorial team of the *Journal of Ethnic and Migration Studies* that contributed with important support and advice that was vital for the successful production of this publication.

Notes

[1] Although the increasing development of legal powers to revoke citizenship in some countries, as the UK, is likely to expand 'deportability' to citizens too (see e.g. Rooney (2014)).

[2] For the full programme of the workshop, please see http://www.nomadit.co.uk/easa/easa2012/panels.php5?PanelID=1120

[3] Although the advantages of multi-sited fieldwork have long been recognised, research methodologies which follow the 'dynamics of people, things, or thoughts' (Marcus 1995; Falzon 2009) still struggle with the limits of research funding politics. In the specific case of deportation, researchers often struggle too with access to certain research locations (see, e.g. Meissner and Hasselberg 2012).

[4] We need to be aware of the fact that the opposition between *country of origin and country of destination*, normally a crucial principle of order in the field of international migration, is reversed through the process of deportation. This reversal does not only refer to space and direction, but likewise to the experience of the (un)expected outcome of migration (see Drotbohm 2014).

References

Aas, K., and M. Bosworth, eds. 2013. *The Borders of Punishment: Migration, Citizenship, and Social Exclusion*. Oxford: Oxford University Press.

Achermann, C. 2012. "Excluding the Unwanted: Dealing with Foreign-national Offenders in Switzerland". In *Politik zwischen Inklusion und Exklusion*, edited by I. Ataç and S. Rosenberger. Göttingen: Vandenhoeck & Ruprecht.

Alpes, M. J., and A. Spire. 2013. "Dealing with Law in Migration Control: The Powers of Street-level Bureaucrats at French Consulates." *Social & Legal Studies* 23 (2): 261–274. doi:10.1177/0964663913510927

Anderson, B., M. J. Gibney, and E. Paoletti. 2011. "Citizenship, Deportation and the Boundaries of Belonging." *Citizenship Studies* 15: 547–563. doi:10.1080/13621025.2011.583787.

Bigo, D. 2008. "Globalised (In)security: The Field and the Ban-opticon". In *Terror, Insecurity and Liberty: Illiberal Practices of Liberal Regimes after 9/11*, edited by D. Bigo and A. Tsoukala, 10–49. London: Routledge.

Bloch, A., and L. Schuster. 2005. "At the Extremes of Exclusion: Deportation, Detention and Dispersal." *Ethnic and Racial Studies* 28: 491–512. doi:10.1080/0141987042000337858.

Bosworth, M. 2008. "Border Control and the Limits of the Sovereign State." *Social & Legal Studies* 17 (2): 199–215. doi:10.1177/0964663908089611.

Bosworth, M. 2011. "Deportation, Detention and Foreign-national Prisoners in England and Wales." *Citizenship Studies* 15: 583–595. doi:10.1080/13621025.2011.583789.

Castañeda, H. 2010. "Deportation Deferred: "Illegality," Visibility, and Recognition in Contemporary Germany." In *The deportation regime. Sovereignty, Space and the Freedom of Movement*, edited by N. De Genova and N. Peutz, 245–261. Durham: Duke University Press.

Coutin, S. B. 2003. "Suspension of Deportation Hearings and Measures of 'Americanness.'" *Journal of Latin American Anthropology* 8: 58–94. doi:10.1525/jlca.2003.8.2.58.

Coutin, S. B. 2007. *Nations of Emigrants. Shifting Boundaries of Citizenship in El Salvador and the United States*. Ithaca, NY: Cornell University Press.

Coutin, S. B. 2014. "Deportation Studies: Origins, Themes, and Directions." *Journal of Ethnic and Migration Studies* 41 (4): 671–681. doi:10.1080/1369183X.2014.957175.

Das Gupta, M. 2014. "'Don't Deport Our Daddies': Gendering State Deportation Practices and Immigrant Organizing." *Gender and Society* 28 (1): 83–109. doi:10.1177/0891243213508840.

De Genova, N. 2002. "Migrant 'Illegality' and Deportability in Everyday Life." Annual Review of Anthropology 31: 419–447. doi:10.1146/annurev.anthro.31.040402.085432.

De Genova, N. 2007. "The Production of Culprits: From Deportability to Detainability in the Aftermath of Homeland Security." *Citizenship Studies* 11: 421–448. doi:10.1080/13621020701605735.

De Genova, N., and N. Peutz, eds. 2010. *The Deportation Regime. Sovereignty, Space and the Freedom of Movement*. Durham: Duke University Press.

Dreby, J. 2012. "The Burden of Deportation on Children in Mexican Immigrant Families." *Journal of Marriage and Family* 74: 829–845. doi:10.1111/j.1741-3737.2012.00989.x.

Drotbohm, H. 2011. "On the Durability and the Decomposition of Citizenship: The Social Logics of Forced Return Migration in Cape Verde." *Citizenship Studies* 15: 381–396.

Drotbohm, H. 2012. "'It's Like Belonging to a Place that has Never Been Yours.' Deportees Negotiating Involuntary Immobility and Conditions of Return in Cape Verde." In *Migrations: Interdisciplinary Perspectives*, edited by R. Schröder and R. Wodak, 129–140. Wien: Springer.

Drotbohm, H. 2013. "Deportation. An Overview." In *Encyclopedia of Global Human Migration*, *Hrsg*, edited by I. Ness, 1182–1188. Oxford: Blackwell.

Drotbohm, H. 2014. "The Reversal of Migratory Family Lives: A Cape Verdean Perspective on Gender and Sociality Prior and Post Deportation." *Journal of Ethnic and Migration Studies* 41 (4): 653–670. doi:10.1080/1369183X.2014.961905.

Ellermann, A. 2009. *States against Migrants. Deportation in Germany and the United States.* New York: Cambridge University Press.

Falzon, M. 2009. "Introduction: Multi-sited Ethnography. Theory, Praxis and Locality in Contemporary Research." In *Multi-sited Ethnography. Theory, Praxis and Locality in Contemporary Research*, edited by M. Falzon, 1–24. Farnham: Ashgate.

Fekete, L., and F. Webber. 2009. "Foreign Nationals, Enemy Penology and the Criminal Justice System." *IRR European Race Bulletin* 69: 2–17.

Feldman, G. 2011. *The Migration Apparatus: Security, Labor and Policymaking in the European Union.* Palo Alto, CA: Stanford University Press.

Fischer, N. 2014. "The Management of Anxiety.An Ethnographical Outlook on Self-mutilations in a French Immigration Detention Centre." *Journal of Ethnic and Migration Studies* 41 (4): 599–616. doi:10.1080/1369183X.2014.960820.

Galvin, T. M. 2014. "'We Deport Them but They Keep Coming Back': The Normalcy of Deportation in the Daily Life of 'Undocumented' Zimbabwean Migrant Workers in Botswana." *Journal of Ethnic and Migration Studies* 41 (4): 617–634. doi:10.1080/1369183X. 2014.957172.

Gibney, M. J. 2008. "Asylum and the Expansion of Deportation in the United Kingdom." *Government and Opposition* 43: 146–167. doi:10.1111/j.1477-7053.2007.00249.x.

Golash-Boza, T. 2014. "Forced Transnationalism: Transnational Coping Strategies and Gendered Stigma among Jamaican Deportees." *Global Networks* 14 (1): 63–79. doi:10.1111/glob.12013.

Golash-Boza, T., and P. Hondagneu-Sotelo. 2013. "Latino Immigrant Men and the Deportation Crisis: A Gendered Racial Removal Program." *Latino Studies* 11: 271–292. doi:10.1057/lst.2013.14.

Guild, E. 2009. *Security and Migration in the 21st Century.* Cambridge: Polity Press.

Hagan, J., K. Eschbach, and N. Rodriguez. 2008. "U.S. Deportation Policy, Family Separation, and Circular Migration." *International Migration Review* 42 (1): 64–88. doi:10.1111/j.1747-7379.2007.00114.x.

Hall, A. 2012. *Border Watch. Cultures of Immigration, Detention and Control.* London: Pluto Press.

Hasselberg, I. 2013. "An Ethnography of Deportation from Britain." Doctoral Thesis, University of Sussex. http://sro.sussex.ac.uk/43788/.

Hasselberg, I. 2014a. "Whose Security? The Deportation of Foreign-national Offenders from the UK." In *The Anthropology of Security: Perspectives from the Frontline of Policing, Counter-terrorism and Border Control*, edited by M. Maguire, C. Frois, and N. Zurawski, 139–157. London: Pluto Press.

Hasselberg, I. 2014b. "Balancing Legitimacy, Exceptionality and Accountability: On Foreign-national Offenders' Reluctance to Engage in Anti-deportation Campaigns in the UK." *Journal of Ethnic and Migration Studies* 41 (4): 563–579. doi:10.1080/1369183X.2014.957173.

Inda, J. X. 2006. *Targeting Migrants. Government, Technology and Ethics.* Oxford: Blackwell.

Inda, J. X. 2013. "Subject to Deportation: IRCA, 'Criminal Aliens', and the Policing of Immigration." *Migration Studies* 1 (3): 292–310. doi:10.1093/migration/mns003.

Kalir, B. 2014. "The Jewish State of Anxiety: Between Moral Obligation and Fearism in the Treatment of African Asylum Seekers in Israel." *Journal of Ethnic and Migration Studies* 41 (4): 580–598. doi:10.1080/1369183X.2014.960819.

Kanstroom, D. 2007. *Deportation Nation: Outsiders in American History*. Cambridge, MA: Harvard University Press.

Kanstroom, D. 2012. *Aftermath. Deportation Law and the New American Diaspora*. Oxford: Oxford University Press. doi:10.1093/acprof:oso/9780199742721.001.0001.

Khosravi, S. 2010. *'Illegal' Traveller. An Auto-ethnography of Borders*. Basingstoke: Palgrave Macmillan.

Lucht, H. 2012. *Darkness before Daybreak African Migrants Living on the Margins in Southern Italy Today*. London: University California Press.

Marcus, G. E. 1995. "Ethnography in/of the World System: The Emergence of Multi-sited Ethnography." *Annual Review of Anthropology* 24 (1): 95–117. doi:10.1146/annurev.an.24.100 195.000523.

Meissner, F., and Hasselberg, I. 2012. "Forever Malleable: The Field as a Reflexive Encounter." In *Where Is the Field? Exploring Migration through the Lenses of Fieldwork*, edited by H. Snellman and L. Hirvi, 87–106. Studia Fennica Ethnologica. Helsinki: Finnish Literature Society.

Nyers, P. 2003. "Abject Cosmopolitanism: The Politics of Protection in the Anti-deportation Movement." *Third World Quarterly* 24: 1069–1093. doi:10.1080/01436590310001630071.

Peutz, N. 2006. "Embarking on an Anthropology of Removal." *Current Anthropology* 47 (2): 217–241. doi:10.1086/498949.

Peutz, N. 2007. "Out-laws: Deportees, Desire and 'The Law.'" *International Migration* 45 (3): 182–191. doi:10.1111/j.1468-2435.2007.00415.x.

Peutz, N., and N. De Genova. 2010. "Introduction." In *The Deportation Regime. Sovereignty, Space, and the Freedom of Movement*, edited by N. De Genova and N. Peutz, 1–32. Durham, NC: Duke University Press.

Pratt, A. 2005. *Securing Borders. Detention and Deportation in Canada*. Vancouver: UBC Press.

Rooney, C. 2014. *Stateless Terrorists: Citizenship in an Age of Risk*. Accessed February 17, 2014. http://bordercriminologies.law.ox.ac.uk/citizenship-in-an-age-of-risk/.

Schuster, L., and N. Majidi. 2014. "Deportation Stigma and Re-migration." *Journal of Ethnic and Migration Studies* 41 (4): 635–652. doi:10.1080/1369183X.2014.957174.

Talavera, V., G. Nunez-Mchiri, and J. Heymen. 2010. "Deportation in the US-Mexico Borderlands: Anticipation, Experience, and Memory." In *The Deportation Regime. Sovereignty, Space and the Freedom of Movement*, edited by N. De Genova and N. Peutz, 166–197. Durham, NC: Duke University Press.

Vigneswaran, D. V. 2013. "Making Mobility a Problem. How South African Officials Criminalize Migration." In *The Borders of Punishment: Criminal Justice, Citizenship and Social Exclusion*, edited by K. F. Aas and M. Bosworth, 111–127. Oxford: Oxford University Press.

Walters, W. 2002. "Deportation, Expulsion, and the International Police of Aliens." *Citizenship Studies* 6: 265–292. doi:10.1080/1362102022000011612.

Webber, F. 2012. *Borderline Justice. The Fight for Refugee and Migrant Rights*. London: Pluto Press.

Wicker, H.-R. 2010. "Deportation and the Limits of "Tolerance:" The Juridical, Institutional and Social Construction of 'Illegality' in Switzerland." In *The Deportation Regime. Sovereignty, Space and the Freedom of Movement*, edited by N. De Genova and N. Peutz, 224–244. Durham, NC: Duke University Press.

Willen, Sarah S. 2007. "Toward a Critical Phenomenology of "Illegality": State Power, Criminalization, and Abjectivity among Undocumented Migrant Workers in Tel Aviv, Israel." *International Migration* 45 (3): 8–38. doi:10.1111/j.1468-2435.2007.00409.x.

Zilberg, E. 2004. "Fools Banished from the Kingdom: Remapping Geographies of Gang Violence between the Americas." *American Quarterly* 56: 759–779. doi:10.1353/aq.2004.0048.

Balancing Legitimacy, Exceptionality and Accountability: On Foreign-national Offenders' Reluctance to Engage in Anti-deportation Campaigns in the UK

Ines Hasselberg

This paper addresses the lack of collective political action and engagement in protests and anti-deportation campaigns (ADCs) on the part of foreign-national offenders facing deportation from the UK. Taking ADC guidelines from migrant support groups, and drawing on ethnographic fieldwork conducted in London, I show that the circumstances of foreign-national offenders, and in particular their own understandings of their removal, appear incompatible with open political action and with the broader work of ADC support groups. The findings presented throughout this paper make the case that foreign-national offenders have conflicting notions about their deportation and their 'right' to protest and campaign against it, revealing how perceptions of legitimacy impact not only on how policies are lived and experienced but also on the scope for political action on the part of those who are experiencing those policies.

During a focus-group discussion conducted in London among foreign-national offenders facing deportation from the United Kingdom (UK), Maria, one of the participants, wondered if the others would wish to join her in forming a campaign to lobby for their rights and added 'and if you guys know other criminals please let me know'. Participants, Maria included, immediately broke out laughing, and one replied, 'Yeah, we're going to stand in Parliament screaming "Justice for Criminals!"' Laughter resumed.

This paper seeks to address the lack of engagement in open forms of political action by foreign-national offenders facing deportation from the UK. Participants in

---

Ines Hasselberg is a Postdoctoral Research Fellow at the Centre for Criminology, University of Oxford.

the above discussion, as with most others interviewed in the course of this research, certainly felt they were being wronged. They recognised they had committed a crime, accepted their conviction and the time they spent in custody. But they questioned the state's legitimacy in deporting them and thus separating them from their families. They believed their rights had been violated and that they were being consecutively punished for an offence for which they had already served time. And yet, Maria's suggestion seemed nothing but an absurdity to them. I will examine here on why this was so.

The data presented here are drawn from a research project that examined how deportation and deportability translate into social reality and the lives of those who it affects the most. Over the course of field research conducted in London in 2009, I closely followed 18 deportation cases. I also attended numerous deportation and bail hearings, volunteered with several migrant support groups, and engaged with legal caseworkers, migrant support groups, immigration judges, court clerks and other removable migrants[1] and family members.[2] The foreign-national offenders participating in this study did not form a homogenous group. They came from different countries, migrated at different phases of the life cycle, and varied greatly in cultural and religious background as well as in age groups and time of residency in the country. Whereas the majority was struggling financially at the time of field research, mostly due to their deportability,[3] prior to conviction their financial situations also varied greatly. In the midst of all these variations, the obvious link between participants was their relationship to the state. Yet, they shared other features. They were all well established in the UK. They felt their lives and families were settled and none foresaw moving out of the country in the short term. Also significant, this group of foreign-national offenders all agreed to participate in the research.

Having just outlined the context of the research, I will now move to frame it along matters of contestation, membership and migrants' political action. I will then address the question this paper seeks to answer. While there are many forms of open and collective political action, I will focus here on anti-deportation campaigns (ADCs) because they suitably illustrate why foreign-national offenders seldom participate in open forms of political action, like protests and demonstrations. Taking ADC guidelines from migrant support groups, I argue that the circumstances of foreign-national offenders, and in particular their own understandings of their removal, appear incompatible with open political action in general and with the broader work of ADC support groups in particular. I show that perceptions of legitimacy impact not only on how deportation policy is lived but also on the scope for political action on the part of those who are experiencing that policy.

Membership, Contestation and the Criminalisation of Migrants

Anderson, Gibney, and Paoletti (2011) make the case that deportation is constitutive of deservability to membership. Deportation constructs citizenship (Walters 2002) because 'every act of deportation might be seen as reaffirming the significance of the unconditional right of residence that citizenship provides' (Anderson, Gibney, and Paoletti 2011, 548). Deportation complies with public expectations and electoral politics, it assures the voting public that the problem has been identified, and is being addressed through state authority (Gibney and Hansen 2003; Bosworth 2008; Leerkes and Broeders 2010). In seeking to expel the unwanted deportation reveals 'citizenry as community of value as much as community of law' and this is where the symbolic and definitive power of deportation lies (Anderson, Gibney, and Paoletti 2011, 548). Deportation thus has the potential to be divisive (Anderson, Gibney, and Paoletti 2011; Freedman 2011; McGregor 2011) as the grounds of who belongs, and who should decide on who belongs, are contested not only between the state and the migrants but also between different actors of the public (see also Kalir, 2014).

Conflicts are brought about during ADCs. Where people may in general and abstract terms want stricter migration control, when faced directly (through a neighbour or colleague) with the harsh reality of deportation, they may seek to prevent particular migrants from being deported (Ellermann 2009; Freedman 2011). It is in this sense that Gibney (2008) argues that deportation invites contestation. But who is worthy of contestation? ADCs may make use of human rights language, but mostly they deploy ideas of integration, belonging and 'the good citizen' to underline the contribution of removable migrants to their community and the society at large:

> by privileging subjective identification over human rights considerations, the criteria may be insensitive to the costs of deportation for those who are deemed unworthy of membership. The violation of the norms and values of the community can come to justify ignoring any other claims the non-citizen may have for not being deported. (Anderson, Gibney, and Paoletti 2011, 560)

In fact, as explored here, foreign-national offenders with no asylum claim seldom campaign against their deportation. Normative expectations around behaviour deem them less worthy than others (Anderson, Gibney, and Paoletti 2011; Anderson 2013) and 'the good citizen' argument is hardly convincing. As Bosworth further points out:

> deportation raises questions about the commitment of a liberal state to human rights and to values like respect, the right to family life and security. It also disrupts social relationships, since non-citizens have often become part of British communities, whatever their immigration status. Few qualms exist, however, when the state deals with those convicted of criminal offences. Foreign offenders have limited numbers of supporters either in prison or in the community outside their immediate family. (2011, 591)

Current reliance on criminal justice and punitive rhetoric about the dangers embodied in foreign citizens is used in policy to secure the border both in the UK and elsewhere (Inda 2006; Bosworth 2011; Khosravi [2011] 2010). The increasing tendency towards governance through criminal law is prevalent in the management of migration (Stumpf 2006), through the practices of detention, bail, reporting and deportation, which not only allow close monitoring of migrants but also reinforce the notion that the public needs protection from them. The policing and criminalisation of migrants thus sends the message that foreigners pose a risk to society.

But while policy is developed and applied it may not be carried through to the end. There is an 'increasing inability of states to conduct the kind of mass deportation campaigns they claim to aim for' (Paoletti 2010, 13). Most migrants participating in this study, for instance, were appealing their deportation for over 2 years by the time I finished fieldwork. The non-deportability of some migrants (Paoletti 2010) leaves them in a legal limbo where they are not included in the host society even if they are physically present, as they are prevented from active participation. This was particularly felt among research participants: not being able to work or actively plan their future and carry on with their lives, their existence in the UK is effectively interrupted even if they are still in the country (Hasselberg 2013).

It should be made clear at this point that British immigration legislation distinguishes administrative removal from deportation. They both entail the expulsion—or intention to expel—foreign nationals from the UK, but the grounds for, and protections against each differ in significant ways. Administrative removal refers to migrants who have no legal entitlement of stay in the UK.[4] Deportation, on the other hand, refers to individuals whose expulsion from the UK the Secretary of State deems to be conducive to the public good, whether or not they hold leave to remain. Broadly speaking, this means that a foreign national with leave to remain is deportable from the UK if convicted to a 12-month sentence or longer.[5] Upon serving the sentence, migrants may be detained in an Immigration Removal Centre while their deportation files are processed. Deportation may be appealed at the Immigration Tribunal[6] on human rights grounds. The migrant, if detained, may also apply at the Immigration Tribunal for bail, which may be granted under certain conditions. Reporting to the Home Office (at designated reporting centres) monthly or weekly is usually part of the terms of bail. The terms of bail remain in place until the migrant is either detained again for removal or has his or her deportation appeal granted. Deportation cancels leave to remain and unlike administrative removal, has an enduring legal effect, meaning that it entails a ban on return—it prohibits the deportee from re-entering the country as long as the order is in force, a period between 3 and 10 years. This is of particular importance to migrants who are thus prevented from returning to the UK to visit family and friends after deportation takes place.

When migrants are confronted with the Home Office's intent to deport them, they are confused, surprised and some even shocked. As they grasp their new circumstances, uncertainty prevails as to whether or not they will remain in the UK and the degree of damage to their present and future lives. When filing the notice of appeal with the Immigration Tribunal, migrants become appellants and new routines enter their daily lives. It is important to bear in mind that foreign-national offenders are not just imprisoned and deported. Between imprisonment and deportation, migrants and their families live in a limbo where their lives are unsettled, ungrounded and uncertain. Some might lose their right to work, most will be subjected to some form of state surveillance, and all will experience long-term uncertainty. Appealing deportation is a long process marked with extreme anxiety and nervousness both for the migrants appealing deportation and their families. Family members are not just affected by the prospect of family separation. They are involved in making appeals, providing statements and attending court hearings whether or not they are giving evidence. They fill in the migrant's tasks and role when they are in detention, and together they share the material and emotional burden of the deportation process.

Overall, research participants felt that they were being punished consecutively: they had served their time in prison but rather than moving on with their lives as a British national would, they find themselves facing expulsion from their country of residence and under constant restrictions and surveillance.

The criminalisation of immigrants in liberal democracies and elsewhere has been examined and discussed in a comprehensive body of literature on the legality and social legitimacy of such practices (Kanstroom 2000; Morawetz 2000; De Genova 2002; Nyers 2003; Maira 2007). These debates are intrinsically connected with notions of citizenship, entitlements and justice. Stumpf (2011) argues that the convergence of criminal and immigration law also reduces migrants' lives and existence to a particular point in time—that of criminal or immigration offence:

> This extraordinary focus on the moment of the crime conflicts with the fundamental notion of the individual as a collection of many moments composing our experiences, relationships, and circumstances. It frames out circumstances, conduct, experiences, or relationships that tell a different story about the individual, closing off the potential for redemption and disregarding the collateral effects on the people and communities with ties to the noncitizen. (Stumpf 2011, 1705)

In the UK, deportation and related practices of surveillance are indeed a straightforward consequence of a criminal conviction. But while the decision to exclude migrants is reduced to that particular moment of their lives, when deciding on deportation appeals the Immigration Tribunal does bear in mind the 'circumstances, conduct, experiences, or relationships that tell a different story about the individual' that Stumpf writes about above. That their lives were now dominated by that one moment in time when they were convicted was in fact all too present in research participants' lives. Having become labelled as offenders, which, coupled with being foreigners, not only subjected them to deportation and state surveillance but also prevented them from openly resisting and protesting for their rights.

Migrants and Political Agency

As Laubenthal argues in her study of pro-regularisation movements in three European countries, the political agency of undocumented migrants was often left unexamined:

Existing research on illegality has focused on the lack of political, social, and economic rights of illegal migrants that follows from their illegal status and impedes the possibility of their collective self-organization. (2007, 102)

In fact, the literature on the state of exception, derived from the work of Agamben (2005), on which many studies of migrant illegality and deportability draw, leaves little space for resistance or contestation. In recent years, numerous studies attempting to apply Agamben's biopolitics of states of exception to contemporary deportation systems have revealed both that authority is not necessarily overly centralised (Landau 2006; Sutton and Vigneswaran 2011) and that there is in fact scope for resistance and contestation (Abu-Laban and Nath 2007; Nyers 2008; Ellermann 2009, 2010; McGregor 2011; Rygiel 2011; Tylor 2013). Even in confined spaces such as Immigration Removal Centres, there is room for political action. In these settings, as the agency of detained migrants is limited, acts of protest, resistance and contestation tend to take the form of hunger strikes (see e.g. McGregor 2011), self-harm and suicide attempts (Nyers 2008; Fischer 2014) or the destruction of identity documents (Ellermann 2010). Confinement may also have a politicising effect in detainees, through the realisation that they are rights-bearing subjects (Peutz 2007) who upon release may pursue open political action (McGregor 2011). Furthermore, the unprecedented mobilisation of undocumented migrants in the USA, in 2003 and 2006, has also worked to challenge the notion that the undocumented, by way of their illegality and rightlessness, are devoid of political visibility and agency (De Genova 2009, see also De Genova 2010).

Immigrants' political action is seldom enacted in isolation. As Laubenthal (2007) argues, immigrants' movements count on the support of other more secure actors: citizens, non-governmental organisations, trade unions, religious groups, etc. Equally, protest and campaigning against deportation and removal is not just in the hands of removable migrants themselves. On the contrary, civil rights groups have been increasingly active in contesting both individual cases of deportation and removal policies more generally, grounding their claims on human rights conventions safeguarding the right to protection in the case of asylum seekers (Walters 2002; Nyers 2003; Heyman 2007) and the right to private and family life in the case of deportation of long-term migrants following criminal convictions (Dembour 2003; Human Rights Watch [HRW] 2007; Steinorth 2008). In the UK, many advocacy and migrant support groups advocate for migrants, support their campaigns and contest immigration policies (Sen 2000; Bhattacharyya and Gabriel 2002). Trade unions often lend support to campaigns against the deportation of their members. Several groups specifically support migrants in campaigns against their removal from the UK; for example, the National Coalition of Anti-Deportation Campaigns, the Southall Black Sisters, No One Is Illegal (NOII) and Women Asylum Seekers Together, among many others. While the approach that these support groups take towards protest and campaigning has an impact on foreign-national offenders' ability to protest, this paper is mainly concerned with migrants' own perception of protest, and not with the actions of organised groups.

Lack of Protest and Participation in Campaigns

When I probed my informants on protest and other forms of resistance, their first reaction was invariably a surprised 'protest'?! It was obvious they had not considered it. Most research participants were in fact reluctant to consider any kind of protest or collective political action. I met David for a follow-up interview at a café close to the reporting centre where he had to report weekly on Wednesday mornings. David had been appealing his deportation for 2 years by the time I interviewed him. He arrived in the UK with his wife and his oldest son in the 1990s, escaping the civil war that wrecked their country. His two younger children were born in the UK:

> I see it as unfair but I have never thought in protesting or doing like a demonstration. (…) And participating in a protest could turn against me, I don't know. Then again I never saw any protest like that. And when there are any protests, do they solve things? Does the government ever change things when people protest? (…) I see it as unfair, but I also see my hands tied. Who is going to protect me? Because, imagine, the way things go if all those immigrants you see there [reporting centre] everyday, if we all get together, and together we demonstrate, that would be a massive thing right? But we are all afraid that it might go against us, so that is not going to happen. (David)

David centres here on one of the main issues given by research participants to justify their lack of protest. There is a strong sense that collective forms of political action like protest and demonstrations not only have no impact on government decisions, but might actually result in the participants' detention or the acceleration of their removal—most research participants feared the repercussions of becoming 'inconvenient' to the Home Office. This last point is particularly relevant when it comes to individual forms of open protest such as ADCs.

Campaigning means, above all, going public. The power of individual campaigns lies in the 'everyday world of local politics' (Bhattacharyya and Gabriel 2002, 150). It is through media publicity that individual campaigns gather wider community support. Leading an ADC involves actual political action, such as speaking in public, distributing leaflets and letters, demonstrations, pickets, meetings and so forth. It also means actively involving migrants' families and friends. It is demanding and time-consuming. For the research participants this was problematic, as being in the appeals system and complying with the conditions of bail was already too much to handle and most felt they had no energy left to fight on another front. Most importantly, however, they had no wish to divulge publicly that they are facing deportation from the UK, nor that they had been convicted of a criminal offence. They are well aware that for them protesting means putting themselves publicly into the 'foreign criminal' category. Trude was distressed by the deportation of her son-in-law to West Africa and what her daughter and grandson were going through. She wanted to go out, set-up a campaign and protest on his behalf but he would not have it:

> He just thinks it's his business and he doesn't want everyone to know so I don't know. He might think differently if he think it can help us getting him back but I wouldn't know where to start it or where to go or anything.

Trude leads us to yet another reason contributing to the lack of protest: even when there is will, there is a lack of know-how and organisational support. ADC support groups acknowledge that most people do not know how to go about protesting and campaigning and need support in that regard—hence the services these groups provide. Most produce brief guidelines on how to campaign and some logistical support. In 2007, NOII published a 23-page leaflet entitled *Campaigning against Deportation or Removal. Building an Anti-Deportation Campaign. A Practical and Political Guide to Fighting to Remain in this Country*. Most advocacy groups will refer migrants to it. The guide provides practical advice on how to start up and maintain a successful campaign, and what pitfalls to avoid; it lists the advantages of campaigning for the right to stay; and details some principles that all campaigns should adhere to. But whereas most ADC organisations give support to campaigns against any and all deportations, the words *prison, sentence, conviction* or *offender* are absent from their campaign material even though specific sentences or even sections are devoted to *asylum seekers, undocumented migrants* and migrants living *underground*. Maria, one of the few research participants who at one point considered open political action[7] became very aware of this:

> Every single organisation that I have approached deals with refugees, nobody deals with ex-offenders. Because it seems to me that there is a need but no one is catering for the kinds of need that I have. No one. So it really is ironic. (…) People don't protest because they are scared. And I am scared. But I'm reaching the point where I have nothing to lose, there is nothing for me to be scared about now, because ex-offenders need to have some level of equality over here. (…) I would be happy to take part in for it but I don't know anybody that I could link with … 'cause I was hoping that I could link with another campaign so I could link my campaign but it just isn't anything out there. (…) I want to protest, I do wanna protest, but how can I get off the ground? How do I do that? Because I am not … I have never done it so I don't know how to start it. And I don't know how to do it basically.

Maria came to the UK as a child, over 40 years ago. For her lack of organisational know-how was compounded by the fact that she could not find any other deportees to join her. As she says, she had nothing to lose and she felt strongly about the rights of former offenders. Most others however, had a more complicated take on this matter. Present throughout participants' narratives of deportation, and surveillance in particular, is the notion that as foreigners and criminals they do not get second chances. For participants, *once a criminal, always a criminal* is the Home Office's stand on the matter. For instance, the mother of Jerome, a 17-year-old boy facing deportation following a drug-related charge, was appalled that instead of developing efforts to rehabilitate her teenage son, the Home Office was only concerned to deport him.

Research participants felt that they were being doubly punished because they combine in a single person two dreadful categories—those of 'foreigner' and 'criminal'. Because they have been convicted of an offence *and* they are foreign, they have to endure this extra round of punishments. Participants are fully aware that British citizens convicted of offences also face difficulties upon release from prison due to their criminal record, e.g. when seeking to secure employment or accommodation. But for them the point is that British citizens get to move on with their lives despite those difficulties, whereas in their own cases the legacy of the criminal record prevents them from moving on. They have to endure another round of courts, this time immigration courts, and be subjected to a whole new set of surveillance practices that again bring their lives to a halt. Their status as foreigners becomes ever more important after criminal conviction, as they have forfeited their right to be in the UK:

> What was I told? I forfeited my rights to being in this country by committing a crime, (…) And why couldn't I be forgiven? [*starts crying*] Why am I simply being looked at as a foreign criminal? Why? (…) In a way the needs that I need to be catered for are needs under the law so basically there has to be somebody to kick off about the fact that 'you know what? Just because you committed a crime does not mean you are defected for life' (…) When does a person stop being an ex-offender? I mean, please, somebody let me know. How many good deeds do I have to do to make up for my one bad deed? No matter which way we look at it, is this not a Christian country? And are we not supposed to forgive? It's those kinds of moral questions that I would like to have addressed. (Maria)

The feeling arising from the perception that wrong is being done to them should not be underestimated. In deportation, this is exacerbated because it is compounded by (i) a sense of powerlessness to do anything about it and (ii) awareness that public opinion is not on their side. So if, on the one hand, migrants felt that they had been punished already for their criminal offence, on the other they were all too aware that it was their actions that led to their immigration predicament and hence felt accountable for it.

ADC support groups are happy to help and assist foreign-national offenders in protesting against their deportation, just as they do for failed asylum seekers and other deportable migrants. But the work of these organisations goes beyond the individual campaigns they support: they lobby the government and work as pressure groups in an attempt to challenge, if not change, current immigration policies. Individual campaigns are the base for and link to broader campaign work over wider immigration issues (Sen 2000; Bhattacharyya and Gabriel 2002). For instance, individual ADCs can challenge the notion of 'public interest' by emphasising the financial independence of the migrants and their many contributions to the community: 'Mocking the immigration regulations by introducing alternative ideas about what constitutes the public good became a standard tactic in anti-deportation campaigns in the Midlands and beyond' (Bhattacharyya and Gabriel 2002, 158). For this purpose, and also to ensure that a particular ADC is successful it is deemed essential that migrants' campaigns conform to two related tenets: in the words of the NOII guidebook, (i) *Demand support—don't beg for it* and (ii) *Don't argue your case is exceptional!* These tenets, even if phrased differently elsewhere, are present in most ADC organisations' written materials, and are crucial in understanding why foreign-national offenders rarely campaign.

Demand Support—Don't Beg for It

The idea underlining the first tenet is that migrants should seek solidarity because they are the subjects of unreasonable immigration policies. They should not seek pity because they are not responsible for their imminent removal. This is captured in the NOII leaflet:

> You are not to blame for the situation you are in. The fault is totally with the Home Office and its immigration laws. Therefore do not feel ashamed! None of this is your fault! (NOII 2007, 7)

For foreign-national offenders, this is a particularly troublesome point, and who is responsible for their deportation is, more often than not, a difficult issue for them. While they may consider the Home Office's policies as 'over the top', they are also very aware that deportation arose from their own actions—it is a direct result of their conviction, for which they are accountable:

> I have never thought about it [protest], but I see that my case is a bit disgraceful because I had the documents [Indefinite Leave to Remain] and that document is being taken away from me because of my actions, I committed a crime right? Then there are those people who have not committed any crime and they are going through the same thing. (David)

Even if the deportation process and its associated living conditions are deemed to be a hard and unfair second punishment, foreign-national offenders did commit an offence and they feel responsible and accountable for it:

> I think I am still paying for the things I did, (...) I have to accept that. That is why I endure this punishment on me. But then I also think this is too much punishment. Or maybe I just don't want to see it, just don't want to change. But I make my own destiny. I am the one who has to think before doing stuff. (Andre)

Remember here the focus-group extract that opens this paper—that small episode illustrates how aware participants are that they have in fact committed an offence and that their status as 'criminals' does not allow them to protest for their right to stay. Justice, they feel, is for the victim and the innocent, not for the criminal. It is in this sense that it is very difficult for research participants to take the ADC support groups' approach of 'demanding' support for their cause and placing full responsibility on the Home Office over their deportation. Ultimately, participants acknowledge their part in it. However, acknowledging their role in the events leading to their deportation is not tantamount to considering deportation and related policies (detention, reporting, etc.) as legitimate punishments. While they feel they have only themselves to blame for being put into a situation where they are abused, the abuse is recognised as such and never legitimised.

Family members tend to feel the same and often have conflicting feelings regarding their relatives' entitlement to stay. Take Tania's words on her partner's deportation following a drug-related conviction:

> Because of his drug convictions I feel like a hypocrite [protesting on his behalf] but I would quite happy support other people. (...) I think it's quite difficult really because I know that there's a lot of people here that should not be here and there's a lot of people here that commit crimes and shouldn't be here. And if I would say that if a person has committed a crime they shouldn't be here, then look at how difficult it is for me. I'm against drugs, against crime, but my child's father ... can you imagine how I feel? (...) I feel like a complete bloody hypocrite! But then I look at my daughter and I just think she deserves the choice to grow up with her dad, she does. (Tania)

Tania is faced with a dilemma in wanting her partner to remain in the UK while at the same time believing that those who commit crimes should be deported:

> I don't know, I just think there are so many people who want to come here, why give an opportunity to someone who has committed a crime as serious as that, over somebody else who all they want to do is stay over with their families? So ... I don't know. (Tania)

She is not alone here—this is a feeling prevalent not only among relatives but also among deportable migrants themselves. Their deportation narratives are narratives of exception, which brings us to the second tenet of ADCs.

Don't Argue Your Case Is Exceptional!

This second tenet seeks to assert that all cases deserve solidarity and thus to avoid divisions deriving from speculation over who is more worthy of remaining in the UK:

> Many campaigns try to argue that their case is 'different' or 'worse' or 'more desperate' than other cases. This is what the Home Office want us to do! The Home Office wants campaigns to argue in public as to who is more 'exceptional' or more 'worthy'. The Home Office wants this because it leads to division and not unity. (NOII 2007, 8)

An ADC, then, should argue that immigration laws overall are cruel and unfair and not that they are just being misapplied to a particular individual or family. Instead of arguing that the Home Office has failed in their specific case, ADCs should aim to reveal the tremendous misery that all others in the same situation are facing, i.e. that it is the policy in itself that is failing. This allows anti-deportation organisations to lobby on wider immigration issues. But research participants were not necessarily against deportation policies per se and do consider themselves as exceptional cases, an exemplified here in the words of George, from Latin America, who had been living in the UK for 19 years at the time of the interview. He has four children, three of which born in the UK. We always met at the hospital where at the time his premature son was in recovery:

> As a person, as a father, as a citizen, from here or from there, I think these polices [of deportation] are necessary. I think yes, there are some people who deserve being deported. (...) Some people only have bad intentions. And I have met some people like this. And when I heard they were facing deportation I thought to myself 'I hope they get deported' because you're thinking about your children. (...) So yes, they should deport people, but dangerous people, people that already have records of being criminal. (...) People should be deported according to the severity of the crime but you also have to respect the rights of the persons, and you should investigate better the background of the person. Because we are all subject to make mistakes in life, no one is perfect. But yes, they should deport people. Honestly, yes. But not me, I don't want it.

Research participants are thus not against immigration policies that aim to deport those with criminal convictions. They are just against their own deportation. It follows then that if the policy is deemed legitimate, exceptionality becomes the only basis to argue against their deportation. But arguing that one's deportation is wrong and the policy in general is adequate is, however, incompatible with the broader work of ADC support groups. This is not to say that only foreign-national offenders take issue with non-exceptionality and that other deportable migrants who have not been criminally convicted will necessarily accept this tenet [see e.g. Tylor (2013) and Webber (2012) on matters of stigma and resistance of asylum seekers and undocumented migrants]. The point here is that a gap exists between foreign-national offenders' understanding of their right to campaign and the broader advocacy work of most ADC support groups.

Contestation and Deservability

The findings presented thus far make the case that foreign-national offenders have conflicting notions about their deportation and their 'right' to protest and campaign against it. As the above quotes reveal, research participants tended to favour deportation policies, contesting only the 'unsatisfying' consideration of the merits of their particular cases, or the broad applicability of such policies. This apparent contradiction is not limited to deportable migrants. Ellermann's (2009) study is revealing of how the dynamics of migration control vary over the policy cycle: as mentioned above, even those who might be in abstract terms in favour of austere border control may develop efforts to prevent the deportation of a particular individual or family that is somehow part of their daily lives (see also Anderson, Gibney, and Paoletti 2011; Freedman 2011). Relevant here are the arguments, discussed earlier, of Paoletti (2010) and Anderson, Gibney, and Paoletti (2011) on deportation as a practice that does not only accentuate the divide between those who belong and those who do not, but also can act as a space of contestation among the public, and between citizens, migrants and the state, over who has the right to decide on who belongs. This contestation is:

> a key and everyday feature of the many local anti-deportation campaigns that currently operate in support of individuals and families facing expulsion in liberal democratic states like Britain. Although often used by governmental elites as a way of reaffirming the shared significance of citizenship, deportation, we suggest, may serve to highlight just how divided and confused modern societies are in how they conceptualise membership and in who has the right to determine membership. (Anderson, Gibney, and Paoletti 2011, 548)

But whereas failed asylum seekers and other deportable migrants can argue for their cases emphasising both their need for protection and their contribution to society in general and their local communities in particular, criminal offenders are less deserving through society's lens of normative behaviour (Anderson, Gibney, and Paoletti 2011). This is not to say that there are no foreign-national offenders leading ADCs. During the course of my research, I came across a handful of online petitions, and associated ADCs, involving migrants with criminal convictions. All of these, however, concerned return to 'unsafe' countries, allowing an emphasis on vulnerability and need of protection. These petitions also used careful wording in justifying or minimising the offences, which were in all cases first offences of minor severity, as exemplified in the petition of Marika, a British army soldier of Fijian nationality, facing deportation 'to a country undergoing a military coup' after being convicted of assault following a 'trivial bar fight' where he acted in 'self-defence' after being 'discriminated against and verbally abused'.[8] Campaigning successfully demands not only public support, but also that foreign-national offenders re-create their own understanding of their deportation and their rights. This is also true of other forms of open and collective political action.

I have detailed in this paper how research participants considered deportation to be a legitimate technique of state control, contesting only the broad applicability of the policies or the assessment of merit in their own case, meaning that they contest only their deportation and not necessarily that of others, and how that reduces their scope for open political action. It should be made clear, however, that this is not tantamount to say that foreign-national offenders lack political agency. They may lack political visibility, but they are not passive subjects waiting to be removed. Quite the contrary, they fought hard to stay in the UK. Through due course, migrants challenged at the Immigration Tribunal the Home Office's intention to deport them, and in complying with the restrictions that deportability imposes on their lives, they sought to challenge the very notion that they are a risk to society and should hence be removed from it. It is also important to note that in this context compliance with such state orders is no easy task—it results in significant human and material costs, an issue I explore in more detail elsewhere (Hasselberg 2013).

Coutin argues that 'the stripping away of a prior legal identity is a violent act' (2010, 205). Most migrants participating in this research project had leave to remain prior to conviction and they felt that their criminal conviction in particular was not serious enough to warrant the cancellation of their right to reside in the UK— meaning that they felt worthy of membership. Although acknowledging that a criminal offence is a serious matter, migrants also emphasised their conduct as hard-working, tax-paying residents prior to conviction. Participants also felt that their conduct following release from prison was a testament that their record as residents in the UK should not be reduced to the particular moment of their criminal conviction (cf. Stumpf 2011). They also strongly felt the weight of their new label as 'offenders', purportedly undeserving of second chances. It is then through due process and compliance with state orders that foreign-national offenders seek to assert their deservability to membership (Hasselberg 2013), and not through protest and other public forms of political action. Thus, it is suggested here that feeling worthy of membership is not tantamount to having a political face to claim that membership— whereas research participants felt deserving of membership they did not feel deserving of fighting publicly for their right to stay.

This paper showed that perceptions of legitimacy influence not only how given policies are lived and experienced but also the scope for political action that people allow themselves. Perceptions of justice and legitimacy in the context of deportation are far from clear-cut and are often conflicting (see also in the volume the papers by Kalir, Fischer, and Drotbhom). Whereas lack of participation in collective forms of political action such as protests and demonstrations is attributed mostly to the belief that these are futile exercises bearing no consequence other than perhaps putting migrants on a tighter spot (remember the words of David earlier on), lack of engagement in personal campaigns is mostly related to foreign-national offenders' understanding of their own deportation. Admitting responsibility over criminal conviction, believing in the overall legitimacy of deportation policies and knowing they lack public sympathy work to prevent foreign-national offenders from engaging in open and individual forms of political actions such as campaigning.

This raises important questions that point to a diversity of normative canons born out of the deportation process (Drotbohm and Hasselberg 2014). On the one hand, there are advocacy imperatives that rely on the non-exceptionality tenet. On the other hand, the claim of exceptionality is the one that makes sense for those whose understandings of the legitimacy of deportation policies and of their own deportation are conflicting. This point is of particular relevance to ADC support groups. Emphasising, especially in written materials, their will to assist foreign-national offenders in campaigning against deportation and fighting to stay, may in itself be a much needed encouragement. ADC support groups are unlikely to change their premises, which appear incompatible with the way research participants understood their own removal. Yet, reinforcing their right to campaign alongside other deportable migrants might challenge foreign-national offenders to rethink the exceptionality of and the accountability for their removal. Understanding how foreign-national offenders perceive their own deportation may assist ADC support groups in devising other means to cater to this segment of the deportable population and show their support.

Acknowledgements

Findings in this paper are drawn from my doctoral research carried out at the School of Global Studies, University of Sussex, and fully funded by Fundação para Ciência e Tecnologia. I am grateful to Heike Drotbohm, Sarah Turnbull, Fran Meissner and the anonymous reviewer for commenting on earlier drafts of this paper.

Notes

[1] The situation of research participants as foreign-national offenders facing deportation differs from other populations of removable migrants in that most had leave to remain, do not fear for their lives if returned to their countries of origin, and have a strong sense of entitlement to remain in the UK.

[2] See Meissner and Hasselberg (2012) for a discussion of access and research locations, and Hasselberg (2013, 44–50) for a discussion on the ethical issues arising from adopting different positionalities in the field.

[3] Mostly due to the costs of legal representation, but also in many cases through forfeiting their right to work.

[4] That is migrants that have overstayed; breached a condition of leave to enter or remain; sought or obtained leave to remain by deception; had their indefinite leave revoked because they have ceased to be a refugee; or are family members of the above (UKBA undated).

[5] Immigration policy and legislation has changed in many significant ways since the time of fieldwork in 2009, and more changes are likely to come about with the new Immigration Bill. These changes have sought to both curtail appeal rights (and access to legal aid) and increase state powers in deporting people.

[6] There have been multiple reforms to the Immigration Tribunal system. At the time of research, in 2009, immigration appeals were hear at the single-tier Asylum and Immigration Tribunal, which was subsequently reverted to a two-tier system in February 2010. To avoid confusion over terminology, I chose here to refer to it only as Immigration Tribunal.

[7] Perhaps not coincidentally, Maria had exhausted all her appeals and by then she knew her deportation was only a matter of time.

[8] Quoted from Marika's petition, which is available at http://www.gopetition.com/petitions/stop-the-deportation-of-an-ex-british-army-soldier.html [last accessed May 21, 2012].

References

Abu-Laban, Y., and N. Nath. 2007. "From Deportation to Apology: The Case of Maher Arar and the Canadian State." *Canadian Ethnic Studies* 39 (3): 71–98. doi:10.1353/ces.0.0049.

Agamben, G. 2005. *State of Exception*. Chicago, IL: University of Chicago Press.

Anderson, B. 2013. *Us and them? The Dangerous Politics on Immigration Control*. Oxford: Oxford University Press.

Anderson, B., M. J. Gibney, and E. Paoletti. 2011. "Citizenship, Deportation and the Boundaries of Belonging." *Citizenship Studies* 15: 547–563. doi:10.1080/13621025.2011.583787.

Bhattacharyya, G., and J. Gabriel. 2002. "Anti-deportation Campaigning in the West Midlands." In *Rethinking Anti-racisms from Theory to Practice*, edited by F. Anthias and S. Lloyd, 149–165. London: Routledge.

Bosworth, M. 2008. "Border Control and the Limits of the Sovereign State." *Social & Legal Studies* 17 (2): 199–215. doi:10.1177/0964663908089611.

Bosworth, M. 2011. "Deportation, Detention and Foreign-national Prisoners in England and Wales." *Citizenship Studies* 15: 583–595. doi:10.1080/13621025.2011.583789.

Coutin, S. B. 2010. "Confined within: National Territories as Zones of Confinement." *Political Geography* 29: 200–208.

De Genova, N. 2002. "Migrant 'Illegality' and Deportability in Everyday Life." *Annual Review of Anthropology* 31: 419–447. doi:10.1146/annurev.anthro.31.040402.085432.

De Genova, N. 2009. "Conflicts of Mobility, and the Mobility of Conflict: Rightlessness, Presence, Subjectivity, Freedom." *Subjectivity* 29: 445–466. doi:10.1057/sub.2009.22.

De Genova, N. 2010. "The Queer Politics of Migration: Reflections on 'Illegality' and Incorrigibility." *Studies in Social Justice* 4 (2): 101–126.

Dembour, M.-B. 2003. "Human Rights and National Sovereignty in Collusion: The Plight of Quasi-nationals in Strasburg." *The Netherlands Quarterly of Human Rights* 21 (1): 65–98.

Drotbohm, H. 2014. "The Reversal of Migratory Family Lives. A Cape Verdean Perspective on Gender and Sociality Prior and Post Deportation." *Journal of Ethnic and Migration Studies* 41 (4): 653–670. doi:10.1080/1369183X.2014.961905.

Ellermann, A. 2009. *States against Migrants. Deportation in Germany and the United States*. New York: Cambridge University Press.

Ellermann, A. 2010. "Undocumented Migrants and Resistance in the Liberal State." *Politics & Society* 38: 408–429. doi:10.1177/0032329210373072.

Fischer, N. 2014. 'The Management of Anxiety. An Ethnographical Outlook on Self-mutilations in a French Immigration Detention Centre." *Journal of Ethnic and Migration Studies* 41 (4): 599–616. doi:10.1080/1369183X.2014.960820.

Freedman, J. 2011. 'The Réseau Education Sans Frontières: Reframing the Campaign against the Deportation of Migrants." *Citizenship Studies* 15: 613–626. doi:10.1080/13621025.2011.583793.

Gibney, M. J. 2008. "Asylum and the Expansion of Deportation in the United Kingdom." *Government and Opposition* 43 (2): 146–167. doi:10.1111/j.1477-7053.2007.00249.x.

Gibney, M. J., and R. Hanson. 2003. "Deportation and the Liberal State: The Forcible Return of Asylum Seekers and Unlawful Migrants in Canada, Germany and the United Kingdom." *New Issues in Refugee Research*, Working Paper 77.

Hasselberg, I. 2013. "An Ethnography of Deportation from Britain." Doctoral Thesis, University of Sussex. http://sro.sussex.ac.uk/43788/.

Hasselberg I. 2014. "Balancing legitimacy, exceptionality and accountability: on foreign-national offenders' reluctance to engage in anti-deportation campaigns in the UK." *Journal of Ethnic and Migration Studies* 41 (4): 563–579. doi:10.1080/1369183X.2014.957173.

Heyman, J. McC. 2007. "Grounding Immigrant Rights Movements in the Everyday Experience of Migration." *International Migration* 45 (3): 197–202. doi:10.1111/j.1468-2435.2007.00417.x.

Human Rights Watch (HRW). 2007. *Forced Apart. Families Separated and Immigrants Harmed by United States Deportation Policy*. Human Rights Watch. Accessed April 23, 2008. http://www.hrw.org/reports/2007/us0707/.

Inda, J. X. 2006. *Targeting Migrants. Government, Technology and Ethics*. Oxford: Blackwell.

Kalir, B. 2014. "The Jewish State of Anxiety: Between Moral Obligation and Fearism in the Treatment of African Asylum-seekers in Israel." *Journal of Ethnic and Migration Studies* 41 (4): 580–598. doi:10.1080/1369183X.2014.960819.

Kanstroom, D. 2000. "Deportation, Social Control and Punishment: Some Thoughts about Why Hard Laws Make Bad Cases." *Harvard Law Review* 113: 1890–1935. doi:10.2307/1342313.

Khosravi, S. [2011] 2010. *'Illegal' Traveller. An Auto-ethnography of Borders*. Basingstoke: Palgrave Macmillan.

Landau, L. B. 2006. "Immigration and the State of Exception: Security and Sovereignty in East and Southern Africa." *Journal of International Studies* 34: 325–348.

Laubenthal, B. 2007. "The Emergence of Pro-regularization Movements in Western Europe." *International Migration* 45 (3): 101–133. doi:10.1111/j.1468-2435.2007.00412.x.

Leerkes, A., and D. Broeders. 2010. "A Case of Mixed Motives? Formal and Informal Functions of Administrative Immigration Detention." *British Journal of Criminology* 50: 830–850. doi:10.1093/bjc/azq035.

Maira, S. 2007. "Deporting Radicals, Deporting La Migra. The Hayat case in Lodi." *Cultural Dynamics* 19 (1): 39–66. doi:10.1177/0921374007077268.

McGregor, J. 2011. "Contestations and Consequences of Deportability: Hunger Strikes and the Political Agency of Non-citizens." *Citizenship Studies* 15: 597–611. doi:10.1080/13621025. 2011.583791.

Meissner, F., and I. Hasselberg. 2012. "Forever Malleable: The Field as a Reflexive Encounter. In *Where Is the Field? Exploring Migration through the Lenses of Fieldwork. Studia Fennica Ethnologica*, edited by H. Snellman and L. Hirvi, 91–109. Helsinki: Finnish Literature Society.

Morawetz, N. 2000. "Understanding the Impact of the 1996 Deportation Laws and the Limited Scope of Proposed Reforms." *Harvard Law Review* 113: 1936–1962.

No-One Is Illegal (NOII). 2007. *Campaigning against Deportation or Removal. Building an Anti-deportation Campaign. A Practical and Political Guide to Fighting to Remain in this Country.* www.noii.org.uk.

Nyers, P. 2003. "Abject Cosmopolitanism: The Politics of Protection in the Anti-deportation Movement." *Third World Quarterly* 24: 1069–1093. doi:10.1080/01436590310001630071.

Nyers, P. 2008. "In Solitary, in Solidarity: Detainees, Hostages and Contesting the Anti-policy of Detention." *European Journal of Cultural Studies* 11: 333–349. doi:10.1177/13675494080 91847.

Paoletti, E. 2010. *Deportation, Non-deportability and Ideas of Membership.* Working Papers Series No. 65, Refugee Studies Centre, University of Oxford.

Peutz, N. 2007. "Out-laws: Deportees, Desire and 'The Law.'" *International Migration* 45 (3): 183–191. doi:10.1111/j.1468-2435.2007.00415.x.

Rygiel, K. 2011. "Bordering Solidarities: Migrant Activism and the Politics of Movement and Camps at Calais." *Citizenship Studies* 15 (1): 1–19. doi:10.1080/13621025.2011.534911.

Sen, P. 2000. "Domestic Violence, Deportation an Women's Resistance: Notes on Managing Inter-sectionality." In *Development and Management*, edited by D. Eade, 178–183. London: Oxfam in Association with The Open University.

Steinorth, C. 2008. "Uner v The Netherlands: Expulsion of Long-term Immigrants and the Right to Respect for Private and Family Life." *Human Rights Law Review* 8 (1): 185–196. doi:10.1093/ hrlr/ngm043.

Stumpf, Juliet P. 2006. "The Crimmigration Crisis: Immigrants, Crime, and Sovereign Power." *American University Law Review* 56: 368–419. doi:10.1093/hrlr/ngm043.

Stumpf, J. P. 2011. "Doing Time: Crimmigration Law and the Perils of Haste." *UCLA Law Review* 58: 1705–1748.

Sutton, R., and D. Vigneswaran. 2011. "A Kafkaesque State: Deportation and Detention in South Africa." *Citizenship Studies* 15: 627–642. doi:10.1080/13621025.2011.583794.

Tylor, I. 2013. *Revolting Subjects. Social Abjection and Resistance in Neoliberal Britain.* London: Zed Books.

Walters, W. 2002. "Deportation, Expulsion, and the International Police of Aliens." *Citizenship Studies* 6: 265–292. doi:10.1080/1362102022000011612.

Webber, F. 2012. *Borderline Justice. The Fight for Refugee and Migrant Rights.* London: Pluto Press.

The Jewish State of Anxiety: Between Moral Obligation and Fearism in the Treatment of African Asylum Seekers in Israel

Barak Kalir

Since 2005 around 60,000 asylum seekers, mostly from Eritrea and Sudan, have entered Israel by crossing the border from Egypt. Notwithstanding the Jewish history of persecution, and Israel being a signatory to the UN Convention for the protection of refugees, modern Israel systematically refuses to grant a refugee status to asylum seekers. Since 2012, the tenacious hostile approach of Israeli policy-makers and state-agents towards asylum seekers has resulted in an outburst of racist verbal and physical attacks against them. This article analyses the socio-legal location of asylum seekers in Israel by examining how their position is articulated by different parties, deploying competing discourses of human rights, citizenship, security and sovereignty. The article advances that appeals—mostly made by critical non-governmental organisations (NGOs), journalists and academics—to human rights, Jewish morals and historic sensitivities are beguiling; while they arouse hopes for compassion and moral obligation, they are also used by mainstream Israeli politicians to justify the exclusion and deportation of so-called 'African infiltrators'. A hegemonic ideology of 'fearism'—which brands the Israeli national narrative and informs the notion of citizenship among Jewish Israelis—leads to the construction of asylum seekers as abject Others, who pose a threat to the Jewish state and to Jews' own right for secured citizenship.

Introduction

'Israel is a Wonderful Country for Refugees. In Theory', this was the headline of a newspaper article in May 2006, discussing the recommendations of a special advisory

---

Barak Kalir is an Associate Professor of Anthropology at the Department of Sociology and Anthropology, University of Amsterdam, Amsterdam, the Netherlands.

committee, appointed by the government, for examining Israel's overall migration policy. One of the committee's recommendations was for Israel to expand the definition of refugee-ness and to establish an effective status determination procedure that privileges asylum seekers in case of doubt about the rigorousness of their claim. In 2006, the number of asylum seekers in Israel was estimated at a few hundred and was not yet seen as a major public issue. The chairman of the committee, Amnon Rubinstein, a distinguished professor of law and a former Minister of Education, told the journalist that 'towards the refugees we hold a special obligation. We know how it was when Jews knocked on locked doors. We carry this luggage on our backs' (Wurgaft 2006). When asked about the possibility of lodging asylum seekers in residential camps 'like in Europe', professor Rubinstein replied: 'God forbid. This will be a black day for the state of Israel. What they have there [in Europe] is practically camps. We can never allow ourselves to have camps'. Notwithstanding the committee's firm position, the journalist, Nurit Wurgaft, a longstanding advocate of human rights, expressed in the title of her article the scepticism she felt about the chances of the committee to change the exclusionary and rigid ethno-religious Israeli migration regime.

By 2012, the number of asylum seekers in Israel reached a total of around 60,000 and the issue of their treatment became the source of fierce political and public debates. Israel holds one of the world's worst records when it comes to the granting of refugee status to those who escape religious and ethnic cleansing in the Sudan or oppression under the authoritarian regime in Eritrea (Feldinger 2012).[1] In 2012, Israel invested around half a billion US dollar in fencing its border with Egypt to prevent asylum seekers from entering the country. It also constructed the biggest detention camp in the Western world to accommodate 10,000 asylum seekers. The Israeli Prime Minister, Benyamin Netanyahu, unreservedly declared that 'this phenomenon is very serious and threatens the national security (...) 60,000 infiltrators could become 600,000, and could bring about the elimination of Israel as a Jewish and democratic state' (Nesher 2012).[2] A few days later, the journalist Nurit Wurgaft (2012) called in an op-ed to stop the racist campaign against African asylum seekers:

> In our [Israeli] history classes, we learned that anti-Semitism flourished in countries where leaders preferred, instead of dealing with economic crisis, to scapegoat a distinctive minority: Jews. These days, when politicians and mayors feed a nasty wave of lies and racist defamations, I wonder whether we all attended the same school.

Most striking in this rapid change of formulating Israel's approach towards asylum seekers—from openness and tolerance to exclusion and hostility—is the way in which the Jewishness of the Israeli state has been used for warranting both opposing stands. The Israeli political and public debate on the treatment of asylum seekers is saturated with references to a Jewish history of persecution, by the exponents of the exclusionary regime as well as by its critics [mostly non-governmental organisations (NGOs)]. In this article, I depict and analyse the exclusionary Israeli institutional treatment and deportation regime of asylum seekers, as well as the attempts by NGOs to promote more inclusive and human rights-based policies. While the focus in studying modern regimes of deportation is often set on the fear they generate in an already highly vulnerable and marginalised population of illegalised subjects (De Genova 2002), my goal here is to analyse how the production of fear in the first place permeates and legitimises the construction of asylum seekers as deportable abject Others by the receiving nation and state.

The article aims to resolve two paradoxical dynamics evident in the treatment of asylum seekers in Israel. First, the fact that a Jewish state—justified and founded against the backdrop of the historical exclusion and tragic persecution of Jews on ethnic and religious grounds—is institutionally treating asylum seekers inhumanely, drafting draconian laws against their free movement and basic human rights. Second, the fact that human rights discourses and appeals to the moral obligation of Jews towards persecuted Others, as promoted by Israeli NGOs, appear not only to be waywardly ineffective in changing the government's exclusionary approach, but also there are signs that they exacerbate this very exclusionary tendency among many politicians and the public at large.

The article contends that the Israeli exclusionary institutional approach is intimately determined by an entrenched anxiety that underlies and informs the construction of non-Jewish Others, as abject figures whose presence allegedly poses an existential threat to the Jewish state. The source for this anxiety is located largely in the Jewish history of persecution that is believed to be remediated, in the aftermath of the Holocaust, by the establishment of a Jewish state in Israel. The Zionist-Israeli narrative makes explicit the idea that only a formidable Jewish state can secure the rights of Jews as equals in the world. It is for this historical truth, so goes the national narrative, that Israel is morally justified to guard its Jewishness, refusing to be swayed by human rights discourses and UN Conventions that demand more inclusive approaches towards non-Jewish migrants and asylum seekers.

In many ways, the hostile Israeli state's framing of undesired migrants and asylum seekers is symptomatic of a global trend towards a 'heightened anxiety about the "Other", who is perceived as a threat or someone who is dangerous to the security of the nation' (Kapur 2003, 10). Indeed, in the post 9/11 era, in the USA, Australia and countries across Europe, there is a detectable effort to discredit asylum seekers: at best, as economic migrants who are associated with criminality, abuses of the welfare system and the undermining of the national social fabric; at worst, as posing potential terror threats to the national security (Andreas and Snyder 2003; Baldaccini, Guild, and Toner 2007; Basaran 2008; Pace 2010). Notwithstanding the move towards the securitisation of migration (Bigo 2002), and the evocations of national security to fence off foreigners, it is only remote voices, mostly located at the extreme far-right and/or openly racist end of the political spectrum, that refer to the presence of undocumented migrants and asylum seekers as constituting an *existential threat* to the receiving state.

It is therefore notable that in Israel, a country with a mighty military establishment, where asylum seekers have never been involved in terrorism or any other activity that pertains to national security, mainstream politicians regularly refer to an existential threat to the Jewish state that is looming due to the presence of a relatively small number of asylum seekers. In Israel, as elsewhere, there are many attempts to defame asylum seekers as bogus, criminal, violent and parasitic in their relation to the society and state. Nevertheless, these attempts in Israel are habitually subsumed under the greater allegation of posing an existential threat. The prominence of a reference to an existential threat is therefore, I argue, only decipherable against the backdrop of the Jewish history and the 'founding trauma' of Israel (LaCapra 2001) as constituting a homeland and a guarantor of rights for Jewish citizens (Willen 2010).

Several Israeli NGOs assist asylum seekers and lobby the government to promote their rights. As in many other countries, a human rights discourse underlies the motivation and ideological orientation of many NGOs working with asylum seekers. More specifically, in an attempt to generate humanitarian compassion among politicians and to mobilise public opinion, Israeli NGOs regularly evoke the Jewish moral obligation to combat all forms of ethnic and religious persecution ('Never Again'). While there have been some strategic gains in pressing the moral obligation of Jews, and by extension of the Jewish state, towards those who escape persecution, there can be little doubt about the overall failure of a human rights discourse and humanitarian compassion to resolve the crisis of asylum seekers in Israel. In fact, I argue that references to the Holocaust have unintentionally implied a comparison, even a competition, between the victimhood of Jews throughout history and that of contemporary asylum seekers from Africa. Shrewd Israel politicians have manipulated this comparison to debunk the plight of African asylum seekers and to supercharge the political and public debate with a Zionist narrative that champions the need to secure the rights of Jews at all costs.

The article proceeds with a theoretical section that is followed by a description of the Israeli policy towards asylum seekers and the attempts by NGOs to counter it. It then offers an ethnographic vignette to illustrate the harsh daily realities of refugees from Africa, before moving to depict the ways in which the Jewish history of persecution is being employed in the discourses of NGOs as well as in the militant approach of mainstream politicians.

Compassion vs. Rights: How 'Fearism' Curtails Political Recognition of Others

The Israeli case study provides an extreme, but by no means unique, illustration of a larger failure of human, universal and fundamental rights to form the basis for a post-national regime of citizenship (Jacobson 1996; Joppke 1998; Soysal 1994) for undocumented migrants and refugees in a world that is premised on territorial sovereign states and their corresponding national(ised) communities (Berezin 2009; Chavez 2008).

Human rights are not, as utopian assertions will have us believe, foregoing or superimposed on citizenship rights; much to the contrary, it is a global regime of citizenship, anchored in territorial nation states that serve as the first grid for entitlements for individuals, who are always primarily seen as belonging to a particular nationality (Arendt 1951). It is by an appeal to humanitarian morals that a room is being created for the treatment of individuals on a different ground, that is, as humans rather than nationals. Yet this room is always conditional because it is ratified and secured by each nation state that has agreed, in principle, to recognise this exceptionality. Nation states are then left to strike a specific balance between what they consider to be their commitment to the exceptional room for human rights, and their obligations within a regime of citizenship towards their own nationals.

Undocumented migrants and asylum seekers are bringing to a stark relief the inherent tension in striking this balance. As Agamben (1994) argues: 'If in the system of the nation-state the refugee represents such a disquieting element, it is above all because by breaking up the identity between man and citizen, between nativity and nationality, the refugee throws into crisis the original fiction of sovereignty'. For if a nation state was easily acknowledging the claims of all asylum seekers, and including them within its regime of citizenship, then it would be blurring the distinction between its own nationals and, potentially, the rest of the world's population. We thus enter the realm of symbolic power, whereby states—which are able to fashion the dominant visions and divisions in society, through their control over categorisation, education and policing—are forced to make the point that politically recognising asylum seekers can only be done on exceptional humanitarian grounds (Ticktin 2006). This exceptionality reinforces the *de facto* moral geography in which regimes of citizenship are always located on a higher plain than that of human rights.

In the context of the *sans papiers* movement in France, Miriam Ticktin (2006) highlights an important distinction between human rights discourses that are grounded in law and humanitarian discourses that appeal to ethical and moral obligations to help the powerless. As Ticktin shows, it is often because human rights organisations achieve very little by trying to advance legal claims that fall on 'deaf state ears' that 'humanitarianism is forced to take on a primary role in government, largely subsuming a system based on rights' (2006, 35). Ticktin rightly alerts us to the sinister logic of humanitarianism with its appeal for compassion on the basis of exceptional circumstances. This type of humanitarianism depoliticises migrants and their legal claims, falls short of questioning the existing logic of states' regime of rights and reproduces and even augments the structural violence against marginalised subjects.

Fully sharing Ticktin's critique on humanitarian discourses that fashion exceptionalism, I want to highlight an additional adverse effect of humanitarianism that feeds an ideology of Othering. The implications of the inherent tension between a regime of citizenship and a global discourse of human rights are often manifested in the monstrous construction of the Other in the image of the bogus asylum seeker and 'failed' refugee. Nation states exclude abject Others (Kristeva 1993; Nyers 2003) by their very inclusion, as those who stand outside the political realm and whose presence threatens to undermine the very distinction and legal border between the inside/outside of the sovereign state. The anxiety that the abject Other generates in those who find themselves on the inside of the national community, always arbitrarily defined (Balibar 2002), helps to produce and to perpetuate the fiction of tangibility of 'us' and 'them' (Isin 2000).

The production of anxiety towards non-national Others is therefore a crucial ingredient in the modern sense-making of national belonging. As Zembylas (2010, 32) contends, there is 'a new kind of global imaginary [that] is being shaped by the fear of the Other or what Fisher (2006) has termed fearism, that is, 'a process and discourse hegemony [which] creates an experience of fear that is normalized ... keeping the cultural matrix of "fear" operative and relatively invisible'. While fearism mostly feeds on powerful global processes—the retraction of the caring state under neoliberal ideologies (Wacquant 2010) and the widely experienced ontological insecurity that typifies a growing inability among many ordinary citizens to understand and plan their lives in a 'liquid modern age' (Bauman 2006)— we should empirically study the manner in which it ties in with the particular histories and national narratives of each state.

In Israel, the production of fearism is intimately intertwined with the compulsion to translate economic and political issues into their implications for the security of the nation and state. Zionism determined the historic mission of Israel, in its capacity as a Jewish state, to protect all Jews in general and against the perceived imminent Palestinian/Arab threat in particular (Newman 2000; Yiftachel 2006). Since mid-1990s, when Israel began to import non-Jewish labour migrants to replace its cheap Palestinian workforce, it adopted a harsh, exclusionary and exploitative institutional approach, categorising foreign workers as aligned with the threatening group of non-Jewish Others (Kemp 2004; Kalir 2012). This militant approach grounds the Israeli deportation regime that 'successfully' removed more than 100,000 non-Jewish migrants since the mid-2000s (Kalir 2010).

Already by the late 1990s, there were signs in Israel that 'a decreasing number of its citizens identify with the single, socially constructed, national ethos of Zionism' (Newman 2000, 305, see also Ram 1998). While Zionism is certainly by now only one source for identity formation among Jewish Israelis, it is nevertheless, I argue, that the cultural matrix of fear that is at the core of the Zionism-cum-security mind-set has remained firmly operative and always ready to be re-enacted. It is this fertile potential to sway the Israeli public opinion against non-Jewish Others, under the pretext of security threats, that has been unleashed in the debate around asylum seekers from Africa, largely by the invocation of the Holocaust and the notion of victimhood by politicians and NGOs alike.

The Anti-Asylum Israeli Policy

In this article, I refer categorically to those who reach Israel from Eritrea and Sudan as asylum seekers. This is not a straightforward choice of terminology in the Israeli context. In fact, it is a major point of contention, resulting from Israel's decision to prevent Eritreans and Sudanese to submit their asylum applications. Instead, Israel opted to apply a 'temporary protection' to the entire group of Eritreans and Sudanese. Importantly, the average international recognition rate of asylum seekers from Eritrea and Sudan is 84.5% and 74.4%, respectively [United Nations High Commissioner for Refugees (UNHCR) 2011]. By imposing its 'temporary protection' on Eritreans and Sudanese, who comprise around 80% of the total population of asylum seekers[3], Israel not only avoids awarding many of them a refugee status, but also, and more importantly for its institutional approach, can maintain that the vast majority of them are not refugees but rather economic migrants.

Under the 'temporary protection', around 35,000 Eritreans and 15,000 Sudanese are not ensured of basic economic and social rights; they do not receive work permits, health insurance, social benefits or any provisions for shelter and food. After they cross the border from Egypt, most asylum seekers are stopped by the Israeli Army and brought to the *Saharonim* detention camp in the Negev Desert, where they undergo a procedure for verifying their country of origin, checking their medical state (mostly for detecting contagious diseases) and registering them in a database. Most are then released from detention and are dropped at the central bus station of a nearby city, *BeerSheva*, with a bus ticket voucher that can take them to south Tel Aviv.

The Interior Ministry issues those who fall under the 'group protection' a temporary renewable visa for three months that formally does not allow its holder to be employed. Following a petition by NGOs, the Israeli High Court ruled that those who receive 'temporary protection' have the right to work in order to ensure their basic livelihood. However, many Israeli employers are still hesitant in providing work to Eritreans and Sudanese, not least because the Interior Ministry issued confusing statements about the legality of such employment. Many employers thus treat asylum seekers as undocumented migrants, leading to widespread exploitation and systematic violation of basic labour rights. As a result, poverty among Eritreans and Sudanese is widespread and drives most of them to reside in inhumane conditions in public parks or rundown apartments, mostly in poor neighbourhoods in south Tel Aviv. Deprived of access to public health care services, Eritrean and Sudanese must either depend on the limited assistance offered by Israeli NGOs (especially the open clinic of Physicians for Human Rights—Israel), or do without until their situation deteriorates to an acute state, and then be treated by emergency units in hospitals.

Amnesty International and two local Israeli NGOs have charged that 'the collective protection currently imposed on Eritreans and Sudanese is in its essence a deferred deportation order'.[4] They cite the Israeli Parliament's Information Centre, stating that 'Israel is the only developed country that uses temporary collective protection as an alternative to granting asylum on an individual basis'.[5] Indeed, the legal instrument of 'temporary protection' was devised for dealing with an abrupt and massive flow of people fleeing their countries seeking shelter elsewhere. Under these circumstances, a receiving state might not have the manpower and material infrastructure to process the applications of individual asylum seekers and can thus apply a 'temporary protection' as a first and interim step in providing refuge to large groups. In Israel, the inflow of asylum seekers from Africa was neither massive nor abrupt, and thus, as noted by the UNHCR, Israel could and should establish an orderly procedure for verifying the individual status of all asylum seekers (Efraim 2012a).

In 2009, days before Israel inaugurated its new refugee status determination (RSD) unit, Yaakov Ganot, the head of the Population Administration in the Interior Ministry, voiced the official view: 'I would say that 99.9% [of Eritrean and Sudanese] are here for work. They are not asylum-seekers, they are not at any risk' (Wurgaft 2009). In the three years that followed, this sceptical institutional approach prescribed a reality in which the RSD unit not only processed around 14,000 asylum applications but also granted an asylum status only to 22 applicants (Nesher 2013).[6] Many Israeli and international NGOs have heavily criticised the unlawful and unprofessional ways in which the RSD unit deliberately works to fail the application of asylum seekers (e.g. HMW 2012a).

The manufactured reality of there being hardly any refugees in Israel clearly results from institutional arrangements set forward by the state (temporary protection, highly restrictive RSD unit, mighty detention/deportation regime, etc.). This reality, in turn, provides politicians with the legitimisation, and for some also the vindication, for insisting that most asylum seekers are labour migrants. This circular logic is at the heart of the Israeli legal terminology and popular rhetoric that define asylum seekers as 'infiltrators'. The term 'infiltrators' comes from the Prevention of Infiltration Law that was passed in 1954, at a time when armed Palestinian groups entered Israel from Egypt and Jordan to attack Israeli targets. Palestinian infiltrators were criminalised and faced up to five years in prison for crossing the border illegally. The term 'infiltrators' thus carries a highly negative meaning that is linked in the Israeli mind-set to national security and terrorism, and using this term defames an entire population. Yet referring to asylum seekers as 'infiltrators' is widespread among mainstream politicians (including the prime minister), the media and by now also many ordinary Israeli citizens. It is very indicative of the Israeli 'security disposition' that the term became vernacular, although not a single asylum seeker from Africa has been implicated in any terrorist activity after crossing into Israel.

In January 2012, the Israeli parliament passed an 'anti-infiltration bill' that allowed authorities to detain all irregular border-crossers, including children, for three years prior to their eventual deportation. The new law has been heavily criticised by many in and outside Israel, but was nonetheless put into effect. After legal appeals by NGOs, the Israeli high court overturned the anti-infiltration law in September 2013, ruling that the imprisonment of asylum seekers is in contradiction to the right for freedom. The court decision led Israel to rapidly build an 'open detention centre' to which those who were imprisoned can be transferred. The new 'open detention centre' (*Holot*) is supposedly complying with the right for freedom, although it is located in the middle of the desert and, as became quickly known from various reports, offers inhumane living conditions to the asylum seekers who lodge there (HMW 2014).

Israel has reiterated its explicit intention to eventually deport those who currently receive 'temporary protection'. Israel secretly negotiated deals with several states in

Africa to relocate Eritreans and Sudanese to these third countries in return for money, aid and other goods (Efraim 2013). In 2012, only weeks after South Sudan declared independence, Israel removed the collective protection of South Sudanese and began deporting them to 'their' country. Israel ignored all international studies that indicated the life-threatening situation in South Sudan, and the fact that all Western countries refrain from repatriating South Sudanese. In June 2012, the Israeli Interior Minister celebrated the deportations to South Sudan with the following statement to the press:

> In having to choose between being called "enlightened and liberal" but not having a Jewish and Zionist state, and being called 'endarkened and racist' but being a proud citizen, I choose the second option. The era of slogans has ended, now the era of actions has begun (Weiler-Polak 2012a).

Putting aside here the multiple and evident ways in which racism is implicated in the Othering and treatment of non-Jews in Israel (HMW 2012b; Willen 2007), it is clear that institutionally, Israel is not busy with providing refuge to asylum seekers but with detaining and deporting them back as soon as possible. It is also apparent that in the dominant Israeli state discourse, a global human rights regime is posed as being mutually exclusive with a national regime of citizenship rights.

An Eritrean 'Infiltrator' in the Jewish State

I met Simon for the first time outside the *Saharonim* detention camp in the Negev Desert.[7] Simon and three of his friends were escaping the blowing wind inside a sheltered bus station. They came to *Saharonim* to visit their respective detained relatives, who were caught by the Israeli army after crossing the border from Egypt.

Simon's wife and daughter have been detained for a month now, but Simon has not yet been allowed to meet them. Detainees can receive visitors every Thursday, however, there are around 2000 detainees and only a few visitors are allowed in each week.[8] Simon called the *Saharonim* administration to arrange for a meeting with his family, but to no avail. Although he left Tel Aviv at 5 am to be there early on, he never made it inside the camp and after waiting six hours a guard told him to try again in two weeks.

Simon has never seen his daughter Winta. He fled Eritrea when his wife Selam was eight-months pregnant. The Eritrean army called on Simon to join the ranks for what would have been a lifelong military service under the internationally condemned authoritarian Eritrean regime. Refusing obligatory conscription usually leads to arrest and imprisonment. Simon first crossed the border to neighbouring Sudan where he had to pay US$6000 to human smugglers for transporting him across Egypt to the Sinai desert and then over the border to Israel.

After working in Israel 16 hours per day for three years, Simon saved enough money to pay smugglers to bring over his wife and daughter to Israel. The price for such a smuggling operation has steadily increased, and in 2012, it cost up to

US$20,000. Simon could find smugglers who offer their services for less money, but these smugglers were not trustworthy, and the risk was higher that his family would become victims to many of the potential abuses on the journey.

Simon calls Selam and Winta every day on the phone. He speaks softly to his daughter whom he has never met. 'She is angry with me' he tells me, 'she doesn't like it in *Saharonim*. There is nothing for her to do there. She is crying and shouting a lot and is asking all the time why they have to be there. She wants to go back to Eritrea'. Selam was diagnosed with 'something in her stomach', as it was explained to Simon, and she first needs to complete a medical treatment before she can be released. While Simon was told repeatedly by the *Saharonim* administration that his family would soon be released, Salem and Winta eventually remained in detention for 10 months in which Simon showed up in *Saharonim* every Thursday, but was never allowed in.

In the bus station outside *Saharonim*, Simon and his friends are waiting for the bus to take them to south Tel Aviv. I approach them, asking in Hebrew whether they want a hitch to Tel Aviv. They look at me suspiciously; being a white-skin Israeli, I could easily be taken for being a state agent. I tell them that I have been refused entry to the camp and am heading back to Tel Aviv. After some quick whispers, they faintly thank me, and we get into the car. They then ask me how much I will charge them for the ride. I say that this ride is free and explain about my academic work and interest in understanding their situation in Israel. The ride to Tel Aviv is long, and after a while, the four men ease a bit in their seats. They speak Hebrew well and tell me that they were worried to accept my offer because they know of stories about Israeli or Palestinian people who give asylum seekers a ride and then drive to the border with Egypt, threatening to push them back to Egypt unless they pay some money. Some asylum seekers who accepted a ride were also robbed, kidnapped for ransom or killed for their organs. 'Everything can happen to us, you see, and nobody will do anything about it. Nobody will even know about it', Kidane summarises the state of fear underlying their precarious existence in Israel.

Simon who sits in front tells me about his dire life in Eritrea. Simon is very skinny and his eyes are deeply sunk behind pronounced cheekbones. His appearance communicates a combination of fragility and unmistaken determination. His father died in the war with Ethiopia when Simon was a small boy. His mother took care of Simon and his sister with some help from an uncle, who fled to the USA and has been sending her money regularly. When it became clear that Simon could no longer escape military conscription, his mother, although old, unemployed and dependent on Simon, urged him to flee the country. His uncle helped Simon to pay for the smuggling operation to Israel, after it proved to be impossible to get Simon to the USA.

Simon is fluent in Hebrew, which he learned mostly at the different working places where he has been employed. For the past two years, he works in the kitchen of a bohemian restaurant in Tel Aviv. Missing a day of work every week to visit *Saharonim* is very costly for Simon, who desperately needs money for his own subsistence as well as for supporting his mother in Eritrea and for paying US$4000 to an Israeli lawyer who promised to get Salem and Winta out of detention.

The Israeli 'Crystal Night': Racist Incitement and Attacks on 'Infiltrators'

In April 2012, Molotov bottles were thrown into three different houses of asylum seekers in south Tel Aviv. One of the houses was functioning as a crèche for asylum seekers' children. While the perpetrators were not caught, the police believed they were part of a small but growing number of residents who resorted to violent attacks against asylum seekers and their properties.

Two weeks later, Simon and I went to visit the crèche, which is located in a one-story house at a quiet residential street. The burned walls in the small front yard are testimony to what happened there. Inside there are several baby-beds in a middle-sized room and toddlers crawl and play on the floor. Blessing, a 30-year-old Nigerian asylum seeker, who runs the crèche for the last two years, lives in the back room of the house with her husband and two children. She tells us about the traumatic night, while serving the children lunch.

> I want to leave Israel, but I can't go anywhere. I can't go back to Nigeria and I can't get to Europe. I have to stay and work here, but I'm scared. The children are asking me 'when are they going to kill us?' what should I say? I don't know what to say. We used to play in the front yard but they are now afraid to go out. I also try not to go out of my apartment. I do the shopping quickly and come back. I close the door of the crèche and then also the door of my room at the back. If someone rings the bell at night, I don't come to open it'. I ask Blessing whether the arson was preceded by threats from neighbours. 'Not at all. The neighbours were the ones who saw the fire first and came down to stop it and called the fire-fighters and police. I always had a good relationship with them. There were never any problems.

Indeed, since the arrival of thousands of asylum seekers in 2006 and up until early 2012, only a handful of violent incidents were recorded in south Tel Aviv. Importantly, south Tel Aviv has hosted the poor, underclass residents of the city for decades. The area suffers from persistent neglect of its deteriorated public infrastructure and is notorious for the presence of drug dealers and street prostitution. In the 1980s and 1990s, Palestinian collaborators with the Israeli army have been relocated from the Occupied Territories to the neighbourhood. Since the mid-1990s the area has become the 'capital' of undocumented migrants who arrived from countries worldwide in search of a better life (Kalir 2010). The inflow of Eritreans and Sudanese is thus the most recent layer in this overpopulated and underinvested part of the city, where the Israeli inhabitants carry grim grievances against the municipal and national authorities. Given the dire circumstances in which different populations in south Tel Aviv are forced to live and make a living, one might actually point out the impressive calmness that characterises public life in the neighbourhood.

The rise in violent attacks against asylum seekers cannot be seen separately from the rise in the militant and racist rhetoric employed by Israeli officials and politicians. An anti-'infiltrators' rhetoric has characterised the approach of Israeli public figures since the issue first surfaced as a major 'problem'. In 2010, for example, Prime Minister Netanyahu stated that 'infiltrators cause cultural, social and economic damage, and pull us towards the Third World ... [they] threaten to wash away our achievements and damage our existence as a Jewish democratic state' (Goldstein 2010). A few weeks later, the Justice Minister, Yackov Ne'eman, voiced his concern: 'The state of Israel is facing an existential threat in light of infiltrators ... we are hopeful that we will eventually implement legislation ... to protect the residents of Israel from the grave phenomenon of infiltration' (Zitun 2010). The Interior Minister, Eli Yishai, urging parliament to approve a budget for fencing the border with Egypt, proclaimed that 'the fact that only 0.01% of the infiltrators are refugees while the rest are migrant workers poses an existential threat to Israel' (Weiler-Polak 2010).

In May 2012, the rhetoric took on a marked warlike tone. After four Eritrean men were arrested on suspicion of sexually assaulting a 19-year-old Israeli woman, the Interior Minister told a radio station that: 'Most of the African infiltrators are criminals. I would put all of them, without exception, into a prison or other holding facility' (Weiler-Polak 2012a). Only days later, Prime Minister Netanyahu univocally framed the 'problem' in a cabinet meeting: 'This phenomenon of illegal infiltrators from Africa is extremely serious and threatens Israel's social fabric and national security' (Nesher 2012). A day later an anti-'infiltrators' demonstration was organised in south Tel Aviv by national and local politicians in protest against the 'unbearable situation'. Some of the speakers included politicians from non-coalition extreme right parties, like Michael Ben Ari (National Union) who exclaimed: 'For three years women have not been able to go to the market without having their purses stolen. Girls can't play. Young men can't find jobs'. He then led the crowd in chanting 'Sudanese to Sudan'. Yet it was MP Miri Regev from the ruling Likud Party, a former Brigadier General and chief spokesperson of the Israeli army, who inflamed the atmosphere, shouting from the podium at the tempestuous crowd: 'The Sudanese people are a cancer in our body'. Minutes later the crowd started collectively shouting slogans like 'Blacks out' and then many rushed in rage through the streets of south Tel Aviv beating up anyone who looked like an African 'infiltrator' (including some Jewish-Israeli citizens of Ethiopian decent), setting on fire waste bins and throwing bricks and bottles against shops and bars associated with asylum seekers.

Many in Israel were shocked by what some journalists and NGOs called the 'crystal night of refugees in Israel', drawing a provocative reference to the *kristallnacht*, the coordinated pogrom against Jews throughout Nazi Germany on the night of 9 November 1938. The racist pogrom was condemned by many public intellectuals, NGOs and politicians. The chairman of the Israeli social movement Peace Now, Yariv Oppenheimer, asked the Attorney General to launch an investigation against MP Regev and other politicians for racist calls and incitement to violence. In the following days, many activists and concerned citizens initiated all sorts of actions to support asylum seekers, for example, organising anti-racism marches and accompanying asylum seekers' children to schools.

Nevertheless, some politicians, who had previously exercised inflamed rhetoric, appeared unfettered by the events and continued their lashing at 'infiltrators'. One day after the pogrom, MP Danon from the ruling Likud Party posted on his Facebook page: 'Israel is at war. An enemy state of infiltrators was established in Israel, and its capital is south Tel Aviv. The infiltrators are a blow to the state. We must stop, arrest and deport them from Israel before it will be too late'. A week after the pogrom, the Interior Minister was presented with police data, showing that crime rates among 'foreigners' in Israel stood at 2.04% compared with 4.99% among Israelis (and this without controlling statistically for the underclass position and dire situation of most asylum seekers in Israel). In response the Minister charged: 'Many women in Tel-Aviv were raped by [African] foreigners but are afraid to complain [to the police] about it, so that they won't have to deal with the stigma of carrying AIDS' (Yerushalmi 2012). Since the 'crystal night' a few more houses of asylum seekers have been attacked, and many asylum seekers have been beaten up for no reason by racist Israelis on the streets of south Tel Aviv, Jerusalem and other cities (HMW 2012b).

The militant Israeli approach towards asylum seekers is ideologically constructed by Jewish-Israeli politicians who perceive and present asylum seekers as posing an existential threat to Israel. In the following section, I demonstrate how appeals by NGOs to the Jewish history in order to generate compassion towards asylum seekers unwittingly compound militant views among many in Israel.

The Dual Jewish History: National Anxiety and Moral Obligation

Since asylum seekers started reaching Israel, new NGOs have been established and existing NGOs have reoriented their efforts to assist asylum seekers in different ways (see Yaron, Hashimshony-Yaffe, and Campbell 2013). NGOs provide asylum seekers medical care, legal assistance, food and clothes, social care, linguistic and professional training, shelter and many more services that the state fails to secure for them. NGOs also carry the flag when it comes to fighting for an asylum policy that is in line with human rights standards and international conventions to which Israel is signatory. This is being done in multiple ways, including legal appeals to the High Court against anti-'infiltrators' government legislations and police actions, drafting and publishing reports and policy recommendations, collaborating with international NGOs and inter-governmental organisations to pressure Israel to comply with international standards and mobilising a public campaign for the fair treatment of asylum seekers (street demonstrations, newspaper articles, cultural events, public dialogues, etc.).

A discourse of human rights underlies the motivation and ideological orientation of Israeli NGOs working with asylum seekers. However, most NGOs base the rationale, if not the obligation, for their support of asylum seekers on the Jewish history of persecution and the Jewish legacy of morality and humanism. Thus, for example, the mission statement of the 'Hotline for Migrant Workers', a central NGO assisting and campaigning for asylum seekers, reads as follows: 'We see as vital the proper treatment of non-Jews amongst us (...) as part of the humanistic and universal values that Judaism teaches and on which the State was founded'. Moreover, the powerful biblical verse— 'You shall not wrong a stranger or oppress him, for you were strangers in the land of Egypt' (Exodus 22:20)— adorns almost every published report that the NGO produces. When the executive manager of another important NGO, 'African Refugee Development Centre', was selected as one of the 12 Young Israelis of the Year by the Jerusalem Post, a special announcement followed in the yearly report of the NGO, stating that the manager, Nic Schlagman, 'is very much connected to Jewish history and believes that our history obligates Israel to treat those who seek protection within our borders with dignity and respect'.

This sense that the Jewish history commends a moral obligation especially of Jews when it comes to asylum seekers is also found outside Israel. 'Right Now' is a US-based NGO comprised of Jewish Americans. In a petition that called on Israel to stop detaining asylum seekers, it was stated: 'As Jews we know that it is our duty, our obligation, to treat others as we would want to be treated in a foreign land, especially if they are people who have been oppressed, like we were so many times in our long history'.

Even within the militant Israeli political arena, the few politicians who seek to condemn the racial incitement against asylum seekers find themselves falling back on the Jewish history for making their case. After the 'crystal night of refugees in Israel', Yair Lapid, a leading politician from the new liberal, centre-right party *Yesh Atid*, posted on his Facebook page:

> I support the arrest and deportation of infiltrators … however, when I see a pogrom led by inciters like MPs Regev, Danon and Ben Ari, I wonder how they have the nerve to call themselves 'Jews'. They don't understand the meaning of 'Jewish morals' or collective Jewish memory, nor do they understand the meaning of Jewish existence. (Somfalvi 2012)

While Yair Lapid clearly shares the general government militant line against 'infiltrators' but disputes the rhetoric, other MPs, like Dov Hanin from the leftist party *Hadash* who calls for a completely different policy in favour of asylum seekers and against their demonisation, also points to the Jewish history: 'The Jews were refugees themselves, how quickly we forgot our history' (Lior 2010).

While many Jews resist a comparison between the Holocaust and any other genocide, using the Holocaust for generating compassion for the cause of asylum seekers in Israel has at times been a successful, albeit partial and problematic, strategy (Paz 2011; Willen 2010). Yet the invocation of the Jewish history inadvertently reactivates the Israeli 'founding trauma', and it thornily feeds an entrenched sense of fearism among Jewish-Israeli citizens. A poll by the Israel Democracy Institute and Tel Aviv University revealed that 52% of Jewish Israelis agree with the statement made by MP Regev about 'unauthorised Africans' being a cancer in the body of Israel.

Some NGOs activists reflected in interviews with me on the 'strategic limits' of using the Holocaust in public debates and on the unintended ways in which it can inflame such discussions. Yet it is very likely that the 'Holocaust discourse, as a fundamental pillar of the Israeli society, will continue to shape people's interpretive readings and the state's responses to asylum-seekers' (Paz 2011, 14).

In the past two years, protests against asylum seekers have been sporadically held in south Tel Aviv. In these protests people commonly carry posters with slogans that unmistakably communicate their sense of fear, or even anxiety, which are rooted in the historic sense of Jewish victimhood: 'We are scared', 'Israel is no longer our home', 'We became a persecuted minority in our own neighbourhoods', 'It is not racism, it is survival', 'If we won't act, we'll become the aliens'. Another common type of slogans shows much antagonism towards a human rights discourse: 'The UN and human rights tarnish the law in Israel', 'Human rights not on our account'.

Israeli NGOs whose loyalty is perceived to be with asylum seekers rather than the Israeli state are also increasingly being demonised. NGO activists are regularly scolded by politicians and citizens during anti-'infiltrators' protests. Some activists receive hate letters and menacing phone calls, while others have been physically attacked during the 'crystal night' and on other occasions (Weiler-Polak 2012b). The incitement against those who (dare) put human rights before the perceived good of the nation state are condemned publicly, even in the Israeli parliament, as was the case when MP Yulia Shamalov-Berkovitch from the centre party Kadima, charged during a discussion on African asylum seekers that 'All human rights activists should be imprisoned and transported to camps we are building' (Efraim 2012b). She further referred to Israelis who assist asylum seekers as 'hypocrites' that incite and pit Jews against Jews. What we see here is the expansion of fearism to engulf not only the figure of the abject Other but also that of the messenger who delivers the 'bad news' to the sovereign.

Concluding Remarks

The hostile Israeli approach towards asylum seekers is rooted in an ideology of fearism. Asylum seekers have neither been involved in terrorism nor do they pose a risk to the health and personal security of Israeli citizens more than any other subgroup in Israel. Nevertheless, their presence has been defamed and painted in dangerous colours by many Israeli politicians, civil servants and journalists. The pervasive Israeli fearism is rooted in a Zionist narrative that, hinging significantly on the tragic history of Jewish persecution and an entrenched sense of historic victimhood, sacralises the need to protect Israel at all costs from non-Jewish Others. While national security is evoked by many states to justify a move towards the securitisation of migration, Israel has been going to great lengths to frame the presence of asylum seekers as posing an *existential threat* to the Jewish state.

Israeli NGOs that attempt to raise awareness to the plight of asylum seekers are caught discursively between a rock and a hard place. To foster compassion and empathy for asylum seekers, NGOs use the same historic sensitivities ('Never Again') which shrewd politicians employ for cultivating fearism. Referencing the long Jewish history of persecution and of seeking shelter as refugees, NGOs create, unintentionally, a perilous competition around the notion of victimhood. The Israeli national narrative is uncompromising in seeing the injustice that has been done to Jews historically as the justification for a Jewish state that guarantees dignified citizenship primarily for Jews. This unbending commitment of Israel to its Jewish citizens depoliticises the structural injustice that is inflicted on asylum seekers. More specifically, a legalistic universalist discourse of human rights in support of asylum seekers is constructed as operating in a zero-sum fashion with the particularism of securing rights for Jewish-Israeli citizens.

We witness here how the very notion of justice becomes relative for those whose subjectivity has been formed in and out of the political and ideological realm of a particular nation state. For many in Israel, universal justice means for Israel to guarantee the rights of Jews in a way that allegedly has never been achieved elsewhere in the world. For many others, mostly outside Israel, universal justice means for Israel to provide shelter to those who are currently escaping persecution.

Yet if the historic victimhood of Jews was sufficient to justify the exclusionary Israeli policy towards non-Jewish asylum seekers, then why do Israeli politicians invest so much in dehumanising and demonising the figure of the asylum seeker as a dangerous 'infiltrator'? Why is there a need for creating this abject phantasm out of the Other? In approximating an answer to these questions, I take my cue from Coutin (2014) who urges us to consider 'what investments, whether material or psychological, require stigmatized others in order to exist?' In Israel, the fantasy of the dangerous abject Other who allegedly threatens the existence of the Jewish state is necessary in maintaining another fantasy: that which proclaims Israel as the only safe haven for Jews in the world. This fantasy, which is at the base of the Israeli production of fearism, consequentially justifies exclusionary politics and an enormous material investment in a mighty military apparatus.

While the Israeli case study certainly has its particularities, there is a lesson here for other societies that currently experience two not unrelated social dynamic: the retraction of the 'caring state' and the increased presence of asylum seekers and undesired Others. In such cases, states are poised to nurish and sustain the fantasy of the dangerous Other, as they stand to gain threefold: economically, by rendering the Other deportable and evermore exploitable in the national labour market; politically, by justifying investments in the state apparatus and by appearing, even if only symbolically, as 'acting though' and protecting the nation; and ideologically, by distracting attention from the increasingly precarious position of many citizens who, in comparison with the abject Other, can still console themselves as privileged members of the state.

Notes

[1]   Multiple factors have led to an increased number of African asylum seekers reaching Israel since 2006: an Egyptian crackdown on asylum seekers in 2006 pushed many of them to Israel; before the heavy fencing of the border in 2012, crossing from Egypt to Israel was relatively easy; a burgeoning smuggling network, mostly operated by Bedouins, rendered this route popular and initially also cheap in comparison to routes taking asylum seekers to Europe; Sudanese and Eritrean asylum seekers in Israel sent money and know-how to their relatives and friends, encouraging them to come to Israel.

[2]   All translations from Hebrew to English are mine.

[3]   According to the Israeli records, out of 58,088 'infiltrators', 56.46% are Eritreans and 25.91% Sudanese (Israeli Ministry of Interior 2012). Notably, the word 'infiltrators' appears in the original government document.

[4]   See 'Recommendations to the government of Israel', November 2012. Available at: http://www.asylumseekers.org/uploads/4/7/0/6/4706099/recommendations_to_the_goi.pdf

[5]   Idem.

[6]   Although asylum applications of Sudanese are not processed by the RSD, in 2007 Israel decided, exceptionally, to grant temporary residency to 452 people from Darfur (ACRI 2009).

[7]   My research on the situation of asylum seekers from Africa is part of more than a decade-long ethnographic research on the lives of non-Jewish migrants in Israel. Gathering data for this article was done during five short fieldwork stints, each of around two weeks, conducted from February 2012 until June 2013.

[8]   In 2013, around 2000 African nationals were held in detention, of which around 1100 were Eritreans and 600 were Sudanese; about 1750 were held under the anti-'infiltration' bill. Most detainees are in Saharonim: 1630 altogether (1416 men, 203 women and 11 children; HRW 2013; Lior 2013).

References

ACRI. 2009. "Asylum Seekers and Refugees in Israel: August 2009 Update." http://www.acri.org.il/pdf/refugees0809en.pdf.

Agamben, G. 1994. *We Refugees*. Translated by M. Rocke. www.egs.edu/faculty/Agamben/agamben-we-refugees.html.

Andreas, P., and T. Snyder. 2003. *The Wall Around the West: State Borders and Immigration Controls in North America and Europe*. Lanham: Rowman and Littlefield.

Arendt, H. 1951. *The Origins of Totalitarianism*. New York: Harcourt Brace.

Baldaccini, A., E. Guild, and H. Toner. 2007. *Whose Freedom, Security and Justice? EU Immigration and Asylum Law and Policy*. Oxford: Hart.

Balibar, E. 2002. *Politics and the Other Scene*. London: Verso Books.

Basaran, T. 2008. "Security, Law, Borders: Spaces of Exclusion." *International Political Sociology* 2 (4): 339–354. doi:10.1111/j.1749-5687.2008.00055.x.

Bauman, Z. 2006. *Liquid Fear*. Cambridge: Polity.

Berezin, M. 2009. *Illiberal Politics in Neoliberal Times: Culture, Security and Populism in the New Europe*. Cambridge: Cambridge University Press.

Bigo, D. 2002. "Security and Immigration: Toward a Critique of the Governmentality of Unease." *Alternatives* 27 (1): 63–92.

Chavez, L. 2008. *The Latino Threat: Constructing Immigrants, Citizens, and the Nation*. Palo Alto, CA: Stanford University Press.

Coutin, S. B. 2014. "Deportation Studies: Origins, Themes, and Directions." *Journal of Ethnic and Migration Studies* 41 (4): 671–681. doi:10.1080/1369183X.2014.957175.

De Genova, N. P. 2002. "Migrant 'Illegality' and Deportability in Everyday Life." *Annual review of Anthropology* 31: 419–447. doi:10.1146/annurev.anthro.31.040402.085432.

Efraim, O. 2012a. "Infiltrators Imprisonment Plan Unrealistic." *Ynet*, July 4.

Efraim, O. 2012b. "Kadima MK: Send Human-rights Activists to Prison Camps." *Ynet*, May 29.

Efraim, O. 2013. "Israel to Deport African Migrants to Uganda." *Ynet*, August 29.

Feldinger, L. G. 2012. "Seeking Asylum? No Spirit of Geneva Here." *Haaretz*, September 30.

Fisher, R. M. 2006. "Invoking 'Fear' Studies." *Journal of Curriculum Theorizing* 22 (4): 39–71.

Goldstein, T. 2010. "PM: Infiltrators Pull Us towards Third World." *Ynet*, January 21.

HMW. 2012a "Until Our Hearts Are Completely Hardened: Asylum Procedures in Israel." http://www.hotline.org.il/english/pdf/asylum_procedures_2012_eng.pdf.

HMW. 2012b. "'Cancer in Our Body': On Racial Incitement, Discrimination and Hate Crimes against African Asylum-seekers in Israel." http://www.hotline.org.il/english/pdf/Incitemen tReport_English.pdf.

HMW. 2014 "'From One Prison to Another': Holot Detention Facility." http://hotline.org.il/en/ publication/holotreporteng/.

HRW. 2013. "Israel: Detained Asylum-seekers Pressured to Leave." http://www.hrw.org/news/2013/ 03/13/israel-detained-asylum-seekers-pressured-leave.

Isin, E. 2000. *Democracy, Citizenship and the Global City*. New York: Routledge.

Israeli Ministry of Interior. 2012. *Data on Foreigners in Israel*. (Hebrew). http://piba.gov.il/ PublicationAndTender/ForeignWorkersStat/Documents/mer2012.pdf.

Jacobson, D. 1996. *Rights Across Borders: Immigration and the Decline of Citizenship*. Baltimore: Johns Hopkins University Press.

Joppke, C. 1998. *Challenge to the Nation State, Immigration in Western Europe and the United States*. Oxford: Oxford University Press. doi:10.1093/0198292295.001.0001.

Kalir, B. 2010. *Latino Migrants in the Jewish State: Undocumented Lives in Israel*. Bloomington: Indiana University Press.

Kalir, B. 2012. "Illegality Rules: Migrant Workers Caught Up in the Illegal but Licit Operations of Labour Migration Regime." In *Transnational Flows and Permissive Polities: Ethnographies of Human Mobilities in Asia*, edited by B. Kalir and M. Sur, 27–54. Amsterdam: Amsterdam University Press.

Kapur, R. 2003. "The 'Other' Side of Globalization: The Legal Regulation of Cross-Border Movements." *Canadian Women's Studies* 22 (3–4): 6–15.

Kemp, A. 2004. "Labour Migration and Racialisation: Labour Market Mechanisms and Labour Migration Control Policies in Israel." *Social Identities* 10 (2): 267–292. doi:10.1080/1350 463042000227380.

Kristeva, J. 1993. *Nations without Nationalism*. New York: Columbia University Press.

LaCapra, D. 2001. *Writing History, Writing Trauma*. Baltimore: John Hopkins University Press.

Lior, I. 2010. "Thousands in Tel-Aviv Protest Plan for Refugee Detention Facility." *Haaretz*, December 24.

Lior, I. 2013. "Israel Admits Asylum Bid Filed by Africans Still Pending, Despite Vowing 'Swift' Review." *Haaretz*, May 29.

Nesher, T. 2012. "Netanyahu: Israel could be Overrun by African Infiltrators." *Haaretz*, May 21.

Nesher, T. 2013. "From 14.000 Applications in 4 years, only 22 People Recognized as Refugees." *Haaretz*, February 13.

Newman, D. 2000. "Citizenship, Identity and Location: The Changing Discourse of Israeli Geopolitics." In *Geopolitical Traditions: A Century of Geopolitical Thought*, edited by K. Dodds and D. Atkinson, 302–331. London: Routledge.

Nyers, P. 2003. "Abject Cosmopolitanism: The Politics of Protection in the Anti-deportation Movement." *Third World Quarterly* 24 (6): 1069–1093. doi:10.1080/01436590310001630071.

Pace, M. 2010. "The European Union, Security and the Southern Dimension." *European Security* 19 (3): 431–444. doi:10.1080/09662839.2010.534462.

Paz, J. 2011. "Ordered Disorder: African Asylum-Seekers in Israel and Discursive Challenges to an Emerging Refugee Regime." *New Issues in refugee Research*, Research Paper No. 205. UNHCR: Geneva.

Ram, U. 1998. "Citizens, Consumers and Believers: The Israeli Public Sphere between Capitalism and Fundamentalism." *Israel Studies* 3 (1): 24–44. doi:10.2979/ISR.1998.3.1.24.

Somfalvi, A. 2012. "Lapid: Rightist MKs Don't Understand Jewish Morality." *Ynet*, May 24.

Soysal, Y. N. 1994. *Limits of Citizenship: Migrants and Postnational Membership in Europe*. Chicago: University of Chicago Press.

Ticktin, M. 2006. "Where Ethics and Politics Meet." *American Ethnologist* 33 (1): 33–49. doi:10.1525/ae.2006.33.1.33.

UNHCR. 2011. *Statistical Yearbook.* http://www.unhcr.org/globaltrends/2011-GlobalTrends-ann ex-tables.zip.

Wacquant, L. 2010. "Crafting the Neoliberal State: Workfare, Prisonfare and Social Insecurity." *Sociological Forum* 25: 197–220.

Weiler-Polak, D. 2010. "Eli Yishai: Infiltrators Pose Existential Threat to Israel." *Haaretz,* October 22.

Weiler-Polak, D. 2012a. "Increasing Worries among Migrants: 'Afraid to Get Out of Our House.'" *Haaretz,* June 11.

Weiler-Polak, D. 2012b. "Threats Made against South Tel-Aviv Aid Workers after Yishai Remarks." *Haaretz,* May 17.

Willen, S. S. 2007. "Toward a Critical Phenomenology of 'Illegality' : State Power, Criminalization, and Abjectivity among Undocumented Migrant Workers in Tel Aviv, Israel." *International Migration* 45 (3): 8–38. doi:10.1111/j.1468-2435.2007.00409.x.

Willen, S. 2010. "Darfur through a Shoah Lens: Sudanese Asylum-seekers, Unruly Biopolitical Dramas, and the Politics of Humanitarian Compassion in Israel." In *A Reader in Medical Anthropology,* edited by B. Good, M. Delvecchio, S. Willen, and M. Fischer, 505–521. Malden, MA: Blackwell.

Wurgaft, N. 2006. "Israel Is a Wonderful Country for Refugees. In Theory." *Haaretz,* May 22.

Wurgaft, N. 2009. "The New Refugee Status Determination Unit Starts Its Work." *Haaretz,* June 19.

Wurgaft, N. 2012. "The Lies That Inflame Baseless Hatred in Israel." *Haaretz,* May 28.

Yaron, H., N. Hashimshony-Yaffe, and J. Campbell. 2013. "'Infiltrators'or Refugees? An Analysis of Israel's Policy towards African Asylum-Seekers." *International Migration* 51: 144–157. doi:10.1111/imig.12070.

Yerushalmi, S. 2012. It's Us or Them. *Maariv,* June 1.

Yiftachel, O. 2006. *Ethnocracy: Land and Identity Politics in Israel/Palestine.* Philadelphia: University of Pennsylvania Press.

Zembylas, M. 2010. "Agamben's Theory of Biopower and Immigrants/Refugees/Asylum-seekers: Discourses of Citizenship and the Implications for Curriculum Theorizing." *Journal of Curriculum Theorizing* 26 (2): 31–45.

Zitun, Y. 2010. "Justice Minister: Illegal Aliens Existential Threat." *Ynet,* September 2.

The Management of Anxiety.
An Ethnographical Outlook on
Self-mutilations in a French Immigration
Detention Centre

Nicolas Fischer

This contribution examines the management of self-mutilations of detained immigrants awaiting deportation in French immigration detention centres. Drawing on ethnographic data, it analyses the struggles opposing members of detention staff over the prevention of self-inflicted wounds and the regulation of immigrant anxiety. They unfold around a contradiction: detention centres are not only a violent police institution, but also a 'humanitarian' realm, where extreme suffering calls for immediate relief. I first describe the 'risk assessment system' organised inside the detention centre to prevent mutilations through medical expertise. I then focus on practical dilemmas faced by Human Rights advocates operating inside detention centres.

In April 2005, a young Rumanian awaiting deportation in the French detention centre of Le Sernans locked himself in his bedroom on the day he was to be forcibly boarded on a flight to Bucharest, and deliberately wounded his hand. He was finally arrested by a team of eight policemen but kept screaming and struggling to escape them. He nonetheless received emergency care from the local medical staff who bandaged his cuts, but the police officer leading the day's escorts to the airport refused to take him, fearing his condition might lead to a stroke or heart attack. As a result, the young man was not boarded on the flight—but he was put in police custody and prosecuted for having intended to avoid deportation, a misdemeanour that could cost him a few months in prison (Fieldnotes, 26 April 2005).

Nicolas Fischer is a tenured researcher at the Centre de recherches sociologiques sur le droit et les institutions pénales (CESDIP), Université de Versailles Saint-Quentin, Guyancourt, France.

This case I personally witnessed while doing fieldwork in immigration detention highlights the paradoxical dimension of this institution. Detention centres have been officially used since 1981 in France, to lock up foreign nationals who face deportation, either for being unauthorised immigrants or because they committed a criminal offence on the French territory. On the one hand, these centres obviously are repressive devices: although they are not formally penal, they confine detainees for a maximum of 45 days, and keep them under close watch until they are either set free on the French territory, of boarded forcibly on a flight to their country of origin. From deprivation of freedom and sometimes poor sanitary conditions to forced removal, these police-run locations are thus designed to enforce a variety of physical constraints and degradations on the detainees—as reminded by the brutal arrest of the young Rumanian. On the other hand, this case however points at another dimension of the 'physical' policing of detained immigrants: while being objects of restraint, they remain eligible for a basic but effective protection of their physical integrity. Whether it is intended or accidental, any serious injury is then supposed to be treated—as was the case for the young man's wound. His case hints as well to the legal and political issues behind this concern: immigrant repression here is not illegitimate per se—it is at the core of the policemen's mission—but it happens in a democratic realm where protective legal provisions exist, and may be actually enforced by a set of state and non-state actors. As the police official of the centre argues, a serious medical problem in detention may then result in a variety of complications—administrative investigation, legal action or activist contention against possible police brutality and the quality of police 'management' of the detained population. The conclusion of the case however brings repression back in: the young man's action is indeed legally qualified as a rebellion against his deportation order, and penalty sanctioned as such.

In this contribution, I will further analyse the paradoxical logics of this body repression *and* protection inside French immigration detention centres (known as *Centres de rétention administrative*), and focusing on the same issue of self-inflicted mutilations by detainees.[1] These rather common situations are indeed occasions to witness the collective management of detainee physical integrity inside those centres: problems of self-mutilations are indeed addressed by police officers, but they are also debated and taken care of by other teams of the detention staff—notably medical practitioners, social workers and independent lawyers.

By analysing this peculiar logic of population management, I wish to contribute more broadly to two fields of research. First, I focus on the contemporary debates over immigrant 'camps', which are now described by a growing literature as the sign of a contemporary turn to 'exceptional' immigration policies (Bigo and Tsoukala 2006; Diken and Laustsen 2005). Drawing on Agamben's (1998) classical definition of the camp as the territory where 'exception is the rule', confinement places dedicated to immigration control have thus been described as locations where immigrants, being set aside as unwanted non-citizens (as opposed to penal convicts being jailed after a criminal offence) are still *inside* the French territory, but already *outside* the state legal and political order. Literally stripped of all political relevance or legal protection, they are reduced to the condition of a 'bare life' and thus exposed to unchecked, violent police treatment. Agamben's perspective thus draws on Foucault's analysis on the importance of biopower—e.g. power relations which object is life in its mere biological dimension—and biopolicies—the state administration of this life, declined in a set of public programmes dedicated to the medical, social or humanitarian 'government' of populations (Foucault 2003, 2008). In Agamben's work however, the diversity of contemporary biopolitics in democracies is reduced to one single form of body control—the exceptional use of force over a highly vulnerable body.

Describing the treatment of self-mutilations in French detention centres, I challenge this perspective by first drawing on the work of Didier Fassin (Fassin and Rechtman 2009) and Miriam Ticktin (2006, 2011) to consider that 'bare life' in contemporary France, far from being merely vulnerable, is actually eligible *as such* for a particular form of state protection. Ticktin thus shows how 'humanitarianism'— e.g. the particular concern over body suffering and the moral obligation to immediately relieve it from its pain—is no longer a mere ethical issue but is at the core of contemporary immigration policies, leading for example to granting a residence permit to immigrants infected with a serious disease, or suffering trauma due to various forms of violence or exploitation. To borrow Fassin's concept, the exposed body in France—and more broadly, in a democratic realm—is bearing per se a 'bio-legitimacy' (*bio-légitimité*) which urges state authorities to intervene, relieve physical or psychological suffering, and provide protection whenever a humanitarian emergency is detected (Fassin 2001). Since humanitarian concerns compel the state to provide suffering immigrants with some kind of protection, they are not only central to immigration policies, but they can also be used by opponents or immigrants themselves to create political pressure over state authorities. On the French case, Johanna Siméant (1998, 2009) showed for example how unauthorised immigrants who went on hunger strike deliberately exposed their suffering body and took important risks for themselves in order to obtain a residence permit.

To summarise—quoting again from Fassin (2005a) —contemporary democracies are caught in a major tension between a logic of repression of unauthorised immigration, leading to both deportation of unauthorised immigrants and institutional protection for those of the migrants who are seen as 'vulnerable'. This political relevance of humanitarian concerns in the middle of an otherwise repressive policy brings a crucial objection to Agamben's perspective, if we examine how it affects French immigration detention centres from the inside. In this context, the tension between repression and protection of immigrants is radicalised: detained immigrants are both locked up to be forcibly deported *and* entitled to basic protection of their physical integrity while they are still on the French territory. They can be described as both remote *and* close to nationals, 'since their origin keeps them away, but their residency brings them closer; since they come from abroad, but [still] live here' (Fassin 2005b, 43, *my translation*).

The tension that will be analysed here is thus specific to the case of democracies where, as in France, immigration control is mixed with the political and legal imperative to protect bodies from 'intolerable' suffering, even when these bodies belong to 'abject' individuals (Nyers 2003). As previously hinted, referring to a 'democratic' social and political realm in this case does not only mean that this humanitarian concern exists, but it also implies that this particular political contexts includes non-state actors—Human Rights advocates, politically concerned lawyers, physicians—whose relations to courts and state officials enables them to draw on such a concern to discuss the legitimacy of deportation orders, and effectively influence the enforcement of deportations. This description not only applies to the French case, but it also characterises other democratic states, although legal systems and political organisations may differ (*see* Ellermann 2009, *and for cases inside and outside Europe*, Hasselberg 2014).

In this context, the particular situation of immigration detention makes the political logics of 'humanitarianism' even more complex inside the centres. First, the combination of repression and protection supposes that the detention staff includes other actors than police officers: if all centres are indeed run by the police, their organisation also requires the presence of state medical practitioners and civil servants, as well as independent lawyers from a Human Rights organisation. As I will show, these actors are in charge of enforcing the repressive control or the care and protection of detainees, according to their official mission and a correspondent professional ethos. Second, these professionals can not only coordinate their activities in the ordinary course of detention, but they can also confront each other in problematic or emergency cases—such as cases of self-mutilations—where the police repression and medical or legal protection of the detainee may suddenly be at odds.

In such cases, detention centres appear as scenes of intense and heated debates over the qualification and treatment of deliberate injuries: as violation of the detainees' physical integrity, they have to be cared for by dedicated professionals while they are still under the responsibility of French authorities. However, these injuries are unavoidably disruptions of the general control detention officials are supposed to keep over the detainees: detention centres in themselves are designed to exercise physical force on the confined immigrants in order to deport them and, in the meantime, they are organised to keep this population disciplined, and make it manageable and available for future removal. In this environment, a physical injury not only calls for medical relief, but it also produces an undisciplined body: it can then be strategically used by detainees in order to avoid detention, but on the police's side, it may be seen as a form of subversion, and as such it should be repressed, possibly prosecuted and above all prevented. As I will show, these situations lead to complex debates were protection and repression logics can sometimes become entangled, and were members of the detention staff may have trouble defining the right response and their own position on the case.

Such a statement tends to complexify the 'Agambenian' vision of the camp as a place where the uncontrolled use of force is the only form of treatment experienced by immigrants: detention centres are indeed repressive devices, but this use of force is paradoxically combined with official policies of medical care and protection—in a complex set of biopolicies that may not be reduced to the exceptional violence associated with Agamben's definition of camps.

This remark also brings me to the second field of research I wish to contribute to, on the sociology of emotions and, in that case, of the production and management of anxiety in the centre. As I have just noted, French detention centres are places where the tension between repression and protection of the immigrants is part of the very organisation of the institution, bringing all actors involved—whether the detainees or the members of the staff in charge of managing the centre—to experience a series of contradictions in the way they are treated or in the way they should treat others or respond to a situation. This situation not only provokes moral concern and indignation according to each of those actors' individual sense of justice, but it also leads them to feel a variety of intense emotions among which anxiety is the most important.

To analyse these emotional issues, I draw on the growing literature on the social dimension of emotions (Hochschild 1979; Lutz and White 1986; Turner and Stets 2006). Far from seeing them as mere biological reflexes, these works consider emotions as collective phenomenons provoked, shared or oriented through social processes that are all specific to a certain context. Although various authors have described some of these processes, fewer works have focused on the influence of structural—or in my case, of institutional and organisational—conditions on the production and control of certain types of emotions (see Turner and Stets 2006). A series of studies have described the subversive use of self-mutilations, especially hunger strikes, in detention places (Kiely 2004; Smyth 1987; Sneed and Stonecipher 1989), however focusing on their strategic dimension for the strikers themselves and on the general public emotion over their case. Fewer works have examined the management of these spectacular actions by detention employees, and the control it involves over emotional reactions. On this side, Mark Graham (2002) has notably analysed how the organisation of street-level bureaucracy emotionally impacted the subjectivity of civil servants; while other studies on prison wardens focus on their peculiar position as actors specialised in both the care and surveillance of the detainees, who are daily placed in close contact with them, and who thus regularly have to deal with their distress (Crawley 2011; Liebling and Maruna 2005). An intense 'emotion work' is thus necessary for these actors to curb their affective reactions and adapt them to the behaviour that is required by their institutional role (Hochschild 1979).

Whether they are policemen, nurses or NGO lawyers, members of the detention staff experience rather similar emotional problems when facing detainee self-mutilations. They too are professionals in daily contact with detainees, who collectively discuss the treatment and prevention of self-injuries according to their professional ethos, and whose reactions are then informed by their personal background and the specific professional expertise they can claim on immigrants and detention. In doing this job of assessment and control of self-injuries, they too have to manage emotions, at two distinct levels.

First, as we will see, the assumed anxiety of the detainees is in itself an object of knowledge, of debate and of control: it is a central and controversial issue for all members of the detention staff, whether they have to manage an actual self-mutilation, assess its gravity and collectively decide of the best way to deal with it; or even more when their goal is to prevent self-inflicted wounds. But these situations are also the source of sometimes intense emotions among members of the staff themselves: in this case, anxiety is the result of an institutionally produced contradiction between the professionals' ethos—their conception of their work and the values associated with it—and a situation where humanitarian concerns may require compromises or cooperation with professionals with opposed missions, with paradoxical choices were, for example, accurate protection can only be achieved through repression and the use of force on the immigrant. The second issue is then the management of their own anxiety and emotional reactions by those professionals.

To clarify these issues, I will start by describing the context of immigration detention, insisting on the progressive rise of a concern over immigrant self-mutilation, and the institutionalisation of mechanisms designed to detect and control deliberate injuries. I will then draw on ethnographical data to describe a few of the emotional issues that arise in the everyday enforcement of mutilation prevention and management in detention. I will particularly focus on the peculiar position of independent lawyers from Human Rights organisation Cimade,[2] whose members have been present inside detention centres since 1984.

Organising Repression and Adding Protection: The Development of Immigration Detention in France

Since its official creation in 1981, immigration detention provides a striking example of the tension I was previously referring to: within 30 years, it has turned from a previously small-scale practice to a fully developed, wide-range institution—25 *Centres de rétention administrative* are currently on duty in France, with a maximum capacity of 140 detainees each, and a maximal detention time of 45 days. This dynamics of institutionalisation however implied an increased organisation and monitoring of the conditions of detention. As border control in general, this task is now a collective one involving many state and non-state experts, in a complex use of legal provisions that may repress or protect unauthorised immigrants. Throughout this evolution, instruments of repression and protection of detained immigrants have been combined—each development of confinement practices being seconded by a new addition of legal provisions or 'humanitarian' measures. In this series of transformations, the imperative of preserving the detainee's physical integrity has been a major issue.

Immigration control in France has long been limited to a discretionary policing of immigrants (Lewis 2007). From the early 1970s on, these repressive practices were nonetheless caught in a renewed social, political and legal environment. First, bureaucratic practices were increasingly constrained by an ever-developing national and European legal framework. The main result of this shift was the progressive emergence of an immigration law where mere discretionary power had prevailed. Second, this legal evolution was both a cause and a result of the unexpected intervention of two new sets of actors in immigration control—Human Rights advocates and legal practitioners (Israël 2009).

The global tendency towards more repression of unauthorised immigration was then confronted with an apparently contradictory trend towards more legal protection for immigrants regardless of their legal or social condition, in the name of the 'principles of the Rule of Law' (Joppke 1998). The transformation of immigration detention since the 1970s exactly reflects this tension, but shows as well how repression and protection could finally be combined in a single institution. Throughout this decade, the common police practice of locking up deportable immigrants in informal facilities indeed became subject to intense public contention, forcing state authorities not only to make detention centres legal in 1981, but also to make them perennial, specialised and finally monitored institutions.

As early as 1984, members of Human Rights organisation Cimade passed an agreement with the French Government and started a permanent presence inside detention centres, to officially provide the detainees with legal counsel, and to ensure public monitoring of detention (Fischer 2014). Detention centres now include other professionals: social workers, and a medical staff (mostly nurses attached to the local hospital) who run a small infirmary for everyday care, and notably examine detainees whose condition may prove to be incompatible with detention and require an evacuation to the closest hospital. This last process was involved in the management of self-mutilation in detention—as will become clear in the case of the detention centre I surveyed.

Controlling and Protecting Bodies in a French Detention Centre

In the spring and summer of 2005, I carried out fieldwork in the detention centre of *Le Sernans-Bréville*, located next to the main runways of the international airport of a major French city.[3] This centre was then one of the largest in France, receiving up to 140 detainees at a time, with an occupation rate of more than 80% each year. These characteristics have made Le Sernans an interesting scene for observing of the daily management of deportation.

Centring my research on the tension between repression and protection in the everyday management of the centre lead me to focus on the work of the independent lawyers from Cimade. I then obtained an authorization from the *Préfet* (the local government authority) and was able to access the centre for a five-month period, as a searcher associated with the local team of lawyers. This status allowed me to share the daily life of this team, and of other non-police professionals—nurses, social workers, agents from the Penitentiary who ran the housing services—who worked inside the detainee zone (the main detention zone, where the everyday life of the detainees unfolded—*see below*). My main observation site was the central building of this zone, where all these actors had their offices and joined everyday to take their meals and share moments of rest. While observing the routine interactions between these professionals, I was also able to observe the interviews Cimade lawyers performed with 30–35 detainees each day. I was also able to accompany them on their common tours around the centre, make stations of various length in common parts of the area—such as the mess room or the recreation hall—and interact with the detainees. I completed these observations with in-site interviews with all Cimade lawyers and some of the social workers and nurses.

My focus and conditions of entry however did include some material restrictions: being associated with the Cimade team, I was allowed to accompany them inside the police zone[4]—the second zone located at the gate of the centre, and were police officers had their headquarters—but I was not allowed to remain in the area. This association also implied a set of issues, both methodological—I had to find the proper distance while observing professionals who shared my age, background and political opinions—and ethical—I had to be careful not to divulge information that could prove harmful for either these lawyers or the detainees.

To analyse the management of self-mutilations in this context, I will first briefly describe how the material organisation of the centre socially produced the legal and geographical border between deportable and non-deportable immigrant bodies. I will then turn to the issue of self-inflicted injuries in this particular realm.

Keeping Detained Bodies under Control

Immigration detention can be shortly summarised as an institution that puts bodies under police control by locking them up and keeping them under constant watch. But it can be described as well as an institution of care, were the detainees may and should have access to medical attention from certified professionals, and where serious sanitary problems have to be avoided at all costs—both to preserve public order, and because the material conditions of detention are a constant object of concern for all members of the staff.

At Le Sernans, this tension was inscribed in the organisation of the centre and in its division in two zones. Each newcoming detainee first entered the police zone, and had to go through the single-storey administration building where deportation files were being processed. While progressing through the corridor of this building, immigrants were socially turned into detainees through a series of legal and physical operations. On the left side of the corridor, their deportation file—their legal status—was being processed: police officers checked their official identity, their orders of deportation and the possible legal action taken against them and finally whether they owned a passport or if a consulate-issued pass was required. Computer processing of this information made it possible to follow each case, and add every new development of the process thus dragging unauthorised immigrants out of the social condition of 'nonexistence' they experienced before their arrest (Coutin 2000), and reaffirming state monopoly over the allocation of legal identity and the ability to travel (Torpey 2000). This legal takeover was combined with physical control, performed on the right side of the corridor. Here detainees were submitted to a degradation ceremony (Goffman 1961) and neutralised as bodies: they were searched for any dangerous object, medically checked for contagious illnesses, and finally deprived of most of their personal belongings.[5] While the connections they possessed with their former lives and social identities were thus being severed or put under police control, they were then produced as literally neutralised, harmless and disciplined bodies.

This 'neutralisation' of immigrants as physical bodies authorised their transfer to the detainee zone, where its effects had to be kept unaltered while allowing for the detainees' everyday life to unfold. As a result, the police control of the zone was effective but could remain a distant one. Its goal was to keep detainees constantly visible and physically available for police action. Freedom of movement could then exist in the detainee zone, while being remotely followed by the police: located in a huge outdoor square closed by a double fence of barbed wire, this zone was not supposed to be entered by police officers in ordinary circumstances, but was permanently checked through a network of cameras while its external limit was patrolled and screened from watchtowers. Inside the zone, free circulation enabled detainees to walk in and out of the six single-storey buildings were their bedrooms were located, and to access in turn the administration building where the different forms of relief were concentrated: a dozen employees from the Penitentiary (now replaced by private contractors) managing housing, five social workers, five lawyers from Cimade present two at a time everyday and four nurses from the nearest hospital.

The general organisation of the centre was thus based on a complex logic: the everyday policing of the detainees consisted in an ever-present but remote control rarely involving the use of physical force—and combined with a more humanitarian concern materialised by the presence of various forms of relief, including medical care. This combination was initially imposed by the immigration detention's legal framework, but inside Le Sernans it first relied on the material setting of the two zones—a topographic organisation which enhanced the division of labour and professional roles between members of the detention staff. While police officers were clearly in charge of maintaining order and organising deportations, the medical, social and legal actors gathered inside the administration building in the detainee zone had developed a common identity: being generally devoted to different forms of relief for the detainees, they commonly saw themselves as being 'on their side' and 'closer' to their needs and situation, as opposed to police officers seen as mostly repressive agents. This collective vision was anchored in the spatial division of the centre—police officers being sometimes referred to as 'those of [the zone] over there', while their unannounced appearance inside the administration building was considered as an unnecessary and disturbing 'intrusion'.

In the day-to-day enforcement of detention however, both zones daily communicated and exchanged information, through routine official or informal contacts.

This implies that members of the staff, whatever their disagreements, all shared a common practical interest in maintaining an overall peaceful order inside Le Sernans. By subverting this order and raising complex humanitarian issues, cases of self-mutilations disrupted this stable distribution of roles and positions—and generated concern over the management not only of immigrant but also of staff anxiety.

Anxiety and Suffering as an Issue for Control and Subversion inside the Center

In the context I have just described, the outbreak of self-mutilations opened an emergency situation, upsetting the routinised enforcement of detention and reviving the tension between repression and protection. First of all, it removed a body from this institutionalised order designed both to control and relieve it. In the case of Le Sernans, this lead all professionals of the centre's staff to locally agree on a procedure designed to prevent deliberate injuries by assessing the emotional condition of the detainees—thus converting it into an issue for the management of the centre. In the following section, I will first analyse the particular history of this agreement. I will then describe actual cases of self-mutilations I witnessed, and analyse how these cases upset the routinised enforcement of detention, sparking off a series of emotional debates among the staff over the proper qualification and response to such radical acts.

Preventing Injuries by Assessing Immigrant Anxiety

When I started my research at Le Sernans, debates on self-mutilation already had a local history that was directly related to Cimade lawyers' access to police information inside the centre and its consequences on immigrant anxiety: while police officers held that the disclosure of information on the effective enforcement of deportations could create emotional stress and spark off immigrant mutilations, lawyers argued on the contrary that the withdrawal of information abandoned the detainees to anxious uncertainty and was the main reason for self-inflicted wounds. In 2000, a local agreement was found: Cimade lawyers enjoyed free access to the police files, except for immigrants who were 'presenting a risk of self-mutilation', and for whom an 'emergency procedure' had to enable police officers, Cimade lawyers and members of the medical staff to determine 'the type of information to be disclosed and the proper psychological attention required by the case' (Cimade 2001, 128, *my translation*).

Although this coordinated procedure was not always followed, this collective negotiation granted a social reality to the psychological and emotional state of the detainees and made them relevant in terms of policing of the centre. This peculiar management of 'psychological attention' also unveils the problematic status of the detainees' anxiety and of its control: as the main alleged cause of self-mutilations, anxiety had to be treated from a humanitarian point of view, in order to prevent serious injuries. But as such, it was also a way for police forces to regain control over a undisciplined body: self-mutilation indeed withdraws the body from the common order of immigration detention, where a minimal physical participation of the detained to their own confinement is required no matter how closely they are watched over—detainees have to agree with a logic that not only neutralises them but also keeps them healthy enough to be eventually deported. The deliberate exposure of their own lives then becomes the one form of subversion that seems barely avoidable—and the management of the immigrants' psychology and intimate emotions, a way to turn their self-destructing spirit into a controllable object.

The tension between a logic of control and repression, and another of humanitarian relief and protection, was thus reproduced over the body and its alleged emotional condition. The procedure for preventing mutilations I have just described however remained part of the general organisation of the centre. When self-mutilations actually occurred in *Le Sernans* however, the human and emotional dimensions of each case questioned the very division of labour and roles among the centre staff, creating professional ethical dilemmas that forced some of its members into managing their own anxiety.

Professional and Personal Conflicts over Suffering Detainees

In spite of preventive measures, a few cases of deliberate self-injuries occurred inside Le Sernans at the time of my observations. In those cases, the treatment of the injured body became the actual object of a struggle inside the centre. Its first strategic use concerned the detainees themselves—since deliberately self-inflicted wounds could be a way to avoid deportation by escaping all physical police control, and force the centre's staff into a humanitarian emergency response better than a repressive one. For the staff itself, the struggle involved both the qualification and interpretation of mutilations, and the proper response. For police officers, the main issue was to regain control over the injured and 'undisciplined' bodies, and possibly prosecute the detainees for their act. For non-police members of the staff finally, the questions raised were even more problematic: while considering the detainees' injuries as painful actions that had to be avoided or cured, they remained reluctant to being part of the police control of self-mutilations. This conflict lead to heated debates and personal conflicts, were humanitarian issues this time caused anxiety among the professional themselves.

This type of emotional conflicts were particularly apparent among the team of lawyers from Human Rights organisation Cimade I followed. Its five members (four women, all in their thirties, and a man around forties) were all full-time employees, with a proficiency in law usually equivalent to a master's degree. As legal practitioners and activists, they expressed a general opposition to repressive immigration policies, while agreeing to fight them through legal means exclusively. This notably led them to disqualify alternative forms of opposition to deportations— including those which drew on physical condition, such as hunger strikes.

This professional ethos proved to be problematic when dealing with detainee self-injury, as will become clearer through the case of Mehdi, a Tunisian man in his forties who presented himself one evening to Marion, the young lawyer who ran the Cimade legal clinic at *Le Sernans* that day. Marion already knew Mehdi: he had been locked up in the centre three months earlier, but had cut his own stomach and had been evacuated in emergency to the hospital. There he received medical care and was then prosecuted and sent to prison for four months, his mutilation falling under the indictment of 'obstacle to the enforcement of an order of removal'. After serving his sentence, he was then sent back to Le Sernans, with his deportation order still pending. The following days, he came back to Marion's office and showed more and more anxiety over his deportation: considering what he had done during his former stay in detention, he feared that police officers of Le Sernans might not warn him of his flight schedule and force him to board by surprise. Marion thus went to the police building to have a look at his file. As she came back she reassured him, telling him no flight was ready for him. After he left, she however turned to me:

> In fact I'm kinda upset, because well, there is really no flight for him, but it's explicitly written in his file that if so, he shouldn't be warned. And that really upsets me [...] You see, the right to suicide, it's the basis of freedom, it's a real choice ... And here you feel it's all that's left for them, it's a resistance ... [...] Because here, I got him in front of me, what am I supposed to tell him? I mean today there is truly nothing, but otherwise what should I say? Should I tell him there is nothing while I know it's not true?

'What if he does it again?' I said:

> Well, if he does it again, it sure is tricky, because the first time, he had already done something, he had ... cut himself, not very far you see, but still he had done it. So if he goes further, it sure isn't simple. (Fieldnotes, Le Sernans, 14 March 2005)

This extract gives a more precise picture of the issues involved in the qualification and treatment of detainee suffering, and of the status of anxiety in these issues. Among the detention staff, all agreed on the obligation to protect the physical integrity of the detainee—but this agreement could not prevent professional and personal conflicts. To police officers, humanitarian concerns logically combined with a demand for control: Mehdi was a suffering body to heal, but as such, it was temporarily freed from the day-to-day control of the detention centre and had to be reclaimed—and since his action was deliberate, the act of mutilation could even be labelled as a felony and prosecuted. This mix between care and criminal prosecution was materialised by Mehdi's trajectory: visiting a series of interconnected total institutions, he went from the hospital to prison, before going back to immigration detention. It could also be detected in the way police officers tried to limit Mehdi's emotional distress and prevent any further mutilation by refusing to disclose any information on the deportation schedule: in so doing, they intended to assess the detainee's previous acts and probable emotional state and turn them into points of support to avoid any further subversion, and regain police control over the body. This combination of humanitarianism and repression still seemed coherent with the organisation of detention and the policemen's professional role. The situation appeared to be more contradictory for Marion, the independent lawyer from Cimade. She had to face a tension that first drew on her institutional position: as a member of the staff with an official mission, she had access to police offices and files, and therefore to policing strategies that were not to be revealed to the detainees. But as a practitioner devoted to helping out detainees, she was in daily contact and could achieve complicity with them, sharing their feelings and intentions. Travelling from the detainee zone to the police zone and back, she ended up being in the position Goffman (1956) described as 'intermediary': the position of an actor caught between two non-compatible social arenas, who has to share their secrets and remain loyal to both.

This peculiar situation accounted for Marion's emotional trouble when having to qualify and respond to Mehdi's mutilation. The conflict of loyalties she objectively faced was also a personal one and induced a contradiction in her own professional ethos: Marion thus could not be loyal to Mehdi without agreeing with his determination to expose his life—a logic she could not accept from a humanitarian point of view, and because she privileged legal and safer solutions. In the same way, she had to remain loyal to police officers and help them prevent further mutilation from Mehdi, but this requirement brought her on the policemen's side; a position she could not possibly hold while professing at the same time to approve Mehdi's act as a form of 'resistance' to police control. Presenting self-mutilation as a 'right' gave it more political and legal legitimacy in her own lawyer's value system, but could not prevent her from a feeling of anxiety and helplessness before a choice she could not make.

In this case, the detainee's humanitarian distress then produced anxiety on the part of the lawyer herself. This emotional reaction was furthermore difficult to manage through relevant emotion work (Hochschild 1979) —as in the case of prison wardens who learn to master improper emotions in order to preserve a 'professional' attitude (Crawley 2011). For Marion, the conflict did not oppose her personal feelings to professional demands, but transposed the general tension between repression and protection into her personal sensibility, facing her with a tension between two personal and professional imperatives—one towards the defence of detainees against police repression, and another towards the unconditional preservation of their physical integrity—she could hardly get over. In this case, a critical situation blurred the institutionalised order of the detention centre and the ordinary division of labour among its staff—to a point when missions of repression, control and protection tended to be merged and indiscernible. The second case I wish to describe gives an example of the strategic games that may occur within this framework.

Strategies over a Wounded Body

In the last case I will analyse, the struggle over the proper treatment of a suffering body lasted for an entire day, during which the actors involved all tried to claim control over the detainee's body and the evolution of the situation. It started when Sedik, another Tunisian national aged 38, arrived in immigration detention to be deported after a criminal conviction that had sent him to prison for two years. Although he claimed he had a right to stay in France, he could show no relevant evidence and remained in detention. He subsequently refused to board on a flight to Tunis, was then prosecuted, and spent four months in jail. When he was sent back to Le Sernans, a second flight was scheduled for him and, on the morning of his planned deportation, he covered his body with his own excrements and cut the veins of his arms with a razor blade.[6] Though his wounds were immediately cleaned and bandaged by the centre's nurses, he refused to take a shower and showed everyone the blade he had kept, implying he could actually go further and had to be left alone. The police officials of Le Sernans eventually considered his situation as 'non-emergency' and allowed him to remain in the centre with a still soiled body.

In this condition, he regularly presented himself during the day to the window of the Cimade office, trying to get information on the claim for liberation under custody that the lawyers from the organisation had sent for him to the local administration a few days before—which made the lawyers uneasy, as they knew this liberation had few chances to be granted, while being reluctant to tell him. The day passed on, with all professionals from the detainee zone wondering over the conclusion of the case, and a palpable tension among the detainees. At the end of this same day, Sedik was finally seized by a team of policemen wearing anti-contamination suits, forcibly taken inside the administration building of the detainee zone, and cleaned in the employee's bathroom in an emotionally trying scene that caused one of the nurses to break in tears. One of the Cimade lawyers was herself overwhelmed and retreated to the organisation's office, while her colleague rushed to the police zone to protest, with no effect. Sedik then forcibly embarked on a police van that was to be shipped by ferry to Tunis, due to the obvious difficulties of boarding him on a commercial flight. The staff of the centre later learnt that the local administration had spent the day making arrangements for this unusual deportation. In a later conversation inside the administrative building, the remaining non-police actors bitterly criticised the violence of the action, and the fact it had occurred in their very workplace. One of the Cimade lawyers stated that his organisation could 'lose credibility' among the detainees after this, and that the remaining tension made it possible for the centre to 'explode' (e.g. face a riot) anytime (Fieldnotes, 3 June 2005).

Self-mutilation here opened again a critical period and throughout the day, the issue for all actors involved was thus not only the control of Sedik's body, but also the control of time and of the evolution of the situation. The first strategic move was Sedik's: he adapted his subversion to the regime of control of the centre by producing a visible bodily disorder in the middle of a supposedly carefully policed area. Just as deportable immigrants going into a hunger strike (Siméant 2009), his action materialised and accentuated the signs of state violence on his body, making them more conspicuous: facing expulsion, he literally turned himself into a dejection—or, to quote from Peter Nyers, into an *abject* body (Nyers 2003). But at the same time, this deliberate injury to his own physical integrity temporarily relieved him from police control—his condition made him provisionally undeportable, and the weapon he kept was another guarantee that he would not be seized upon by the police— whose members could not afford the risk that he might inflict himself a more severe injury. He therefore opened for himself a margin of action within the limits of the centre and 'sanctuarised' his own body by threatening to reach a level of violence no law enforcement officer could accept. At the same time, he was able to use emotional responses to his act—a general anxiety among members of the staff due to the uncertain outcome of the situation, and the growing tension among the detained population.

The final part of the case suddenly reversed this logic: Sedik was surrounded by police officers who took entire control of his body and turned it back into a 'sterilised' and harmless object—a sterilisation materialised by the anti-contamination suits they chose to wear—before embarking him on a travel run entirely by police officers, in a police vehicle with no contact with the public. This police seizure went along with an extension of police repression to the whole perimeter of the centre—with officers occupying the detainee zone and using the administrative building, a facility I have already said was the common workplace of non-police professionals, who saw it as a normally repression-free area. This spectacular transgression of the common order of immigration detention generated two sets of emotions. The intervention first caused fear and distress, even bringing to a breakdown, as a reaction to the sudden outburst of police violence in an area where physical force was not supposed to be used, and for legal, medical or social workers whose ethos and formation was foreign to the logics of law enforcement. The aftermath of this police action was then dominated by bitterness and indignation from these same professionals, regarding what they precisely saw as an unjustified use of force, both harming their relationship with the detainees and the very possibility to restore order inside the centre. Sanitary aspects had only been used here as a support of repression—cleaning Sedik to better deport him—leading non-police members of the staff to an emotional claim for the restoration of a logic of protection, and above all of medical and sanitary relief.

Conclusion

Opening this contribution, I first challenged Agamben's classic vision of non-penal detention devices as 'camps' where a single logic of exception and exposition of bare life to unlimited violence may be observed. The empirical data I have retraced here do include critical situations and emergencies where the official and routinised order of things was suspended, and where the professional geography and division of labour inside the centre were upset. But in all cases, this transgression did not lead to an only-violent and repressive episode. The situations I have described underline on the contrary the accuracy of the concept of 'bio-legitimacy' I borrowed from Fassin and Ticktin—which does not mean that detention centres are places where the detainees' physical integrity is always preserved. What better comes out of this analysis is that the definition of this bio-legitimacy, and of the way it should influence deportations, is caught in an irreducible tension between two logics of repression or protection of the immigrants—a tension both Ticktin and Fassin evoke, but which in that case was present in the early definition of immigration detention in France, and is included in the very organisation of Le Sernans through its official rulings, its topographical zoning, and the official mission and professional ethos of its staff members.

This institutionalised combination of repression and protection also accounts for the social production and management of anxiety and other emotions. If immigration detention does indeed include a series of emotionally charged 'humanitarian' issues and debates, these different emotions are generated, curbed or managed according to organisational dimensions of the centres—the topography, official or customary rules and professional ethos I have just referred to. In Le Sernans, concern over body integrity in both a protective and a repressive perspective first lead to an established procedure for preventing self-injuries by controlling immigrant anxiety. In this case, the actors of the centre tried to create an organised control of the distress created by the very logic of deportation among the detainees. But this organised combination of care and policing also lead to anxiety among the very members of the staff—and particularly for independent actors such as Cimade lawyers, who were not civil servants but still worked inside the centre, and whose ethos of defence and protection of the detainees did not allow them to collaborate with police officers, while banning any approval of the detainees' deliberate self-injury as a legitimate strategy of 'resistance'.

The tension between repression and protection was thus transferred from the objective organisation scheme of the centre to the subjective dilemmas of its actors, as each case of mutilation raised issues over their professional identity or the extent of their mission, and each response could be seen both as a way to help the detainee and as a way to restore public order inside the centre. This conclusion first shows the interest of looking at the professional's side of the management of prison mutilations. By directly connecting the production and management of emotions to the institutional organisation of detention and detention management—in other words, by showing how emotional reactions are framed and curbed by the institution—this approach may enable us to propose a political sociology of emotions. Such a perspective is all the more interesting as it is a tendency of contemporary democracies to include more and more independent non-state actors in the enforcement of public action—thus making government regulation more transparent, but bringing more emotional issues into street-level bureaucracy.

Finally, if this particular tendency emphasises the impossibility to describe deportation enforcement in a democratic realm as a mere set of violent 'exceptional' practices, it also underlines, by contrast, the situation of less controlled, socially remote spaces of immigration control were such a tension between repression and humanitarianism does not occur. This is for example the case in Lybian immigrant detention camps were medical care is barely available (also see Galvin on deportations in Botswana 2014). As previously quoted from Fassin (2005b), humanitarian care for suffering immigrants inside contemporary democracies has to be analysed in relation to its 'outside': poorly visible areas where human suffering ceases to be of moral and legal concern.

Notes

[1] I will draw here on material gathered for my Ph.D. dissertation in Political science, forthcoming in a revised version (see Fischer 2014).

[2] Cimade is the acronym for Comité inter-mouvements pour l'aide aux déplacés et aux réfugiés (inter-movement committee for the relief of refugees and displaced persons). Its lawyers share this intervention with representatives of four other organisations since 2010.

[3] For reasons of confidentiality, all real names of persons and locations have been replaced by fictitious names.

[4] Although unofficial, the terms 'police zone' or 'detainee zone' were commonly used by the detention staff.

[5] Detainees actually had access to their luggage during detention. Visits of friends or relatives were allowed under the watch of a police officer.

[6] Although the origin of this blade is unclear, it should be noted that detainees were allowed to shave daily in the centre, under the watch of a police officer.

References

Agamben, G. 1998. *Homo Sacer: Sovereign Power and Bare Life*. Stanford, CA: Stanford University Press.

Bigo, D., and A. Tsoukala. 2006. *Illiberal Practices of Liberal Regimes. The (in)security Games*. Paris: L'Harmattan/Centre d'Etudes sur les Conflits.

Cimade. 2001. *Centres de rétention administrative. Rapport 2000* [Immigration Detention Centers and Locations. 2000 Annual Report]. Paris: Cimade.

Coutin, S. B. 2000. *Legalizing Moves: Salvadoran Immigrants' Struggle for U.S. Residency*. Ann Arbor: University of Michigan Press.

Crawley, E. 2011. "Managing Prisoners, Managing Emotion: The Dynamic of Age, Culture and Identity." In *Emotions, Crime and Justice*, edited by S. Karstedt, I. Loader, and H. Strang, 255–271. Oxford: Hart.

Diken, B., and C. B. Laustsen. 2005. *The Culture of Exception: Sociology Facing the Camp*. Abingdon: Routledge.

Ellermann, A. 2009. *States against Migrants: Deportation in Germany and the United States*. Cambridge: Cambridge University Press.

Fassin, D. 2001. "Quand le corps fait loi. La raison humanitaire dans les procédures de régularisation des étrangers." [When the Body Speaks the Law: Humanitarian Reason in Immigrant Legalization Procedures] Sciences sociales et santé 19 (4): 5–34. doi:10.3406/sosan.2001.1533.

Fassin, D. 2005a. "Compassion and Repression: The Moral Economy of Immigration Policies in France." *Cultural Anthropology* 20 (3): 362–387. doi:10.1525/can.2005.20.3.362.

Fassin, D. 2005b. "L'ordre moral du monde. Essai d'anthropologie de l'intolérable" [The World's Moral Order. An essay in Anthropology of the Intolerable] In Les constructions de l'intolérable. *Etudes d'anthropologie et d'histoire sur les frontières de l'espace moral*, edited by D. Fassin and P. Bourdelais, 17–50. Paris: la Découverte.

Fassin, D., and R. Rechtman. 2009. *The Empire of Trauma: An Inquiry into the Condition of Victimhood*. Princeton, NJ: Princeton University Press.

Fischer, N. 2014. *Le territoire de l'expulsion. La rétention administrative des étrangers dans l'Etat de droit* [Territory of Removal. Immigration Detention and the Rule of Law in France]. Lyon: Presses de l'ENS.

Foucault, M. 2003. *Society Must Be Defended: Lectures at the Collège de France, 1975–76*. New York: Picador.

Foucault, M. 2008. *The Birth of Biopolitics: Lectures at the Collège de France, 1978–79*. Basingstoke: Palgrave Macmillan.

Galvin, T. 2014. "'We Deport Them But They Keep Coming Back': The Normalcy of Deportation in the Daily Life of 'Undocumented' Zimbabwean Migrant Workers in Botswana." *Journal of Ethnic and Migration Studies* 41 (4): 617–634. doi:10.1080/1369183X.2014.957172.

Goffman, E. 1956. *The Presentation of Self in Everyday Life*. Edinburgh: Social Sciences Research Center, University of Edinburgh.

Goffman, E. 1961. *Asylums; Essays on the Social Situation of Mental Patients and Other Inmates*. Garden City, NY: Anchor Books.

Graham, M. 2002. "Emotional Bureaucracies: Emotions, Civil Servants, and Immigrants in the Swedish Welfare State." *Ethos* 30 (3): 199–226. doi:10.1525/eth.2002.30.3.199.

Hasselberg, I. 2014. "Balancing Legitimacy, Exceptionality and Accountability: on Foreign-national Offenders' Reluctance to Engage in Anti-deportation Campaigns in the UK." *Journal of Ethnic and Migration Studies* 41 (4): 563–579. doi:10.1080/1369183X.2014.957173.

Hochschild, A. R. 1979. "Emotion Work, Feeling Rules, and Social Structure." *American Journal of Sociology* 85 (3): 551–575. doi:10.1086/227049.

Israël, L. 2009. *L'arme du droit* [The Weapon of Law]. Paris: Presses de Sciences Po.

Joppke, C. 1998. "Why Liberal States Accept Unwanted Immigration." *World Politics* 50 (2): 266–293. doi:10.1017/S004388710000811X.

Kiely, J. 2004. "Performances of Resistance: Communist Hunger Strikes and Demonstrations in Nationalist Prisons, 1928–1937." *Twentieth-Century China* 29 (2): 63–88. doi:10.1179/tcc.2004.29.2.63.

Lewis, M. D. 2007. *The Boundaries of the Republic: Migrant Rights and the Limits of Universalism in France, 1918–1940*. Stanford, CA: Stanford University Press.

Liebling, A., and S. Maruna. 2005. *The Effects of Imprisonment*. Cullompton: Willan, 209–231.

Lutz, C., and G. M. White. 1986. "The Anthropology of Emotions." Annual Review of Anthropology 15 (1): 405–436. doi:10.1146/annurev.an.15.100186.002201.

Nyers, P. 2003. "Abject Cosmopolitanism: The Politics of Protection in the Anti-deportation Movement." *Third World Quarterly* 24 (6): 1069–1093. doi:10.1080/01436590310001630071.

Siméant, J. 1998. *La cause des sans-papiers* [The Undocumented's Cause]. Paris: Presses de Sciences Po.

Siméant, J. 2009. *La grève de la faim* [Hunger Strike]. Paris: Presses de la Fondation nationale des sciences politiques.

Smyth, J. 1987. "Unintentional Mobilization: The Effect of the 1980–1981 Hunger Strikes in Ireland." *Political Communication* 4 (3): 179–189. doi:10.1080/10584609.1987.9962820.

Sneed, D., and H. Stonecipher. 1989 "Prisoner Fasting as Symbolic Speech: The Ultimate Speech-action Test." *Howard Law Journal* 32 (3): 549–562.

Ticktin, M. 2006. "Where Ethics and Politics Meet." *American Ethnologist* 33 (1): 33–49. doi:10.1525/ae.2006.33.1.33.

Ticktin, M. 2011. *Casualties of Care: Immigration and the Politics of Humanitarianism in France*. Berkeley: University of California Press.

Torpey, J. 2000. *The Invention of the Passport: Surveillance, Citizenship, and the State*. Cambridge: Cambridge University Press.

Turner, J. H., and J. E. Stets. 2006. "Sociological Theories of Human Emotions." Annual Review of Sociology 32 (1): 25–52. doi:10.1146/annurev.soc.32.061604.123130.

'We Deport Them but They Keep Coming Back': The Normalcy of Deportation in the Daily Life of 'Undocumented' Zimbabwean Migrant Workers in Botswana

Treasa M. Galvin

Based on ethnographic fieldwork among 'undocumented' Zimbabwean migrants in Botswana, this paper examines the complex strategies 'undocumented' migrants employ to deal with the threat and occurrence of deportation. In particular, the paper considers the manner in which strategies used to cope with forced repatriation are discernible at different levels, namely in the way official immigration categories and associated terminologies are contested through definitions of self; in the experience of daily life as a constant need to respond to the threat of deportation; and in the process of return to Botswana. Though the event itself is stressful and disruptive, it is not conceptualised as a barrier to migration as a livelihood strategy. The paper shows how 'undocumented' Zimbabwean migrant workers do not experience deportation as a single event but as a constant threat to their transnational livelihoods and an unwelcome interruption to daily life. It reveals that strategies to cope with deportability and deportation can become a normal part of daily life for 'undocumented' migrant workers as they seek to safeguard livelihoods that depend on cross-border mobility.

Introduction

One of the most striking features of current immigration systems is the extent to which changes have occurred in the nature, scope and use of deportation or forced repatriation as a state practice. Yet, despite its global reach, the practice of deportation takes place in specific contexts. Though there is an extensive body of

---

Treasa M. Galvin, is senior lecturer at the Department of Sociology, Faculty of Social Sciences, University of Botswana, Gaborone, Botswana.

literature on the forced repatriation of migrants to the Global South from North America and Europe, deportation as a state practice in Southern African countries remains largely unexplored (see Drotbohm and Hasselberg 2014). This paper seeks to contribute to our understanding of deportation by focusing on the forced repatriation of 'undocumented' Zimbabwean migrant workers from Botswana.

Several case studies highlight the plight of deportees confronted by the disruptive, traumatic and irreversible outcome of deportation as they are returned to countries where they have never lived (Peutz 2006) or which they barely remember (Drotbohm 2012), are excluded from the deporting country for long periods (Zilberg 2004; Coutin 2010) or unable to ever return (Peutz 2006; Willen 2010; Drotbohm 2011). But, to what extent are deportees' experiences shaped by particular socio-economic and political settings? Are there circumstances in which migrants can experience deportability and deportation as simultaneously disruptive and mundane? As stressful and traumatic yet also as routine and ordinary?

Bearing these questions in mind, this paper examines the complex strategies 'undocumented' migrants employ to deal with the threat and occurrence of deportation. In particular, the paper considers the manner in which strategies used to cope with forced repatriation are discernible at different levels, namely in the way official immigration categories and associated terminologies are contested through definitions of self; in the experience of daily life as a constant need to respond to the threat of deportation; and in the process of return to Botswana. The paper also examines the way in which 'undocumented' migrants' sense of injustice is shaped by: stigmatising state labels; experiences of labour exploitation; and their treatment by state officials during apprehension and deportation. Finally, it is argued here that strategies to cope with deportability and deportation can become a normal part of daily life for 'undocumented' migrant workers as they seek to safeguard livelihoods that depend on cross-border mobility.

Migration and Deportation in Botswana

While cross-border migration has long been a feature of countries in Southern Africa, over the past two decades, one of the most significant migration flows has been from Zimbabwe to other countries in the Southern African Development Community (SADC) most especially to South Africa and Botswana.[1] Over this period, the livelihoods of Zimbabweans have been exposed to a series of shocks most notably, high rates of unemployment and a fall in real wages that originated in the country's economic structural adjustment programme (1990s) and more recently the economic crisis linked to hyperinflation, political uncertainty and economic sanctions. In this context, migration is a livelihood strategy and a response to economic and political uncertainties at home and perceived opportunities in neighbouring countries. In Botswana and more generally within the SADC region, Zimbabwean migrant workers display a considerable degree of heterogeneity at a number of levels that include their use of different forms of migration and their official immigration status.

For individuals, migration as a livelihood strategy can be short term in nature or a circular process that becomes semi-permanent or long term. Within the confines of their host societies' immigration laws, they are broadly categorised into 'legal' and 'illegal' immigrants. At present, there are no accurate statistics on the number of 'undocumented' Zimbabweans in Botswana though an increasing number of 'undocumented' Zimbabweans in both South Africa and Botswana (Campbell 2006) are a feature of recent migration flows.

In Botswana, the right to deport migrants has not always been vested in the national authority. Under colonial rule, Botswana authorities did not have the right to deport migrants as control over colonial immigration (to the territory) from countries such as Southern[2] and Northern Rhodesia[3] was vested in the migrant's country of origin (Makgala 2006). This situation changed with the attainment of independence in 1966. The Immigration Act (1966), the Immigration Amendment Act (1991) and the Immigration Act (2011) stipulate the categories of people who can be deported. Though there are no accurate statistics available on the exact numbers of deportees, the government has since then exercised the power to deport migrants and to declare certain individuals 'prohibited' immigrants. Over time, the discourse around and justification for deportation in Botswana have emphasised the recurring themes of national security (Mgadla 2008), the association of migrants with crime, concerns over illegal immigrants (Makgala 2006) and the need to protect the economic interests of citizens as well as political concerns that the country's small and limited economy could not accommodate large numbers of immigrants (Morapedi 2007). Despite the economic growth experienced by Botswana over the past three decades, high levels of poverty, inequality and unemployment have created the sense that citizens have not benefitted from this economic growth (Morapedi 2007). As a result they have become 'extra-critical about entitlements to citizenship and the advantages and privileges that come with it because economic opportunities are uncertain' (Nyamnjoh 2002, 763). In this context, recent migration from Zimbabwe has given rise to anti-Zimbabwean sentiments (Morapedi 2007; Makgala 2006; Nyamnjoh 2002) and to a significant increase in the number of Zimbabweans deported from Botswana.

Among 'undocumented' Zimbabweans, the threat of deportation is ever present and its occurrence is so frequent that it is an intrinsic part of their daily lives. At one level, deportation is experienced as a form of state power over which they have little control. Yet, at another level, it is an aspect of their lives which they seek to manage on a regular basis. Of concern here is how 'undocumented' Zimbabweans deal with the daily threat of deportation in order to secure their transnational livelihoods, and how effective are their strategies as they seek to manage the threat and occurrence of deportation.

The research on which this paper is based stems from a study centred on the health needs of Zimbabwean migrant workers in Botswana, where it became clear from the start that deportation overlapped in significant ways with the health concerns of 'undocumented' migrants. The priorities and daily lives of the participants encouraged the research to expand into a study of resources available to migrant workers and their coping and survival strategies when confronted by deportation as a routine state practice that threatens their cross-border livelihoods. This research was ethnographic in nature, based on in-depth qualitative interviews and participant observation. The opportunities for participation and observation enhanced knowledge of the deportation process, the treatment and experiences of deportees and the difficulties they faced. Over the course of the research (2009–2011) the 25 participants on whose experiences this paper is based were deported to Zimbabwe and had subsequently returned to Botswana. While 20 participants were deported once, 5 were deported on more than one occasion. As a group of 'returnees' they provided valuable insights into what they called the 'U-turn' namely, the process of deportation and the act of return. They spoke openly and freely about their experiences of deportation, their return to Botswana and the strategies they employ to protect themselves from deportation and to reduce its impact. The 17 males and 8 females were in the age group of 16–45 years. While 15 were married, 7 were single and 3 were divorced. At the start of the research, they had been in Botswana for periods ranging from 14 days to 6 years and worked in different sectors of the formal and informal economy such as construction, agriculture and domestic work or were self-employed.

Throughout the course of this work, the descriptive and analytical utility of the terms 'illegal immigrant' and 'undocumented migrant' was constantly called into question. The degree of heterogeneity among 'undocumented' Zimbabweans undermined the value of these terms (De Genova 2002; cf. Malkki 1995) while their movement between the official categories of 'legal' and 'illegal' meant that their immigration status was fluid in nature. Additionally, they did not define themselves as 'illegal' or 'undocumented' or consider their work or livelihoods within the confines of the criminality implied by those terms. 'Migrant worker' and 'livelihood' were the terms that best approximated their heterogeneity and the way they socially constructed and defined themselves and their circumstances.

Throughout this paper, the terms 'undocumented' migrant and 'illegal' immigrant are used in quotation marks to very loosely describe these migrant workers and to refer to official state categories. This is not to lessen the significance of the legal categories 'illegal immigrant' and 'undocumented migrant' or the 'social relation to the state' and 'political identity' that define 'migrant illegality' (De Genova 2002, 4). Rather, I want to draw attention to the ways in which 'undocumented' migrant workers define themselves in opposition to official categories and within alternative descriptive terminology as they interpret and represent their daily experiences in a particular sociocultural setting.

Immigration Status: Dynamic Categories, Contested Values

Zimbabweans are legally allowed to enter Botswana to visit, but not to take up employment, for a period of 90 days in each 12-month period. These 90 days can be used at different times throughout the 12-month period or in one visit. As migrant workers, Zimbabweans largely regard this 90-day permit as a temporary resource to facilitate their mobility as a livelihood strategy. Temporary and circular patterns of migration are easily accommodated within this 90-day period: it enables individuals to avoid the risk of crossing the border at undesignated points, and its annual renewal facilitates re-entry into the country. In relation to both 90-day permits and wider immigration issues, participants do not experience immigration status as a fixed, rigid category constructed within the narrow confines of immigration law. Immigration status is experienced as actual and potential statuses, the dynamic nature of this status and complex processes of change, rather than a single status that could be equated with the official categories of 'legal' or 'illegal' immigrant.

Because of frequent changes in immigration status, in the course of the research, individuals found themselves in different parts of a transnational 'undocumented' cycle. 'Undocumented' Zimbabwean migrants describe three ways in which an individual's immigration status can change depending on the immigration documents they hold at a particular time. One may have no valid Zimbabwean[4] or Botswana documentation; a valid Zimbabwean passport but no residence or work permit in Botswana; and Botswana permits that are expired but valid Zimbabwean travel documents. These are not experienced as three mutually exclusive situations as individuals move from one to another, are in different categories on different occasions or have found that being in one category can give rise to another. Thus, when an individual overstays their 90-day visitor's permit they move between official categories, a move that can be reversed by 'going back home' for a period and re-entering Botswana on another 90-day permit.

In addition, and in their experience, immigration status—which can on occasion be negotiated with state officials—is not always a protection against the arbitrary nature of deportation or a guarantee of an improvement in the condition of a migrant worker, as illustrated by these narratives: 'I was on my way to the immigration to extend my days when they stopped the kombi.[5] … my days don't expire 'til tonight, but they arrested me' (mz14). This migrant was deported three days later and spent a week at home before returning to work in Bostwana. Another migrant told me: 'One policeman was willing to release me, but the other (senior) policeman insisted me to be deported' (mz5). Even when a bribe is successfully negotiated it does not ensure a complete exemption from deportation (see also Sutton and Vigneswaran 2011).

In contrast to their experience of immigration status as fluid and changeable, the status attached to labour migration is constant and shaped by core values in the Zimbabwean cultural landscape. In this context, livelihood strategies are intertwined with the economic well-being of family and kin group members. In the absence of employment opportunities at home, labour migration is an acceptable and valued economic activity. As a result the livelihoods of families revolve around both economic activity in Zimbabwe (farming, informal trading and wage labour) and migrant remittances, a point also noted by Drotbohm (2014) in relation to transnational families in Cape Verde. As a result, the status attached to being a migrant worker is largely dependent on successfully fulfilling one's obligations to family and kin at home. As the values that shape the status of migrant worker are central to participants' self-definition, official immigration categories and associated terminology are experienced as a set of labels that stigmatise and devalue their sense of self and their moral reality. They portray themselves in terms that more closely approximate the fluid and complex nature of their immigration status as part of the condition of the migrant worker. An expired 90-day permit, which is commonly referred to as 'days', is a point of self-description only in opposition to official categories and terminology. Participants describe how 'my papers have expired', 'my days are finished', 'I have no passport ... so, no days. ... but when I get my passport I will have days'.

The label 'illegal' immigrant and its implied criminality is the most fiercely contested of all the official labels and is viewed as inappropriate, illogical and unfair as migrants argue that working and earning a living is not a criminal activity: 'I don't know what is wrong with these people ... I'm not a criminal. ... you know I'm just making a living' (mz8). Aware of local sentiments towards them, both positive and negative, they counteract the label of 'illegal' immigrant and its associated stigma by projecting themselves as more skilled, educated and hard-working than their Batswana counterparts. They find Batswana hostility towards them difficult to understand as they see no contradiction between their livelihood needs and the skills they offer Botswana's economy, as illustrated here in the words of a participant: 'You know, these people don't know it but they need us' (mz8).

Their stay in Botswana is defined as a temporary period of labour migration during which their status as migrant workers and associated obligations and expectations remain constant while immigration status is experienced as flexible and changeable, at times negotiable and contradictory. On the rare occasion when they use official labels, as in the quote below, they do so to internally differentiate among themselves, to reinforce their migrant worker status and to emphasise the normative aspect of their livelihoods and associated values and responsibilities:

> I have a wife and family responsibilities at home. ... These young men do not even send remittances, they just eat [squander] all their money. ... they are just 'illegal immigrants'. (mz8)

Official labels can then be used to describe those whose activities are considered to be outside the normative order and to reassert their identity as migrant workers. However, and though they do not define themselves as 'illegal' immigrants, they are not oblivious to the vulnerability and insecurity that arise from their 'undocumented' status.

Deportability and Vulnerability in Daily Life

Participants differentiate between their sense of deportability when they encounter the condition of deportability and associated forms of control as daily processes of social exclusion. Their sense of deportability is experienced through random police raids in areas where they live, workplace raids, roadblocks, the use of police helicopters to ensure they do not evade arrest and the use of state technology and symbols to differentiate citizens from non-citizens:

> It was stop and search. They said 'Batswana show your Omang [ID cards] … non-Batswana come out … you come out … where are your papers?' An immigration officer was there, they could tell this is a fake stamp … I had them [false papers] but I didn't take them out … you could go to court. (mz8)

Monitoring and control techniques of this nature give rise to difficulties in travelling to and from work, in finding accommodation and restricted movement especially when police raids are taking place. One participant, for instance, attributed his homelessness to constant police raids. Surveillance and control associated with the condition of deportability are experienced as exclusion and marginalisation from services such as banking and health care, where employees constantly ask for 'papers' as proof of eligibility and the inability to report crime. Female 'undocumented' Zimbabweans experience particular anxieties in relation to pregnancy. The use of pre- and post-natal care increases their vulnerability to detection, while giving birth in a hospital where their 'undocumented' status may be discovered is described as extremely stressful.

Although they differentiate between their sense of deportability and the condition of deportability, both are ever present in aspects of their lives. The feeling that they are being singled out as unwanted and problematic increases both their sense of vulnerability and marginalisation:

> You see where we live there are lots of Chinese … But when they come with their raids, they only go to Zimbabwean houses. The way they treat us Zimbabweans … it's bad. (fz6)

Excluded from the protection offered by national labour laws, their working conditions are completely controlled by their employers (Willen 2010) while their vulnerability exposes them to collusion between employers and the state practice of deportation. They recount in detail the behaviour of employers who refuse to pay them knowing that they have no recourse to the law or who call the police to have them arrested and deported when pay day comes. In a manner similar to Fussell's (2011) concept of wage theft, daily work and livelihood strategies are shrouded with uncertainties and anxieties around whether they will be paid: will the employer pay them the amount owed and on time or will he seek to have them deported? While participants are aware of these broader processes of exploitation and speak openly about them, they do not conceptualise them as within their sphere of control. Deportation, when it occurs, interrupts the transnational remittance practices (Hagan, Eschbach, and Rodriguez 2008) that are a central part of their livelihood strategy. As a result, vulnerability and marginalisation easily translate into anxieties about livelihoods that are intertwined with commitments to family at home and the status of migrant worker.

Deportation to Zimbabwe

In response to the perceived threat of 'illegal' immigration from Zimbabwe, deportation as a state practice has become more pervasive and visible in Botswana. In the period covered by the research, there were approximately 103,000 repatriations from Botswana.[6] The extensive nature of deportation is well illustrated by mz17 who describes his arrest and deportation as follows:

> Wednesday 10 am I was caught. Taken to … police station … In two hours we were 70. That's when we knew there was a raid. We were arrested at our work place. They were using helicopters and kombis. So we never had a chance of running away.

The visibility of deportation along with the concentration of resources on Zimbabweans is evident in: constant police raids that target Zimbabweans; the purchase of large 'white bodied prison type vans' specifically to transport 'Zimbabwean deportees'; and the increasing use of the detention Centre for Illegal Immigrants (CII). The CII is located in Francistown, Botswana's second largest city some 82 kilometres from the Ramokgwebana border post with Zimbabwe. While officially this detention centre is called 'The CII', locally it is called *Teronko ya Ma Zimbabwe*, meaning 'a prison for Zimbabweans'. Unwilling to accept official categories and labels that stigmatise and demean, and holding a strong sense that they are not criminals, Zimbabwean deportees refer to the centre as 'Gerald' after the name of the suburb in which it is located. The CII is under the authority of the Department of Immigration and Citizenship and is administered under provisions in the Prisons Act and the general prison code. In contrast to detention centres such as that described by Fischer (2014), there is no provision for non-state actors to provide medical, social or legal services to deportees at the CII. In addition to Zimbabwean deportees, it houses small numbers of asylum seekers and 'undocumented' migrants from other countries.

The increased visibility of deportation is also evident in the setting up, in 2008, by the International Organisation for Migration (IOM), and with the agreement of the Zimbabwean Government, of a 'Reception and Support Centre' (RSC) at the Plumtree border post in Zimbabwe. The RSC also includes offices for the Zimbabwean Ministries of Home Affairs, Foreign Affairs, Public Service and Social Welfare who play a supporting role to the IOM in relation to deportees. When IOM'S RSC was established, Botswana was not a member of IOM.[7] However, an arrangement between the two parties means that all Zimbabwean deportees are taken to the IOM's RSC, although there are no legal or formal links between the CII in Francistown and the IOM's RSC in Plumtree. At the IOM centre deportees are provided with a meal, accommodation overnight (if necessary), a full voluntary health screening, transport to Bulawayo[8] and transport costs to their destinations.

Despite adding to the visibility of deportation, deportees do not associate the IOM's RSC with the stress and anxieties caused by other aspects of the process or experience it as an extension of their detention. Instead, the IOM's RSC represents the end of their ordeal—it has added a structure, services and certainty to the entire process and a space in which deportees feel they are treated humanely, even if its existence does not lessen the overall hardship they experience during deportation.

For deportees, the deportation process is stressful because it is shrouded with uncertainty and a lack of information (Sutton and Vigneswaran 2011). When 'undocumented' migrants are raided and taken by the police, they have little sense of how long the process of deportation will take. During the course of this research, I found deportees being held in the low security prison[9] in Gaborone, in police stations around the city, or taken immediately to the border. On other occasions, they are detained for varying periods of time along the way at the CII in Francistown, as illustrated here:

> I spent 6 nights in a police station in Gaborone ... then on Monday they said I was going home ... that the immigration was coming for me. ... but we did not go to Zimbabwe, we went to ... where we spent a night and then to Francistown where I spent another night. The next day we crossed the border. (mz16)

> They found us after work. They say 'let's go let's go'. I wanted to collect my property ... they say 'no, no, no, don't waste our time' ... They took us to ... police station and put us in a cell. It had no light, toilet, air ... no good. We were 24 in the cell ... all Zimbabweans. ... On Friday we were taken to Gerald. We all went to Gerald together. On Saturday we were taken to IOM. Saturday they deported us. In the cell they gave us porridge only ... sorghum ... one meal a day. In Gerald we got food. There are no beds but blankets. (mz14)

In fact, some of the most difficult, stressful and what are described as unfair aspects of the deportation process arise from their treatment by the police and other officials, when they have to leave their possessions behind, are held in unhygienic conditions and officially classified as prisoners on remand:

> They came to the farm with an aeroplane [helicopter] and a mini bus. The aeroplane was flying on top ... we were 25. My madam was asleep ... they never saw her. They came into the house. They take me in the house. Then they take us to police station in ... We stayed two days, then they take us to Gerald. ... They deported us Saturday. At the police station in ... no food ... we got water from the toilet. We were 25 in a cell ... just women. We just go to the toilet with them waiting for us at the door. Batswana are very rough. Three days ... no food, no bathing. Baby was trying to breast feed ... I don't have enough milk. Police didn't talk to us. (fz5)

To counteract the anti-Zimbabwean sentiments that permeate their interaction with the deportation process migrants utilise knowledge of their limited rights and their self-definition in the face of these sentiments: 'We said deport us ... we cannot be kept in a cell for more than 24 hours'. The policeman said 'You guys must know that you are foreigners' (mz14). When mz16 was in a police station awaiting deportation his relatives came to see him. A police woman told him 'Tell them, you are an illegal immigrant ... Every week we pick them but they just keep come back'. He replied to her 'I have no papers ... no, I have no passport', reasserting his lack of documents while contesting the label of 'illegal immigrant'.

In Botswana, the label 'illegal immigrant' defines the deportee as a participant with few rights or individual needs. Participants describe their treatment at the time of arrest and their journey home as humiliating and demeaning, a point noted by Bloch and Schuster (2005) in relation to more general deportation practices:

> The police came at night when we were asleep at around 1 am. They asked my husband whether he had a permit or passport. He then gave them. Unfortunately ... I had overstayed. They told my husband that they taking me with them. We walked around with them for about five kilometres and I was the only lady and I was not even wearing my underpants. I asked if I could wear it. They refused. I told them that I was tired and I'm pregnant. They told me that my feet were not pregnant but my stomach. I asked to go to the toilet. They refused up until I had to wet on myself. That's when they took me to the toilet. It was now six am in the morning. (fz3)

The type of treatment here described by fz3 is commonly known as 'release yourself', a term used to describe attempts by police officers to solicit bribes from 'undocumented' Zimbabweans.

Deportations from Botswana to Zimbabwe take place overland. Though there are a number of official border crossings between the two countries, the majority of deportees are repatriated through the Ramokgwebana–Plumtree border *post*. The journey from Gaborone to Francistown is over 400 kilometres and *summer* temperatures can reach 30–35°C. En route there is one stop to facilitate a 'rest break' for the driver and other staff but deportees are not allowed out to use toilet facilities or to buy food or liquids. For women with children, this part of the deportation process is particularly stressful and difficult. While in-transit and within the temporary community defined by a common understanding of their predicament, they *devise* strategies to try to alleviate the situation:

> Along the way we had a woman who you know ... had eaten that porridge at the police station before we left. ... and was sick. Just imagine there was no toilet. We had to get a plastic bag for her to use and then just squeeze it through the bars on the window. Just imagine ... the smell and how she felt. (mz17)

The long journey in a confined space gives rise to concerns about the possibility of exposure to individuals with communicable diseases such as Tuberculosis, and fellow deportees who seem too ill to travel. One deportee told me:

> You know there was a man in the truck with us who was very ill ... he was really ill looking ... they should not have brought him. ... He should be in hospital. (fz3)

The CII in Francistown is described as overcrowded, with unwashed blankets, no provision for food for those arriving late in the evening and where children are detained with their parents. For the participants deportation is stressful, disruptive and disempowering but it does not deter them from pursuing their livelihood goals. This is most evident in their strategies to cope with vulnerability on a daily basis and to return in order to secure their transnational livelihoods.

Managing Vulnerability to Deportation

In contrast to other case studies (Drotbohm 2011; Coutin 2010; Peutz 2006; Zilberg 2004), 'undocumented' Zimbabweans are deported 'home' to a familiar environment where their identity is rooted. As deportees they are not declared prohibited immigrants in Botswana or prohibited from re-entry for a specified period. As temporary 'undocumented' labour migrants they do not intend to acquire permanent residence and at the time of deportation have no right of residence to lose. But, similar to other deportees (Drotbohm 2011; Peutz 2006; see also Drotbohm 2014; Schuster and Majidi 2014), deportation has the potential to expose them to the stigma associated with the unsuccessful migrant, as 'home' is also the place where their status as migrant workers is acknowledged, valued and defined. In this context, their coping strategies are designed to avoid deportation and mitigate its impact.

Drotbohm (2014) draws our attention to the works of authors such as Willen (2007) and Ratia and Notermans (2012) who highlight a range of strategies 'undocumented' migrants employ to limit their contact with state officials and to remain unseen. For participants, forms of 'illegal' migration control, such as random police raids in residence, workplace areas and roadblocks, are not viewed as equally disruptive or stressful but each requires its own response and some are more easily dealt with than others. State tactics of monitoring and control of migrants associated with deportability are experienced as the most difficult to strategise around because of its unexpected occurrence. In order to ensure that such practices do not interfere with employment or confine them to local or national spaces, they use a number of strategies specific to their circumstances. To avoid early morning police roadblocks, migrants make arrangements with employers to start work later than normal or, when self-employed, choose their starting time: 'I don't start work until after nine. ... ah, that's fine, you find the roadblocks gone' (fz6). Women who work as house cleaners and live at their employers' gated homes avoid detection: 'When they [the police] ring the bell I tell them there are no Zimbabweans here. ... You see I speak very good English ... so ... they think I am the madam' (fz7). On a number of occasions, when the police called while her employer was at home he paid them a bribe to ensure she was not deported. During festive occasions such as Christmas or when they need to return home for funerals and other family events they cross the border at un-gazetted points; pay a fee (approximately 150 bwp[10]) to bus drivers who negotiate their exit with immigration officials; or pay fines for having overstayed their 90-day permit.

On the other hand, the normalisation of such forms of state control allows for planned and repeated coping and evasion strategies. In dealing with healthcare needs 'undocumented' migrants often rely on self-medication from pharmacies, clinics where the medical staff is sympathetic, use false documents, borrow money to pay for private medical care (where proof of eligibility is less of an issue) and/or utilise the limited rights that characterise their 'territorial personhood' (Coutin 2010; cf. Motomura 2006, 10) to access services such as vaccinations for their children. Pregnant women choose to forego pre-and post-natal care and seek admission to hospital in an advanced stage of labour in order to curtail their contact with a state institution. Similar to their documented counterparts, they travel home to renew specific forms of medication such as anti-retroviral therapy.

Exclusion from banking is not a hindrance to remittance obligations as migrants call upon friends and relatives 'who have papers' to formally send their remittances, send them informally for a fee through bus drivers or arrange for a family member to come and collect the money or goods which they want to send home. Barriers to employment are overcome through targeting specific employers who do not demand work permits and by informal sector employment. 'Immigration consultants' can be paid a fee to negotiate temporary permits that have little bearing on actual employment. This is the case when a farm-worker permit is acquired to work as a house cleaner.

While Walters (2002, 288) notes that deportation is 'constitutive of citizenship', for participants ethnicity and other perceived markers of identity in addition to their non-citizen status are used to conceal their 'illegality'. As a legacy of the colonial era Zimbabwe and Botswana share a long land border whose arbitrary nature separates ethnic groups that are culturally and linguistically similar. In this context, ethnicity can be flexible and manipulated (Barth 1969) to overcome the differentiation between citizen and non-citizen. FZ8 explains that her mother is a Kalanga from Botswana while her father is a Kalanga from Zimbabwe. She herself grew up in Zimbabwe and is a Zimbabwean citizen: 'I have been here almost 6 years. ... when they come [when there is a police raid] I tell them I am Batswana, why do you want to see my papers. Usually they leave me alone'. MZ15 narrates his experiences during his first six months in Botswana in 2010:

> Those people they look at colour ... you see I am light skinned so they think I am one of them. That Christmas I was moving freely in ... they would greet me and I would answer. ... I also learned some Setswana.

Legal routes are also used to temporarily regularise a stay:

> You see I had a boyfriend with papers ... my employer asked me but why do you not just marry him ... it was complicated ... you see he has a wife at home ... but we got married and now I am on his permit. (fz6)

Deportation is experienced as an act of forced removal that causes stress and anxiety. It is also experienced as an event that threatens to disrupt cross-border livelihoods and to expose participants to what Heike Drotbohm, in her contribution to this special issue, terms 'reverse migration'. Immediate re-entry into Botswana and a return to work mean that deportation does not destroy their plans for the future or bring about an irreversible change in their lives (Miller 2012). As with raids and other forms of migrant control, a number of stratagems are used to mitigate the potential impact of deportation. Geographical proximity and a porous border with low levels of security are among the specific factors that facilitate return. Additionally, detention and deportation do not extend beyond Botswana, while their access to travel documents and future movement is not restricted within Zimbabwe.[11] But, return to Botswana is also dependent on individual initiatives. Two different types of vulnerabilities are experienced in this regard: those over which 'undocumented' migrants have no control, such as the conditions while in-transit, and those over which they seek to assert control such as the decision to return. The planning and preparation evident in their daily lives along with the use of social networks highlight how their livelihood strategies take the possibility of deportation into account. Mindful of the ever present threat of deportation they prepare for this eventuality:

> You don't go anywhere without your cell [mobile phone] … in case they catch you. With your cell you can call someone to let them know. And in Plumtree you can sell it to get money. … [to come back]. (fz7)

Mobile phones are of vital importance—they are extensively used to warn others about the location of roadblocks, to keep those who are left behind informed about their movements and to protect employment by informing employers about their situation:

> When they arrested me, I called [employer] to tell her what had happened. I called her when I got to Bulawayo to say that I would go home to see my wife … In a week I was back at work. (mz14)

Participants suggest that for purposes of identification they prefer to carry their national identity card so that in the event of deportation the immigration authorities cannot stamp 'deported' on their passports. Or alternatively, they carry no identification documents so that the authorities cannot establish their true identity when their details are recorded at the CII in Francistown. Temporary travel documents (TTDs) are used to negate the effects of deportation most especially the need to protect future mobility and plans to return:

> My TTD expired in August and I was deported in November. I had a valid passport but I didn't want to spoil it [stamped deported]. (fz2)

Participants belong to networks of common understanding and shared experiences. Given the uncertainties and vulnerabilities that characterise daily life, social networks are essential and can be mobilised in times of crisis. In addition to providing information on state surveillance activities, the whereabouts of deportees, the process of deportation and the means to return, social networks crucially provide an employment safety net whereby friends and family can be substituted for deportees while they are away as well illustrated here by fz6:

> It's not really a problem … my friend and I work in the same place, so if I'm away she does both jobs until I come back. I do the same for her. They don't mind as long as the work is done.

In some instances, this is arranged; on other occasions their temporary replacement is a silent understanding with the employer while in other cases the real reasons for their absence are not revealed. The ability of deportation to disrupt continuity of employment is also offset by: the availability of part-time jobs ('piece jobs'[12]) that are short term and changeable in nature; their willingness to tolerate unsafe working conditions, long hours and lack of benefits; and the continued willingness of employers to hire migrant workers. One Batswana employer seeking work permits for four Zimbabwean herd boys at his cattle post told an immigration officer, 'You know us Batswana, in three months I have had four workers. After a month I go there and I find them at the gate saying they want to go. Now I need workers'.

Vulnerability and past experiences of deportation highlight the need to protect property and can limit the type of possessions bought:

> When I'm in Botswana my property is not something I cry about. It should only be things that you can call a friend and say wrap them and send them. My problem the last time … I had two cars … and needed to call someone to take care of them while I was away. (mz8)

Once in Zimbabwe, they might take time to visit family or immediately activate their plan to return, renew expired travel documents and re-enter Botswana on a 90-day visitor's permit: 'I stayed a few days to get my travel documents, my ETD [Emergency Travel Document] … I'm not jumping the fence again' (mz8). Once again immigration status changes but their status as migrant workers remains constant.

The need to return to Botswana is described in practical, temporary terms such as to collect their possessions, outstanding wages or money they have loaned to others: 'I came back to collect my belongings and collect my money from my employer … then I thought I will see' (mz9). 'I had to collect my money … and at least bring something for my family' (mz12). Returnees hope to continue to meet the social obligations inherent in their status as migrant workers. A return to work ensures that they remain the providers of remittances in contrast to deportees who are forced to become the receivers of remittances (Drotbohm 2011).

Finally, deportation can be used to the advantage of the deportee. Not wanting to spend his money on transport home mz6 recounts:

DEPORTATION, ANXIETY, JUSTICE

> I deliberately surrendered myself to the police and told my friends to bring my goods because I wanted to go home. I did not stay in Zimbabwe. I prefer to work in Botswana. I like Botswana.

This practice has its counterpart in the short visits which deportees pay to family at home before they return. In a similar manner, Schuster and Majidi (2014) describe an Afghan deportee who utilised deportation as an opportunity to inspect his house before returning to Iran as an 'undocumented' migrant. Deportation can then be utilised in practical ways to the advantage of those vulnerable to it.

Conclusion

'Undocumented' Zimbabwean migrant workers do not experience deportation as a single event but as a constant threat to their transnational livelihoods and an unwelcome interruption to daily life. Though the event itself is stressful and disruptive it is not conceptualised as a barrier to migration as a livelihood strategy. In order to contain and manage the threat of deportation, they draw on a range of strategies, resources and capabilities. Their self-definition as migrant workers in opposition to their official immigration status is a striking feature of the way in which they contest deportability and deportation. Though the daily threat of deportation and the event itself exposes their vulnerability, being vulnerable is not equated with powerlessness. Their agency, though limited in scope, lies in individual strategies played out in social and cultural spheres of understanding among themselves and is asserted within limited spheres in order to achieve their primary goals. On a daily basis, they utilise a range of strategies to circumvent surveillance and processes of social exclusion. In the event of deportation, they strategise to return to Botswana in order to secure their threatened livelihoods. In this way, deportation becomes part of the daily lives of 'undocumented' Zimbabwean migrant workers, a hassle but not a barrier to migration, a temporary threat to migrant livelihoods but not the end of those livelihoods.

In order to understand the daily lives of participants, it is necessary to consider deportation as: a process rather than a discrete event; a lived reality that begins before and continues after the act of forced removal; and a practice that impacts on a wide range of people. It has been shown here that, for 'undocumented' Zimbabweans, the success of migration as a livelihood strategy is intertwined with: the need to circumvent deportation, cope with the event (when it occurs) and negate its impact through return migration to Botswana. Equally, deportation is experienced as more than an event in the present. Rather it is linked to earlier historical, socio-economic and political situations while its impact may resonate in the future. Participants' experiences suggest the need for a broader understanding of deportation and a refocusing away from the earlier emphasis drawn from migration studies (see Coutin 2014). Furthermore, the 'U-turn' described by participants suggests that a broader focus should also incorporate the complex factors that give migration and re-migration their enduring character despite state policies on deportation.

In this volume, Schuster and Majidi's (2014) account of irregular Afghan workers deported from Iran who subsequently return to their 'undocumented' status there suggests that the 'U-turn' described by participants is not unique to Botswana or to 'undocumented' Zimbabweans. But specific factors such as geographical proximity, porous borders, state practices that do not restrict deportees from re-entry can facilitate such movements. Equally, when the original causes of migration such as an economic crisis continue to exist, re-migration (after deportation) represents the continued use of migration as a livelihood strategy.

The capacity to live life in a state of vulnerability is not unique to deportable populations. Though the causes of vulnerability vary, on a daily basis large numbers of people cope with lives made vulnerable by a range of social, economic and political events. For participants the threat of deportation is ever present. Their capacity to cope with their vulnerability to deportation requires a set of strategies developed over time that become a normal part of daily life. Arguably, deportable populations everywhere strategise to manage their vulnerability in order to avoid apprehension and secure their livelihoods. Within the broader framework of deportation as a process rather than a discrete event, there is scope for ethnographic research to further explore how the different phases of deportation are experienced and shaped into what constitutes normality in the daily lives of migrants.

Acknowledgements

I would like to thank the Office of Research and Development at the University of Botswana for the original research grant that gave rise to a much bigger study. I would also like to thank the anonymous reviewers for their thoughtful and constructive comments on an earlier draft of this paper. Finally, I would like to thank the editors of this special volume (Heike Drotbohm and Ines Hasselberg 2014) for their encouragement during the preparation of this paper.

Notes

[1]   The number of Zimbabweans who legally entered Botswana increased from 477,000 in 2000 to over one million in 2008. The vast majority were cross-border shoppers and traders who did not over stay the legally allowed time. The number of work permits issued to Zimbabweans increased from 1177 in 2003 to 8779 in 2009 Campbell and Crush (2012).
[2]   Now Zimbabwe.
[3]   Now Zambia.
[4]   Passport or an emergency travel document (ETD) or a Temporary Travel Document (TTD).
[5]   A public transport vehicle.
[6]   Zimbabwe Immigration Statistics 2009–2011.
[7]   Negotiations on membership are still on-going.
[8]   Zimbabwe's second largest city located 98 kilometres from the Plumtree border post.
[9]   Commonly referred to as the 'boys' prison'.
[10]   The Botswana Pula.
[11]   With the exception of those who have outstanding criminal charges.
[12]   Refers to the temporary and irregular work undertaken by 'undocumented' Zimbabweans.

References

Barth, F. 1969. *Ethnic Groups and Boundaries*. Boston, MA: Little Brown & Co.

Bloch, A., and L. Schuster. 2005. "At the Extremes of Exclusion: Deportation, Detention and Dispersal." *Ethnic and Racial Studies* 28 (May): 491–512. doi:10.1080/0141987042000337858.

Campbell, E., and J. Crush. 2012. *Unfriendly Neighbours: Contemporary Migration from Zimbabwe to Botswana*. Cape Town: SAMP (Migration Policy Series No. 61).

Campbell, E. K. 2006. "Reflections on Illegal Immigration in Botswana and South Africa." *African Population Studies* 21 (2): 23–44.

Coutin, S. B. 2010. "Confined Within: National Territories as Zones of Confinement." *Political Geography* 29: 200–208. doi:10.1016/j.polgeo.2010.03.005.

Coutin, S. B. 2014. "Deportation Studies: Origins, Themes, and Directions." *Journal of Ethnic and Migration Studies* 41 (4): 671–681. doi:10.1080/1369183X.2014.957175.

De Genova, N. 2002 "Migrant 'Illegality' and Deportability in Everyday Life." *Annual Review of Anthropology* 31 (1): 419–447. doi:10.1146/annurev.anthro.31.040402.085432.

Drotbohm, H. 2011. "On the Durability and the Decomposition of Citizenship: The Social Logics of Forced Return Migration in Cape Verde." *Citizenship Studies* 15 (3–4): 381–396. doi:10.1080/13621025.2011.564790.

Drotbohm, H. 2012. "'It's like Belonging to a Place That Has Never Been Yours.' Deportees Negotiating Involuntary Immobility and Conditions of Return in Cape Verde." In *Migrations: Interdisciplinary Perspectives*, edited by R. Schröder and Ruth Wodak, 129–140. Wien, New York: Springer.

Drotbohm, H. 2014. "The Reversal of Migratory Family Lives. A Cape Verdean Perspective on Gender and Sociality Prior and Post Deportation." *Journal of Ethnic and Migration Studies* 41 (4): 653–670. doi:10.1080/1369183X.2014.961905.

Drotbohm, H., and I. Hasselberg. 2014. "Editorial Introduction to Deportation, Anxiety, Justice: New Ethnographic Perspectives." *Journal of Ethnic and Migration Studies* 41 (4): 551–562. doi:10.1080/1369183X.2014.957171.

Fischer, N. 2014. "The Management of Anxiety. An Ethnographical Outlook on Self-mutilations in a French Immigration Detention Center." *Journal of Ethnic and Migration Studies* 41 (4): 599–616. doi:10.1080/1369183X.2014.960820.

Fussell, E. 2011. "The Deportation Threat Dynamic and Victimization of Latino Migrants: Wage Theft and Robbery." *The Sociological Quarterly* 52 (4): 593–615. doi:10.1111/j.1533-8525.2011.01221.x.

Hagan, J., K. Eschbach, and N. Rodriguez. 2008. "U.S Deportation Policy, Family Separation, and Circular Migration." *International Migration Review* 42 (1): 64–88. doi:10.1111/j.1747-7379.2007.00114.x.

Makgala, C. J. 2006. "Ngwato Attitudes towards Zimbabwean Immigrants in the Bechuanaland Protectorate in the 1950s." *African Historical Review* 38 (2): 191–206.

Malkki, L. H. 1995. "Refugees and Exile: From 'Refugee Studies' to the National Order of Things." *Annual Review of Anthropology* 24 (1): 495–523. doi:10.1146/annurev.an.24.100195.002431.

Mgadla, P. T. 2008. "'A Good Measure of Sacrifice': Botswana and the Liberation Struggles of Southern Africa (1965–1985)." *Social Dynamics* 34 (March): 5–16. doi:10.1080/02533950802078889.

Miller, O. A. 2012. "Deportation as a Process of Irreversible Transformation." *Journal of Ethnic and Migration Studies* 38 (1): 131–146. doi:10.1080/02533950802078889.

Morapedi, W. 2007. "Post-liberation Xenophobia in Southern Africa: The Case of the Influx of Undocumented Zimbabwean Immigrants into Botswana, C. 1995–2004." *Journal of Contemporary African Studies* 25 (May): 229–250. doi:10.1080/02589000701396330.

Motomura, H. 2006. *Americans in waiting: The lost story of immigration and citizenship in the United States*, 10. New York: Oxford University Press.

DEPORTATION, ANXIETY, JUSTICE

Nyamnjoh, F. B. 2002. "Local Attitudes towards Citizenship and Foreigners in Botswana: An Appraisal of Recent Press Stories." *Journal of Southern African Studies* 28 (4): 755–775. doi:10.1080/0305707022000043502.

Peutz, N. 2006. "Embarking on an Anthropology of Removal." *Current Anthropology* 47 (2): 217–241. doi:10.1086/498949.

Ratia, E., and C. Notermans. 2012. "'I Was Crying, I Did Not Come Back With Anything': Women's Experiences of Deportation from Europe to Nigeria." *African Diaspora* 5 (2): 143–164.

Schuster, L., and Nassim Majidi. 2014. "Deportation Stigma and Re-migration." *Journal of Ethnic and Migration Studies* 41 (4): 635–652. doi:10.1080/1369183X.2014.957174.

Sutton, R., and D. Vigneswaran. 2011. "A Kafkaesque State: Deportation and Detention in South Africa." *Citizenship Studies* 15 (5): 627–642. doi:10.1080/13621025.2011.583794.

Walters, W. 2002. "Deportation, Expulsion, and the International Police of Aliens." *Citizenship Studies* 6 (3): 265–292. doi:10.1080/1362102022000011612.

Willen, S. S. 2007. "Toward a Critical Phenomenology of 'Illegality': State Power, Criminalization, and Abjectivity among Undocumented Migrant Workers in Tel Aviv, Israel." *International Migration* 45 (3): 8–38.

Willen, S. S. 2010. "Citizens, 'Real' Others, and 'Other' Others: The Biopolitics of Otherness and the Deportation of Unauthorized Migrant Workers from Tel Aviv, Israel." In *The Deportation Regime. Sovereignty, Space, and the Freedom of Movement*, edited by N. De Genova and N. Peutz, 262–294. Durham and London: Duke University Press.

Zilberg, E. 2004. "Fools Banished from the Kingdom: Remapping Geographies of Gang Violence between the Americas (Los Angeles and San Salvador)." *American Quarterly* 56 (September): 759–779. doi:10.1353/aq.2004.0048.

Deportation Stigma and Re-migration

Liza Schuster and Nassim Majidi

Many, if not most, of those who are forcibly expelled from the country to which they have migrated will not settle in the country to which they have been returned but will leave again. A recent article examined some of the reasons why this should be so. It was argued that in addition to the factors that had caused the original migration, such as fear of persecution, continuing conflict, insecurity, poverty and lack of opportunity, deportation creates at least three additional reasons that make re-migration the most likely outcome. These were debt, family commitments and the shame of failure and or 'contamination' leading to stigmatisation. In this article, we explore the stigma of failure and of contamination attached to those deported, and the ways in which they respond to and manage this stigmatisation, including by re-migrating. We use Goffman's concept of stigma and the refinement offered by to further nuance understanding of the impact of deportation.

Introduction

Among deportation scholars it has become almost axiomatic that many, if not most, of those who are forcibly expelled from the country to which they have migrated will not settle in the country to which they have been returned but will leave again (Schuster and Majidi 2013; Alpes 2012; Arowolo 2000; Brotherton and Barrios 2009; Dumon 1986; Hagan, Eschbach, and Rodriguez 2008; Saito and Hunte 2007; Zilberg 2007). In a recent article (Schuster and Majidi 2013), we examined some of the reasons why this should be so. Based on our explorations of post-deportation outcomes for Afghans, we argued that, in addition to the factors that had caused the original migration, such as fear of persecution, continuing conflict, insecurity, poverty and lack of opportunity, deportation creates at least three additional reasons that make re-migration the most likely outcome.[1] These were debt, family commitments and the shame of failure and or 'contamination' leading to stigmatisation. The notion of stigma recurs in a number of studies on deportation (Brotherton and Barrios 2009; Galvin, 2014). In some cases, in

---

Liza Schuster is a reader in Sociology at City University London.

particular those deported from the US, those who are forcibly returned are tainted with the stigma of criminality (Brotherton and Barrios 2009; Hagan, Eschbach, and Rodriguez 2008; Drotbohm 2014), but in the case of those deported from Europe, it seems the stigma is more likely to be that of failure.

However, in the literature the stigma of deportation has been described rather than analysed. In this article, we explore the stigma of failure and of contamination attached to those deported, and the ways in which they respond to and manage this stigmatisation, including by re-migrating, and the conditions under which it does or does not arise. We use Goffman's concept of stigma (1963) and the refinement offered by Link and Phelan (2001) to further nuance understanding of the impact of deportation. We argue that families and communities will stigmatise those who challenge their images of migration destinations as lands of opportunity, preferring to believe only those who are lazy, stupid or unlucky (Alpes 2012) will be deported. We further suggest that this stigmatisation acts as an additional pressure to re-migrate. However, while we argue for the existence of a link between stigma and re-migration, we are careful to place stigma within the wider structural framework of physical, economic and social (in)security, and in contextualising stigmatisation, note that it is not inevitable.

Stigma and Migration

Goffman's theory of social stigma defines stigma as an 'attribute that is deeply discrediting' and causes the individual to be classified as different from others, from the norm, undesirable and therefore to be rejected, reducing his/her identity 'from a whole and usual person to a tainted, discounted one' (Goffman 1963, 3). Stigma as a conceptual tool has been used since Goffman's study by researchers to examine the exclusion of a wide range of social groups labelled as other and treated as tainted by those who are 'normal', perhaps most extensively in relation to mental illness (Corrigan, Markowitz, and Watson 2004; Dinos et al. 2004; Rüsch, Angermeyer, and Corrigan 2005), HIV/AIDS (Castro and Farmer 2005; Parker and Aggleton 2003; Alonzo and Reynolds 1995) and disability (Kleinman et al. 1995; Schneider 1988; Fine and Asch 1988). Scholars have also looked at the stigmatisation of migrants, usually in receiving countries and usually those stigmatised not just because of their immigration status, but also because they are engaged in sex work (Lévy and Lieber 2008; Scambler 2007; Pheterson 1993) or HIV positive (Koku 2010). Goffman's work clearly resonates in many areas of research and Link and Phelan (2001) provide an impressive overview of the different contexts in which the concept has been used. Much of this literature has focused on the way these stigmatised groups manage their relationships with the society in which they reside or their rejection by that society (Field 1994; Kusow 2001, 2004).

Work on stigma has largely been in the field of psychology and so perhaps inevitably there is a strong emphasis in studies of stigma on the individual. However, sociological approaches have been recommended and used to understand how structural processes link stigma and discrimination (Corrigan, Markowitz, and Watson 2004). Link and Phelan also stress the importance of moving beyond a focus 'on the perceptions of individuals and the consequences of such perceptions for micro-level interactions' (2001, 366). The micro-level interactions documented here occur within structural contexts of inequality and poverty that construct migration as a solution to individual problems. Goffman highlights the contingent and dynamic nature of stigma, arguing that while it functions in face-to-face interactions, it 'cannot itself be fully understood without reference to the history, the political development and the current policies of the group' (1963, 127). Context is vital in the assigning of stigma-normal categories (Kusow 2001, 180; Goffman 1963, 127) and so we have taken a comparative approach here to illustrate how what is 'normal' and what is 'stigmatised' (and by whom) varies according to geographical, historical and political contexts.

More recently, as the literature on deportation has expanded significantly, authors have examined the stigmatisation of those who are deported (Drotbohm 2011a, 2014; Galvin, 2014; Peutz 2006, 2010; Brotherton and Barrios 2009; Zilberg 2004). Brotherton and Barrios suggest that 'the experience of stigma is probably the most difficult social and psychological issue confronting deportees' (2009, 43). It may be tempting to see deportation as the end of the stigmatising process, the point at which the person tainted by irregular migration status is expelled from 'normal' society. Our interviewees indicated that, in certain circumstances, deportation continues the process of stigmatisation and leads to the deported person being discounted and treated as tainted by failure (Drotbohm 2014), as no longer normal. As we will show, this is particularly the case where deportation challenges a shared understanding (and shared expectations when migration is a collective decision) in the communities to which people are returned, one that people are anxious to hold onto. In the Brotherton and Barrios study just mentioned, Dominican Javier articulates a perspective that could be Afghan: 'They don't believe it can happen to a person. They think I must be stupid because I went there, spent 25 years of my life there and didn't come home rich' (2009, 50) and Drotbohm notes that deportation challenges affirmation of the families' 'transnational relatedness, cross-border solidarity and familial success' (2012, 133).

Link and Phelan identify discrete elements of the stigmatisation process: 'labelling, stereotyping, separation, status loss and discrimination co-occur in a power situation that allows the components of stigma to unfold' (2001, 367). The first occurs when a label is attached to a human difference, the second when negative characteristics are attached to that label and the third when a distance is introduced between 'us' and 'them'. However, stigma is only effective when those labelled suffer discrimination and a loss of status. Link and Phelan (2001) conclude that stigmatisation is entirely contingent on access to social, economic and political power that allows exclusion and discrimination. In the case of certain categories of migrants, labels such as 'illegal' are applied, and characteristics such as criminality associated with them (Khosravi 2009; Palidda 1999; Den Boer 1998; Drotbohm 2014). Because of the consequences of discovery, including detention and deportation, undocumented migrants (i.e. deportable migrants) are forced to separate themselves from 'normal' citizens or to take great care to hide their status (Bloch, Sigona, and Zetter 2009; Alpes 2012; Drotbohm 2014), and may end up being physically separated in detention centres. As such, undocumented migrants are subject to 'the full execution of disapproval, rejection, exclusion and discrimination' (Link and Phelan 2001, 367), which in some cases leads to their physical expulsion from a state. However, we take up the story when those deported arrive in a place that they cannot, or no longer feel that they can, call home.

Methods and Data

The data used in this article was gathered separately by Schuster and Majidi through discrete projects over a period of five years. Although Majidi has conducted both qualitative and qualitative studies, for this paper we used only the qualitative data as this is where the issues and perceptions of shame, failure and stigma arose. Majidi has been conducting field-based research in Afghanistan since 2007 (e.g. for UNHCR, ILO, DfID, IOM, Norwegian Refugee Council) and for her doctoral thesis. Of the 100 returnees interviewed by Majidi in three provinces of Afghanistan (Kabul, Nangarhar and Balkh), 50 had been deported from the UK and assisted through the UK return and reintegration fund (Majidi 2009). Those selected in 2009 were then re-interviewed in 2011 to obtain a longitudinal perspective of their post-deportation experience.

Additionally, we drew on Majidi's previous work for UNHCR and ILO in 2008 with Afghans deported from Iran (2008), in particular the qualitative fieldwork consisting of 50 individual profiles, 20 case studies and 6 focus groups with 103 Afghans deported from Iran. Those people interviewed at the Iranian-Afghan border had been in Iran for periods between 2 weeks and 20 years before being deported. Majidi also mapped out and interviewed the different stakeholders involved on the Afghan side of the deportation and return process—from the people deported, to their families and friends, to the taxi drivers taking them from the border to Herat city, smugglers, hotel owners, national authorities, NGO workers and United Nations agency representatives.

Schuster spent six months in Afghanistan in 2012–13: three in Kabul and three conducting an ethnographic study in Northern Afghanistan studying the impact of deportation on those deported and their families. During the six months in Afghanistan, she stayed with a total of 11 families and visited at least twice with 5 more. All but two of the families with whom Schuster stayed were Hazara, largely because the contacts in Paris who facilitated the family stays were Hazara. Every family she stayed with had close members living and working abroad. Many had lived in Iran (for between 3–14 years) and some had been deported from there.

During the three months in Kabul, Schuster conducted 10 interviews with men who had been deported from Iran, Norway, Germany or the UK, or with their brothers and four interviews and one informal focus group with women in Herat who had been deported from Iran with the assistance of an informal interpreter. All but four of the interviews and one focus group were with men and all of those interviewed who had been deported from Europe or Australia were male. The male bias reflects the reality that the overwhelming majority of deportations are of men. The women who had experienced deportation and who spoke about their experiences had all been deported with their families from Iran.

Analysis

For this paper, we sifted our data separately looking for interviews or conversation where shame or rejection were mentioned explicitly or implicitly by the respondents. The initial coding of the data consisted of a detailed reading of each interview. As particularly themes emerged, we discussed and considered these discretely, before looking for relationships between them. In discussing the analysis of stigma, two caveats need to be flagged. First, the separating out of stigma in this article is artificial as in both data-sets it was intimately linked to issues of debt, lost opportunities and affective ties (Schuster and Majidi 2013), as well as collective decisions and structural factors leading to migration. It is important to stress it was never offered as a primary reason for leaving, but rather something which compounded other difficulties, such as insecurity and destitution. It is isolated here to flag its importance and facilitate the analysis of the role of stigma, but a rounded understanding of the pressures to re-migrate post-deportation or of the impact of deportation would need to treat all of the above and most importantly the question of physical and economic security. Deportation is a complex process that varies depending on a whole gamut of factors, of which stigma is only one and often not the most important one.

We were also aware that, in the formal interviews in particular, there was a very clear power imbalance. This was never completely resolved but we tried to redress this by responding as fully as possible to all questions that were asked and by offering clear explanations of the research and its purpose. O'Connell-Davidson (1998) has noted the problems of giving voice and we ourselves share a certain scepticism about whether that is possible in academic research because there is no single voice to be represented: ethnicity, class, education and especially gender all mediate the experiences of the people we interviewed. As noted by Jacobsen and Skilbrei (2010, 194) 'the accounts of the same person may also be ambivalent and unsettled, containing "several voices" that speak differently in different contexts'. We have tried to reflect this variety in our analysis and choice of quotations.

Afghan Migration and the Stigma of Deportation

For stigma to function there must be a shared understanding of the normal. Afghanistan, located on the Silk Routes of Central Asia, has for centuries witnessed and participated in migratory movements along its highways. However, the last 35 years in particular have seen massive population displacements thanks to the

Soviet invasion (1979–1989), followed by civil war and the rise of the Taliban. With every regime change, some Afghans would return, while others would leave, some more than once and most usually to the neighbouring countries of Iran and Pakistan. The norm has been to use migration as a coping strategy (Harpviken 2009; Monsutti 2005 and more generally, see Cassarino 2004). It is estimated that 76 per cent of Afghanistan's population has experienced displacement (ICRC 2009) and Afghanistan is amongst the countries with the largest proportion of its citizens living outside its borders. Around six million Afghans still reside in the neighbouring countries of Iran and Pakistan and there are significant communities in Australia, Europe and North American, even though since 2002, some 5.7 million refugees have returned to Afghanistan (UNHCR 2013). While Iran and Pakistan host large populations of registered Afghan refugees, there are also hundreds of thousands of undocumented workers vulnerable to arrest and immediate deportation, often followed as soon as practically possible by re-migration (Majidi 2008; Schuster and Majidi 2013). As such, migration is a norm for many Afghans, who share experiences of migration for survival, security, marriage, labour and education and often for a combination of all of these reasons[2] (Monsutti 2005; Stark and Bloom 1985; Massey et al. 2005). Migration is often seen as a necessary and normal, though painful, experience for both the migrant and those left behind (Aranda 2006).

There is extensive literature documenting migrant expectations that their sojourn will be limited and that they will return after a fixed, usually underestimated period (see van den Berg and Weynandt 2012) with capital to invest in businesses or material assets such as houses or cars or the future of their children (Stark 1991)—expectations shared by those they leave behind. There is often the expectation that successful migrants will help other family members migrate through marriage or sponsorship (Cassarino 2004; Drotbohm 2012). Increasingly, the reality is less clear, as expectations and norms of migration are challenged by the restrictions increasingly imposed on migrants by states. Those taking a more structural approach to return migration emphasise the context in which migration occurs and its role in shaping expectations of what migration can do for the individual, their family and the sending and receiving society (e.g. Cerase 1974).

One category of migrant absent from this analysis is, however, the migrant who is deported. Deportation challenges established norms in sending states 'and therefore returnees experience stigma, discrimination and shame due to discrepancies between what is socially expected and what is the actual reality' (Gomes 2012, 2). Those who have been deported from Australia or Europe discredit the dominant shared understanding of migrants as successful adventurers and of those destinations as places where people go to succeed, to improve their own lives and the lives of their families (Galvin 2014). One way to preserve the idea of e.g. Australia or Germany as an ideal destination is to blame the person deported, to label them as criminal, lazy or unlucky. A focus group with young men deported from the UK in Kabul highlighted a common experience: that of having fingers pointed at them, and being labelled 'the deportee' in the respective vernacular [see also Drotbohm (2011b) on those deported to Haiti]. They are then stereotyped as failures, or in an ironic continuation of the pre-deportation stigmatisation, as criminals. Peutz notes in relation to deported Somalilanders that 'the shame associated with their deportation was manifested in speculation regarding the reasons for it' (2006, 224). Often there is little awareness that those who enter without papers are liable to deportation,[3] so there is an assumption that the person deported must have been engaged in criminal activities. Young men in Paris after re-migrating post-deportation spoke bitterly of their families' lack of comprehension of what they had suffered en route to and in Europe (Schuster and Majidi 2013). As noted by Peutz (2006) and Khosravi (2009) often (though not always) the assumption is that they must have been doing drugs or stealing, and the injustice of these suspicions is keenly felt.

In particular for those interviewees deported from Europe, their original decision to migrate so far was determined by the need for collective investment because of the much higher expense involved in travelling outside the region. Often families, friends or acquaintances will have lent money in the expectation that it would be repaid and that they would share in the benefits expected. Hussein's whole family had migrated in stages to Iran, from where they financed the further migration of a brother to Australia and from where Hussein had been deported back to Afghanistan:

> My father borrowed 4,000$ to send my brother abroad. He promised he would send back at least 200$ every month to my father. He is old and cannot work and there is no work for me here. But he sent back only 500$ in the two years he has been away so we have to sell our house to repay the debt. (Hussein 25)[4]

> When he returned he was completely lost—no job, he lived in his brother's house whose situation was already not good, he felt like he was worsening their situation, that he brought his entire family down, instead of making their lives better, as he was supposed to do. He is now back in London. (Interview in 2011 with uncle of a man deported in 2009)

The prolonged absence of a loved one and of a contributor to the family income would have been negotiated with the family. Their deportation, like their migration therefore becomes everyone's business. In Hussein's case, the creditor had publicly abused his father for not repaying the debt, and elders from both families had met together to negotiate the solution—in this case the sale of the family home. While the stigma is centred upon the person deported it often touches the entire family (Drotbohm 2014).

Goffman (1963) argues that those stigmatised must constantly confront the image that others reflect back at them and deal with their rejection by others. In Afghanistan, there is very little privacy, and it is common for family and neighbours to visit when someone returns and ply them with questions. When one returns without money or gifts, it is hard to hide a deportation. After a time, comparisons are made with the migrant members of other families who regularly send back money or equipment, giving rise to the question 'if he could take care of his family, why can't you'? An Afghan in Paris explained to nods of approval 'those words are sharper than blades, and the wounds do not heal' (Nemat 40). Carling and Hernandez-Carratero in the context of Senegalese migrants echo these feelings 'Returnees are not only frustrated and angry but also speak of a sense of shame in relation to having failed and coming home empty-handed' (2008, 4; see also Alpes 2012). This stereotype of the successful migrant leads to rejection and separation from communities and families.

> My income is low here and we are under a lot of pressure. The only worry is that people think that the 'son of ... 'has returned and has money; I have none. My family would have preferred that I had stayed there so that I could send money back. I was, back in the day, a refugee in Pakistan. I am used to moving around. With this type of pressure and having disappointed people around me, I will probably migrate again, especially given how the situation is deteriorating here day by day. (Mohammad Gol, 34)

Tainted by their failure, they suffer an important loss of status. This in turn affects their employment or marriage prospects. Employment is most often found through networks and connections (*wasita*), so a man's reputation is therefore closely linked to his ability to secure a job. Questions will be asked of different family members and friends about the individual's behaviour abroad and the reasons for his return if it is not voluntary and temporary. Similarly, the stigma of failure can make finding a bride difficult. One of the first acts of many young men when they receive papers is to return to Afghanistan to look for a bride, and his capacity to bring his wife abroad with him is an important point in his favour. Having said that, for some of those who have been deported, marriage is seen as a way to bring him back into the fold, of anchoring him, although this necessitates finding a bride price, which will be difficult if family capital was spent on the journey. If this has repercussions for the marriages of other siblings—this will increase resentment within the family.

The dominant discourse generates stereotypes and rejection of those who challenge those stereotypes, leading to a process of exclusion, but also of internalised stigma (Koku 2010; Campbell and Deacon 2006). Our research highlights the impact of internalising negative stereotypes. Fear of rejection by families and communities may lead those deported to avoid rejection by excluding themselves from the labour market and ultimately by excluding themselves from their home society by re-migrating. The cycle of stigma that is generated is in part self-imposed, since the person deported has failed to live up to his own expectations of himself. One coping strategy is to reject Afghan society as tainted, especially by corruption, as discredited and as different from 'normal societies', a common trend among those deported from Europe.

Coping Strategies

Goffman talks of the stigmatised creating a separate system of honour as a way of managing their stigma (1963, and see Kusow 2004). This is difficult for those deported from Europe, North America or Australia—they are too few and too scattered. However, they can and do attempt to reverse the stigma. Becker and Blumer have argued that stigmatisation may be reversed when 'individuals who are labelled in a certain fashion talk among themselves about how they are characterised and collectively engage in a process to offset the label' (cited in Kusow 2004, 194). Those deported from the UK, for example, spoke of the rampant corruption in their country, within the government and within the labour market, to the point that it does not seem worthwhile to them to seek a stable employment.

> I was very unhappy as soon as I came back. People live like animals here and according to rules that I disagree with; I didn't even want to work here. What is the point if you have to pay to get a job? (Mirwais 25)

They are critical of other returnees, who lived in the US and Europe during the years of war, and who returned voluntarily after 2001 with the passport of their country of exile. These are criticised as some of the worse types of leaders: those who have returned to benefit financially and take the money out of the country, to finance their other Western lives.

> How can they build a tall building when I can't even have a mud home? It is not even worth working here. I can buy a job for myself in government if I wanted, but what would be the point? Just the other day someone called me and said that if I paid, I could have a civil servant position. But that does not interest me. If you enter the system, you become as corrupt as them. (Jamshid, 32)

In a form of stigma reversal (Kusow 2004), their experience of life 'over there' is turned into a source of superiority over those who accept how life is 'over here'. There is a disdain for the country of origin, for the society, for way of life and traditions. Rather than directing their frustration, resentment and sense of injustice at the country that deported them, they focus it on the situation in Afghanistan and are sustained by their dreams of returning to, for example, the UK. Ahmad Tamim complained of the overall lack of 'social and cultural environment in this country'.

> There is no infrastructure. People live in tents even in Kabul, they have no culture, no good social understanding of how to behave with each other, and the fact that the army and the police do not behave well with ordinary citizens is a big problem. (Ahmad Tamim 38)

Those deported are forced to reconstruct a spoiled identity (Goffman 1963). Snow and Anderson (1987), writing on the homeless, describe a number of the strategies employed to manage stigmatisation, including hiding identities from the public in order to avoid shame and the process of 'fictive storytelling' or 'narrative embellishment' of the past, present and future to disguise actual identities. In the case of those who have been deported, they may try to hide their deportation in a number of ways. Alpes describes the case of Manuella deported from Swtizerland to Cameroon, who went to stay with a relative in Nigeria until she could re-migrate to Europe (2012). Those deported to Kabul followed similar strategies. In Kabul, the friend of a young man deported from the UK explained:

When Wali was deported, he could not go home. He was ashamed to face his family. He asked us [his friends] for help, so we put together some money for him to go to Pakistan. His family think he is still in England. (Humayun, 31)

In other cases, the individual may return home but change the narrative of deportation—claiming instead to be visiting, while intending to leave again as soon as the money can be raised. It is difficult to manage this deception without the collusion of the immediate family since returning without money and/or gifts to be displayed to other family members is very hard to explain. If the person deported has the resources they can create another life in the country of origin and leave behind their deportation experience. One such example is the owner of KFC (*Kabul Fried Chicken*) who was deported from Britain and was able to combine his experience of working in a chicken restaurant there with funding from his family to create a successful business in Kabul and avoid the stigma of deportation.

A Complication: The Stigma of 'Contamination'

The stigma of deportation is complicated by the stigma of contamination, which can have fatal consequences. In Afghanistan, we found similar responses to those found by Peutz six years earlier: 'those who are returned to Somaliland are potential spoilers of the true culture at home' (2006, 227). The teenagers and young adults who left for Europe at a young age and returned with visible and invisible signs of their cultural change (clothing, behaviour, accent etc.) are sometimes seen by family and or the community as 'contaminated'. In the case of one young man interviewed in 2009 and again in 2011, from Paghman district in Kabul province, his return led to clashes due to the changes he had undergone:

They all bother me because I went to the UK. They say I lost my culture, became a kafir … all sorts of insults. Another deportee—Habib—returned and was killed in our village last year. I left because I no longer felt safe. But now I have no employment, no stable income, no skills, no future and no family by my side. (Najib, 22)

In this case the stigma has to do with the time spent abroad, rather than the simple fact of having been returned against one's will. Deportation exposes and compounds the stigma of contamination, particularly for those without economic or social power. As seen from Najib's comments, this can lead to murder. The stigma of contamination could be mitigated if the person was seen to come back bringing benefits to his family, or if he could present himself as a successful migrant as with the KFC businessman above rather than a failure—although this too has dangers, since we encountered stories of people presumed to have come back with money being kidnapped (Schuster and Majidi 2013).

Peutz (2006) refers to parents who 'deport' their children to Somalia as a way of correcting or containing contamination. Musa (40) in Kabul was concerned about his younger brother Mohamad (30) and appealed to Schuster, who had known Mohamad for about four years, to get him deported back to Afghanistan. Mohamad had spent eight years in Europe, the last four in France. Musa was in despair—his younger brother wasn't studying, didn't seem to be working, had no home, no wife and no children and he had heard that Mohamad was drinking, taking drugs and dating women. Musa himself had recently been deported from Iran, and wanted to see his younger brother before he left again. For Musa, there was no stigma attached to deportation—it could help him save his brother from going to the bad. As we talked, he wept and stroked the photograph of his brother Schuster had brought for him. And yet, if Mohamad was to come back, and against his will, it was hard to see how he would again fit in to life in Afghanistan.

This section highlighted some of the ways in which stigma is a response to the cultural, social and economic shock of deportation. This experience leads many to re-migrate. The longitudinal research completed by Majidi in 2009 and 2011, which found that many had left, generated interviews with their relatives where trauma and stigma were often mentioned, including the unwillingness to adapt to a society that deportees now reject. This sense that the person deported and re-migrating was rejecting society was related to us mainly by family members and friends left behind, who were not prompted for their views on the migrant's decision. Nonetheless, the sense of compassion in these interviews was striking. For example, one young man mentioned sadly that his friend had to leave because he did not feel he belonged anymore. However, in other cases, deportation does not lead to any particular stigma, although it results in re-migration due to the fact that it is a longstanding coping strategy, the 'norm' in Afghanistan. Those deported from Iran, as will be seen in the final section of this paper, are not stereotyped, excluded or rejected. On the contrary, their often violent experiences of irregular migration, difficult working conditions and forced returns, evoke compassion from other Afghans who have witnessed those same conditions (Drotbohm also found compassion for those deported from return migrants to Cape Verde, who understood how precarious life in the US had become (2012, 137)).

The Normalisation of Deportation

As noted by Galvin (2014) most studies of deportation concentrate on deportations from the Global North to the Global South, although there are significant numbers of people deported within the Global South. In some countries, deportation, while still only involving a minority of the population, is such a significant phenomenon that it has become a norm of that society. Similarly to the study of Zimbabwean migrant workers in Botswana, Afghans migrating to Iran are confronted with a 'constant threat' of deportation, an event that is 'simultaneously disruptive and mundane, stressful and traumatic yet also … routine and ordinary' (Galvin 2014) In this scenario, deportation from Iran is lived as a *reverse migration*, when 'achievements of transnational mobility and support capacities are negated', (Drotbohm, 2014). Large numbers of Afghans are regularly forcibly removed from Iran and Pakistan, and increasing numbers from other destinations. In 2011 the government of Iran recorded 211,023 deportations, down from over 400,000 deportations in 2007, but nonetheless a significant number. One of the more surprising findings arising from Schuster's ethnographic work and confirmed by Majidi's field interviews (Majidi 2008), was the lack of stigma attached to deportations from Iran or Pakistan. For those deported from outside the region there is considerable stigma attached to their forced return, and their deportation is experienced as a catastrophe, but for irregular Afghan workers in Iran, deportation has become an occupational hazard. We suggest that this is due to the level of investment these different types of migration require.

It costs on average $400 for an irregular entry to Iran, whereas the trip to Europe will cost as much as $10,000. In addition, upon arrival in Iran, irregular Afghan migrants usually find better-paid employment within a week of their arrival (Majidi 2008) and are able to send money back home within a month. The investment is quickly paid off. We argue that there is no stigma attached to deportation from Iran because of the lower investments, and because of the shared understanding and acceptance of deportation as a reality. It became clear from all the interviews with those families deported from Iran, and from conversations with families and family members in Northern Afghanistan that the potential for stigmatisation was overridden by collective resentment and anger towards Iran because of negative experiences of life in that country and not just of deportation. When during a focus group in Herat one woman said 'we would be happy if America destroyed Iran', the other seven women in the group murmured agreement, while another added:

> Yes, America should attack and destroy all Iranians … I was arrested in the bazaar with my husband. I told them my children [5 & 7 years old] were at home, but they didn't care. They took us to the camp and then to the border … I didn't see my children for two months until my sister brought them to me. (Zeinab 35)

This anger comes from shared experiences of abuse, discrimination and injustice and a feeling of powerlessness vis-à-vis the dominant society. Baba had lived in Iran and been deported to Afghanistan in 2008. He used this as an opportunity to return home to check on his house, before going back without papers to Iran because the rest of the family and work were there—not because he wanted to:

> Here, we say Aqa (sir) or Khanum (madam) or biadar (brother) or khwahar (sister) if we are talking to someone we don't know—but there, they just shout 'Afghan, hey Afghan'. There is no respect. We cannot even buy a sim card—nothing. They can arrest you for nothing. Iranians can beat you and you cannot do anything. If someone beats you—the police will arrest the Afghan'. (Baba 68)

> I was walking in the street and two men called to me 'Afghan, come here'. They made me stand and they robbed my money and my phone and then told me 'get out of our country, Afghan. Why are you here? We don't want you'. And other Iranians just looked and said nothing. (Hussein 25—who was stabbed in the stomach during another attack)

Many of the young men had 'war stories' from their time in Iran, including arbitrary arrest, beatings, detention and robbery. While young men are frequent targets of street crime in many countries, the perception of the young men spoken to was that they were targeted because they were Afghan and because they were Afghan their attackers could act with impunity. All of those interviewed, including Hussein, had experienced the detention centres where those arrested are kept until transported to the borders. Family members in Afghanistan knew of the process, since in many cases, they would have received a phone call from the border to send money so the person or family deported could get back to their province. The Sang Sefid detention centre in Iran is known throughout Afghanistan:

> I spent 8 days at Sang Sefid detention centre with about 1300 people living and sleeping in the same place. I did not receive any food or water, except for times when I was able to pay for it. We were not even allowed to go to the bathroom or to wash ourselves. I had money stolen from me by the Iranian authorities and I suffered verbal abuse, in the form of insults and other dirty comments. (Reza, 25)

> My third arrest and deportation was very difficult. At the detention centre, we received one piece of bread per day, with some rice that no one could possible eat. We had access to water, but there were no clean bathrooms that we could use. The covers were so dirty we could not use them at night. (Morteza, 40)

Like deportation from Europe, deportation from Iran could be traumatic due to the conditions and manner of deportation, but unlike being deported from Europe or Australia, it was rarely stigmatising and did not lead to rejection or exclusion. An indication of the extreme pressures to migrate and the economic necessity to work, is that in spite of the harsh conditions in Iran and the stigmatisation that they do suffer there—so many Afghans return:

> I have been deported three times already. I know a lot of people who get deported and leave immediately the next day to go back. We have no other choice but to try again. (Morteza 40)

> I will most certainly go back to Iran. The same economic problems still exist in Afghanistan; I hear it from other deportees who have returned to Ghazni. Unemployment and inflation are everywhere in Afghanistan. So we will all go back for work to Iran. (Hamid, 36)

What is evident here is that while for most people the action—deportation—leads to the same outcome—re-migration; the route is complex. Re-migration does not inevitably follow deportation, though it is the most probable outcome and the reasons for it include fear, poverty, debt, loss and stigmatisation. Even where, as in the case of deportation from Iran, there is no stigmatisation and a lower level of investment, re-migration is still the most likely outcome if the structural problems such as conflict, oppression and poverty in the country of origin are not addressed. There is no one is a necessary factor, but all are sufficient.

Conclusion

Over a prolonged period of engagement with people directly affected by deportation, the authors were struck first that so many of those who had been deported advanced feelings of shame as reasons for re-migration. However, on closer analysis we found that what we came to understand as a process of stigmatisation seemed to attach more to those who had been deported from further afield, and less to those who were deported from neighbouring states. In this article we have explained this in terms of the level of investment in the project not only by the family of the migrant who has been deported, but also familiarity with conditions in the state from which one is being deported. In other words, stigmatisation may be seen as a way of punishing those who have failed to repay the family's investment and as a way of holding on to the dream of a better life in a distant destination, a dream challenged by deportation. Since a smaller investment is required for migration to Iran or Pakistan, and since there are fewer illusions about life in Iran and Pakistan as compared to life in Australia or Europe, so there is less tendency to punish and greater understanding and sympathy for those deported.

What was particularly striking though was that, regardless of whether one was stigmatised or not, the most common response to deportation was re-migration. Deportation represents at best a temporary set-back, at worst a catastrophe, for the overwhelming majority of those deported and stigmatisation is most likely to occur in the latter case, thus compounding the difficulties experienced by the person deported, and increasing the pressure to re-migrate. There are no easy lessons to be drawn from this analysis, though it confirms findings from other studies examining deportation to and from other states (Alpes 2012; Brotherton and Barrios 2009; Drotbohm 2011a, 2011b; Peutz 2006) that deportation does not deter migration or re-migration, and that its consequences encourage those deported to leave again.

These findings, and those of the other papers in this issue, highlight the importance of developing studies that reflect the complexity of migration: that connect the different stages of the journey; that explore the different actors and structures involved in each stage; and, in particular when it comes to understanding structural factors, takes a comparative approach. This comparative approach allowed us to illustrate how what is 'normal' and what is 'stigmatised' (and by whom) varies according to geographical, historical and political contexts. While a narrow focus is increasingly encouraged in order to generate greater depth, our paper underlines the importance of breadth—of following the migrants and understanding the contexts in which they are embedded. It is only by doing so that assumptions about the efficacy or otherwise of policies can be challenged.

Acknowledgements

Schuster and Majidi are indebted to the editors and to the anonymous reviewers for their insightful and helpful comments, and to Alice Bloch, Milena Chimienti and John Solomos for comments on an early draught.

Schuster is profoundly grateful to all the families who hosted her but especially Hasidullah, his wife, son and grandson who were unfailingly patient and kind with the strange cuckoo in their nest and to the Leverhulme Trust for funding her time in Afghanistan.

Majidi is indebted to the Social Science Research Council's Dissertation Proposal Development Fellowship (DPDF) which funded the second part of the longitudinal study of deportation (2009–2011).

Notes

[1]   Where possible—re-migration from Cape Verde, for example, is physically impossible because of the island's position (thanks to Heike Drotbohm, one of the editors, for this point).

[2]   As others have noted (Van Hear 2009), it is increasingly difficult to disentangle motivations for migration. Many of those we interviewed and spoke with had left Afghanistan because of the different waves of conflict, though the degree of direct menace to individuals varied. Nonetheless, all assumed that they would be able to contribute to the welfare of their families and many that they would be able to bring their family out. In this paper, we do not therefore disaggregate our interviewees/contacts on the basis of immigration status prior to deportation.

[3]   There are many agencies in Afghanistan, especially in Kabul, offering tickets and visas to Australia and Europe for a range of prices and Schuster became used to people asking if she thought that e.g. '$18,000 for a ticket and visa' was a fair price. When she explained that a return ticket from Kabul to Paris and a visa together should cost about $1000 and that any agent that added a fee of $17,000 would be offering services that would not be legal, she was greeted with astonishment and scepticism and asked how they could operate so openly if it was illegal, since many had friends or relations had successfully used these agents—unaware that they might be deported if discovered.

[4]   All names have been changed and the number refers to the speaker's age.

References

Alonzo, A. A., and N. R. Reynolds. 1995. "Stigma, HIV and AIDS: An Exploration and Elaboration of a Stigma Trajectory." *Social Science & Medicine* 41 (3): 303–315. doi:10.1016/0277-9536 (94)00384-6.

Alpes, M. J. 2012. "Bushfalling at All Cost: The Economy of Migratory Knowledge in Anglophone Cameroon." *African Diaspora* 5 (1): 90–115. doi:10.1163/187254612X646189.

Aranda, E. 2006. *Emotional Bridges to Puerto Rico: Migration, Return Migration, and the Struggles of Incorporation.* New York: Rowman & Littlefield.

Arowolo, O. 2000. "Return Migration and the Problem of Reintegration." *International Migration* 38 (5): 59–82. doi:10.1111/1468-2435.00128.

Bloch, A., N. Sigona, and R. Zetter. 2009. *No Right to Dream: The Social and Economic Lives of Young Undocumented Migrants in Britain.* London: Paul Hamlyn Foundation.

Brotherton, D., and L. Barrios. 2009. "Displacement and Stigma: The Social-psychological Crisis of the Deportee." *Crime Media Culture* 5 (1): 29–55. doi:10.1177/1741659008102061.

Campbell, C., and H. Deacon. 2006. "Unravelling the Contexts of Stigma: From Internalisation to Resistance to Change." *Journal of Community & Applied Social Psychology* 16: 411–417. doi:10.1002/casp.901.

Carling, J., and M. Hernandez-Carretero. 2008. "Kamikaze Migrants? Understanding and Tackling High-risk Migration from Africa." Paper presented at Narratives of Migration Management and Cooperation with Countries of Origin and Transit, Sussex Centre for Migration Research, University of Sussex, September 18–19.

Cassarino, J.-P. 2004. "Theorising Return Migration: The Conceptual Approach to Return Migrants Revisited." *International Journal on Multicultural Societies* 6 (2): 253–279.

Castro, A., and P. Farmer. 2005. "Understanding and Addressing AIDS-related Stigma: From Anthropological Theory to Clinical Practice in Haiti." *Journal Information* 95 (1): 53–59.

Cerase, F. P. 1974. "Expectations and Reality: A Case Study of Return Migration from the United States to Southern Italy." *International Migration Review* 8 (2): 245–262. doi:10.2307/3002783.

Corrigan, P. W., F. E. Markowitz, and A. C. Watson. 2004. "Structural Levels of Mental Illness Stigma and Discrimination." *Schizophrenia Bulletin* 30 (3): 481–491. doi:10.1093/oxford-journals.schbul.a007096.

Den Boer, M. 1998. "Crime et immigration dans l'Union européenne [Crime and Immigration in the European Union]." *Cultures & Conflits* 31–32: 101–123.

Dinos, S., S. Stevens, M. Serfaty, S. Weich, and M. King. 2004. "Stigma: The Feelings and Experiences of 46 People with Mental Illness Qualitative Study." *The British Journal of Psychiatry* 184 (2): 176–181. doi:10.1192/bjp.184.2.176.

Drotbohm, H. 2011a. "On the Durability and the Decomposition of Citizenship: The Social Logics of Forced Return Migration in Cape Verde." *Citizenship Studies* 15 (3–4): 381–396. doi:10.1080/13621025.2011.564790.

Drotbohm, H. 2011b. "Deporting Diaspora's Future? Forced Return Migration as an Ethnographic Lens on Generational Differences among Haitian Migrants in Montréal." In *Geographies of the Haitian Diaspora*, edited by R. Jackson, 185–204. Oxford: Routledge.

Drotbohm, H. 2012. "'It's like Belonging to a Place That Has Never Been Yours.' Deportees Negotiating Involuntary Immobility and Conditions of Return in Cape Verde." In *Migrations: Interdisciplinary Perspectives*, edited by M. Messer, R. Schroeder, and R. Wodak, 129–140. Vienna: Springer.

Drotbohm, H. 2014. "The Reversal of Migratory Family Lives. A Cape Verdean Perspective on Gender and Sociality Prior and Post Deportation." *Journal of Ethnic and Migration Studies* 41 (4): 653–670. doi:10.1080/1369183X.2014.961905.

Dumon, W. 1986. "Problems Faced by Migrations and Their Family Members, Particularly Second Generation Migrants, in Returning to and Reintegrating into Their Countries of Origin." *International Migration* 24 (1): 113–128. doi:10.1111/j.1468-2435.1986.tb00105.x.

Field, S. 1994. "Becoming Irish: Personal Identity Construction among First-Generation Irish Immigrants." *Symbolic Interaction* 17: 431–452.

Fine, M., and A. Asch. 1988. "Disability Beyond Stigma: Social Interaction, Discrimination, and Activism." *Journal of Social Issues* 44 (1): 3–21.

Galvin, T. 2014. "'We Deport Them but They Keep Coming Back': The Normalcy of Deportation in the Daily Life of 'Undocumented' Zimbabwean Migrant Workers in Botswana." *Journal of Ethnic and Migration Studies* 41 (4): 617–634. doi:10.1080/1369183X.2014.957172.

Goffman, E. 1963. *Stigma: Notes on the Management of Spoiled Identity*. Englewood Cliffs, NJ: Prentice Hall.

Gomes, M. 2012. "Reframing Reentry: Considerations for Immigrant Ex-offenders Facing Deportation." *Research Notes* 90: 1.

Hagan, J., K. Eschbach, and N. Rodriguez. 2008. "U.S. Deportation Policy, Family Separation, and Circular Migration." *International Migration Review* 42 (1): 64–88. doi:10.1111/j.1747-7379.2007.00114.x.

Harpviken, K. B. 2009. *Social Networks and Migration in Wartime Afghanistan*. Houndmills, Hampshire: Palgrave Macmillan.

ICRC. 2009. *Our World: Views from the Field Afghanistan*. http://www.icrc.org/eng/assets/files/2011/afghanistan-opinion-survey-2009.pdf.

Jacobsen, C. M., and M. L. Skilbrei. 2010. "'Reproachable Victims'? Representations and Self-representations of Russian Women Involved in Transnational Prostitution." *Ethnos* 75 (2): 190–212.

Khosravi, S. 2009. "Sweden: Detention and Deportation of Asylum Seekers." *Race & Class* 50 (4): 38–56. doi:10.1177/0306396809102996.

Kleinman, A., W. Z. Wang, S. C. Li, X. M. Cheng, X. Y. Dai, K. T. Li, and J. Kleinman. 1995. "The Social Course of Epilepsy: Chronic Illness as Social Experience in Interior China." *Social Science & Medicine* 40 (10): 1319–1330.

Koku, E. 2010. "HIV-related Stigma among African Immigrants Living with HIV/AIDS in USA." *Sociological Research Online* 15 (3): 5. doi:10.5153/sro.2170.

Kusow, A. 2001. "Stigma and Social Identities: The Process of Identity Work among Somali Immigrants in Canada." In *Variations on the Theme of Somaliness*, edited by M. Turku Lilius, 152–182. Turku: Abo Akademi University.

Kusow, A. 2004. "Contesting Stigma: On Goffman's Assumptions of Normative Order." *Symbolic Interaction* 27 (2): 179–197. doi:10.1525/si.2004.27.2.179.

Lévy, F., and M. Lieber. 2008. "Northern Chinese Women in Paris: The Illegal Immigration—Prostitution Nexus." *Social Science Information* 47 (4): 629–642. doi:10.1177/05390184080 96451.

Link, B. G., and J. C. Phelan. 2001. "Conceptualizing Stigma." *Annual Review of Sociology* 27: 363–385. doi:10.1146/annurev.soc.27.1.363.

Majidi, N. 2008. *A Research Study on Afghan Deportees from Iran*. Geneva: UNHCR/ILO.

Majidi, N. 2009. *An Evaluation of the UK Return and Reintegration Programme*. London: DFID.

Massey, D. S., J. Arango, G. Hugo, A. Kouaouci, A. Pellegrino, and J. E. Taylor. 2005. *Worlds in Motion: Understanding International Migration at the End of the Millennium*. Oxford: Oxford University Press.

Monsutti, A. 2005. *War and Migration: Social Networks and Economic Strategies of the Hazaras of Afghanistan*. New York: Routledge.

O'Connell Davidson, J. 1998. *Prostitution, Power and Freedom*. Oxford: Polity Press.

Palidda, S. 1999. "La criminalisation des migrants [The Criminalization of Migrants]." *Actes de la recherche en sciences sociales* 129 (1): 39–49. doi:10.3406/arss.1999.3302.

Parker, R., and P. Aggleton. 2003. "HIV and AIDS-related Stigma and Discrimination: A Conceptual Framework and Implications for Action." *Social Science & Medicine* 57 (1): 13–24. doi:10.1016/S0277-9536(02)00304-0.

Peutz, N. 2006. "Embarking on an Anthropology of Removal." *Cultural Anthropology* 47 (2): 217–241.

Peutz, N. 2010. "'Criminal Alien' Deportees in Somaliland: An Ethnography of Removal." In *The Deportation Regime: Sovereignty, Space and the Freedom of Movement*, edited by N. De Genova and N. Peutz, 371–409. London: Duke University Press.

Pheterson, G. 1993. "The Whore Stigma: Female Dishonor and Male Unworthiness." *Social Text* 37: 39–64. doi:10.2307/466259.

Rüsch, N., M. C. Angermeyer, and P. W. Corrigan. 2005. "Mental Illness Stigma: Concepts, Consequences, and Initiatives to Reduce Stigma." *European Psychiatry* 20 (8): 529–539. doi:10.1016/j.eurpsy.2005.04.004.

Saito, M., and P. Hunte. 2007. *To Return or to Remain: The Dilemma of Second-generation Afghans in Pakistan*. Kabul: Afghanistan Research and Evaluation Unit.

Scambler, G. 2007. "Sex Work Stigma: Opportunist Migrants in London." *Sociology* 41 (6): 1079–1096. doi:10.1177/0038038507082316.

Schneider, J. W. 1988. "Disability as Moral Experience: Epilepsy and Self in Routine Relationships." *Journal Social Issues* 44: 63–78. doi:10.1111/j.1540-4560.1988.tb02049.x.

Schuster, L., and N. Majidi. 2013. "What Happens Post-deportation? The Experience of Deported Afghans." *Migration Studies* 1 (2): 241–240. doi:10.1093/migration/mns011.

Snow, D., and L. Anderson. 1987. "Identity Work among the Homeless: The Verbal Construction and Avowal of Personal Identities." *American Journal of Sociology* 92 (6): 1336–1371. doi:10.1086/228668.

Stark, O. 1991. *The Migration of Labor.* Cambridge: Basil Blackwell.

Stark, O., and D. E. Bloom. 1985. "The New Economics of Labor Migration." *The American Economic Review* 75 (2): 173–178.

UNHCR. 2013. *Global Appeal 2013 Update.* http://www.unhcr.org/50a9f82a854.pdf.

Van den Berg, G. J., and M. A. Weynandt. 2012. *Explaining Differences between the Expected and Actual Duration Until Return Migration: Economic Changes (No. 497).* SOEP papers on Multidisciplinary Panel Data Research.

Van Hear, N. 2009. "Managing Mobility for Human Development: The Growing Salience of Mixed Migration." United Nations Development Programme Human Development Reports Research Paper 2009/20. http://hdr.undp.org/en/reports/global/hdr2009/papers/HDRP_200 9_20.pdf.

Zilberg, E. 2004. "Fools Banished from the Kingdom: Remapping Geographies of Gang Violence between the Americas (Los Angeles and San Salvador)." *American Quarterly* 56 (3): 759–779. doi:10.1353/aq.2004.0048.

Zilberg, E. 2007. "Refugee Gang Youth: Zero Tolerance and the Security State in Contemporary US–Salvadoran Relations." *Youth, Globalization, and the Law*, 61–89.

The Reversal of Migratory Family Lives: A Cape Verdean Perspective on Gender and Sociality pre- and post-deportation

Heike Drotbohm

Deportation, as a coerced and involuntary mode of return migration, contradicts common assumptions and understandings of transnational livelihoods. This can be felt particularly strongly in the realm of the family—the social sphere where migration is facilitated and enacted. Drawing on anthropological fieldwork in Cape Verdean transnational social fields, this paper applies a gendered perspective in examining how deportation affects individual positions within transnational families. It studies how female and male deportees try to re-establish their social and affective lives after their return and also takes into account the perspective of family members who continue to live in the (former) destination country and who have to cope with the absence of a deported relative. These findings reveal power relations and social inequalities produced by state removal, unfolding not only between states and non-citizen residents but also among family members whose lives are divided involuntarily by state borders. The article comes to the conclusion that deportation not only 'reverses' the position of migrants in their (alleged) countries of origin but also that these processes of 'reversal' extend to all achievements of migratory family lives—both in the migrants' country of origin as well as in the country of destination.

Introduction

In this paper I will explore the dynamics between deportation and a transnational family life by focusing not only on how family relations are shaped by and adapted to the context of deportation, but also on how they are probed into and questioned

---

Heike Drotbohm is a Guest Professor at the Department of Social and Cultural Anthropology, Albert-Ludwigs-University of Freiburg, Breisgau, Germany.

through the procedure of deportation, in which multiple actors interact. In particular, I am interested in the moral subtext of return migration, which orders the position of individual family members and their moral integrity along lines of gender, generation, support capacities and the (often assumed) reasons for returning.

To date, the nexus between kinship and the regulation of cross-border mobility by state forces has been examined in two different fields of investigation. First, a large body of scholarship has focused on the question of how intimate relationships such as marriage and parenthood adapt to conditions of spatial separation (Parreñas 2005; Baldassar 2007; Drotbohm 2009; Dreby 2010; Carling, Menjivar, and Schmalzbauer 2012). Second, given the increasing number of family members who accompany or follow migrants (or intend to) to the so-called global North, a number of scholars have studied in detail the highly selective procedures of family reunification and the contested meaning of transnational marriage migration (Strasser et al. 2009; Kofman et al. 2011).

Complementing these fields of investigation, I will examine the effect of deportation on migratory families. The truism that the 'family' is not just any kind of social group or network is especially applicable in the context of cross-border mobility. The Universal Declaration of Human Rights declares that 'the family ... is entitled to protection by society and the State', and the Convention on the Rights of the Child stipulates that 'the best interests of the child' need to be considered in states' actions. At the same time, states hold the sovereign right under international law to expel criminal aliens from their territory. Hence, the state act of returning foreign nationals to their countries of origin often implies a fundamental yet irreconcilable contradiction between the individual right to a family and a nation-state's freedom to expel unwanted residents (Morris 2002; Benhabib 2004).

I base my argument on the observation that state removal contravenes cross-border family lives in at least three senses. In the first type of transnational family, migrants are forced to return to their countries of origin and to live with relatives from whom they had been separated before. Seen in this light, deportation entails a kind of 'involuntary' family reunification. In the second type, migrants are deported *after* having succeeded in bringing their relatives to the destination country, and then are forced to leave those relatives behind in the destination country. In such cases, families that have managed to establish their lives in a foreign country are divided by those borders they had already crossed once before. In the third constellation, family members return (or are returned) together with a deported relative. Often, these three social constellations overlap, as a deportee leaves some family members behind in the country of destination and returns to other family members who are still living in the country of origin and family members habitually accompany or visit their deported relative, at least temporarily.

In this article I want to examine in detail how families—deportees as well as their relatives—deal with these unexpected changes. In such situations the composition of families, their often gendered inequalities and the perception of generational relations need to be understood as a moral terrain that is negotiated not only between policy-makers and families but also *within* the families themselves (Grillo 2008). Drawing on insights gained during anthropological fieldwork in Cape Verde as well as among Cape Verdean migrants in the USA, I shall demonstrate that the moral perception of state removal draws on established norms and expectations, often gendered, of cross-border support arrangements, which, under different circumstances, would be important means of demonstrating upwards social mobility in transnational fields. When addressing these issues I do not intend to idealise 'the family' as an institution of love and emotional stability. By applying a constructivist lens to 'kinship', as has been promoted in the context of the 'after kinship' paradigm (Carsten 2000), I rather wish to move beyond a victim perspective and focus on the dynamics between the social power of migration law, personal status and intimate social relations.

In this article, I will examine the social outcome of deportation along different stages along the "deportation corridor" (see Drotbohm and Hasselberg, 2014). I will first summarise important research findings on the social and emotional consequences of deportation and then describe the ethnographic context and research methods. Next, I will reflect on the general meaning of return in this particular cultural field and ask what happens when migrants return empty-handed and are unable to contribute to transnational support practices. Here and in the following section, I will apply a gendered perspective in examining how female and male deportees try to re-establish their social and affective lives after their return. I will then go into the particular difficulties of transnational parenting and illuminate a particular situation that often prevails in so-called mixed-status families. Before concluding, I will reflect on the perspective of those 'remaining behind', who continue to live in the (former) destination country, who have to cope with their own anxieties and develop their own under-standings of 'justice' while facing the unexpected absence of their family member(s).[1]

Research on the Social Outcomes of Deportation Procedures

In the scholarship on the deportation (often euphemistically termed 'repatriation') of foreign nationals by state forces, the adverse consequences on family lives across national borders have not yet received much attention. Nevertheless, studies that have primarily focused on the nexus between citizenship, undocumented labour migration and human rights do shed some light on the social and emotional costs of forced return. The most important scholarly field in this regard deals with processes of 'illegalisation' in the context of immigration. Nicholas De Genova, for instance, has examined the increasing vulnerabilities of labour migrants in the USA, where the distinct category of 'undocumented' goes along with economic exploitability and, more recently, in the context of the increasing securitisation of migration control, with 'illegalisation' (2007, 426). Several authors offer insights into the rising impact of surveillance, which has brought those living in this 'condition of deportability' into a social circumstance characterised by fear of being checked and detection avoidance (De Genova 2002; Coutin 2007). In her research on 'illegal' migrants in Israel, Sarah Willen (2007, 17), drawing on Thomas Csordas, describes 'somatic modes of attention' that arise from aggressive mass deportation campaigns. Under conditions of fear, migrants not only reduce their contact with local officials but also modify their dress codes, daily rhythms and spatial routines in order to remain inconspicuous or even invisible.

These threats and anxieties, generated by 'post-entry social controls' (Kanstroom 2007), affect the emotional conditions within migrant families in particular ways. On the one hand, as Hagan, Rodriguez and Castro have observed among Latinos in the USA, undocumented migrants fear the possibility of being deported and thereby separated from their families even for such banal offences as driving without a driving licence (Hagan, Rodriguez, and Castro 2011, 1382). In an article on deportation procedures in Italy, Ratia and Notermans (2012, 151) observed that the everyday lives of undocumented migrants mainly revolve 'around having to "look out" for the police'. These fears may result in a general attitude of distrust and lead to the migrants' withdrawal from public venues or communal events, which can have an isolating effect on the entire family (Menjívar 2012, 316). Joana Dreby, in her work on Mexican immigrants in the USA, describes constant feelings of insecurity and the impossibility of establishing a 'normal' everyday life under these conditions of stress. She highlights in particular the problematic effect of this culture of surveillance on the perspectives of children, who fear the eventual deportation of their family members or their friends: 'The threat of deportability inspired fears of separation among children regardless of their own legal status or family members' actual involvement with immigration officials. It also resulted in U.S. citizen and immigrant children alike conflating immigration with illegality' (Dreby 2012, 830).

While the threat of deportation in and of itself can have devastating effects on the lives of migrant families, the actual realisation of the deportation procedure can be even more traumatic and often implies permanent changes for both the deportee and his or her family members. Migrants are frequently caught unawares in the course of their everyday activities, for instance, when their papers are checked during police raids at their workplace or in a street control action (Ratia and Notermans 2012; Kanstroom 2012). Thronson (2008, 392) sees in this a conscious strategy on the part of state authorities:

> In fact, the current immigration law enforcement strategy of raiding homes and workplaces relies on the worry and trauma that raids create among parents and children to maximize its impact. Immigration raids sow fear in hopes that immigrants will voluntarily leave the United States.

The arrest and detention of a close family member is then followed by a precarious phase of fear. In many cases this spatial separation of family members happens from one moment to the next. The routine goodbye hug in the morning between a husband and wife may be the last one for an unexpectedly long time or even, in some cases, for the rest of their lives. Deportees are often not given sufficient information on the duration of their detention, fear bad treatment or inadequate health care and can be denied contact with their family members while they are in prison awaiting the continuation of their lawsuits. Ratia and Notermans (2012, 153), referring to Nigerian detainees in Italy, describe this interim phase as being shaped by shame, incomprehension and depression. Family members of detainees share this burden and try to bring about a good ending by investing large sums of money in lawyers and other kinds of legal counsel (Hagan, Rodriguez, and Castro 2011).

The transformative effect of deportation on families accelerates after the de facto return of the person to the country of origin. Comparable to the uncertain condition of detention, in the first phase after this involuntary return the deportee remains 'in limbo', as families have to reorganise their lives in two spatial settings and re-establish their modes of communication and contact, all the while often still hanging on to the hope of an eventual reunification at a later point in time. In addition to these pressing everyday difficulties, the emotional burden may weigh even more heavily because, as Kanstroom (2012, 144) notes, 'A deportation order often means never seeing one's children grow up, not being able to care for one's parents, or not being able to be with a spouse'. Given the organisational, financial and emotional difficulties transnational families may face under these conditions of involuntary return and family separation, how do they rearrange their social interactions and their intimate relationships at both ends of the 'deportation corridor', to use the term presented in the introduction to this special issue?

Ethnographic Context and Research Methods

Most of the deportation research to date has focused either on the situation of family members living in the so-called global North or on the situation of deportees after their return to their alleged 'home' countries. The following exploration of the Cape Verdean case will complement this state of knowledge by bringing both perspectives together. Transmigration has played a crucial role throughout the history of Cape Verde, a West African island nation (Carling and Batalha 2008). For this reason, Cape Verde is an ideal ethnographic field site for studying the social meaning of involuntary return migration. The nine inhabited islands have long served as a trading post between West Africa, Europe and the Americas. Hence, cross-border mobility and global networking early on became the cornerstone of the island nation's economic foundation. The emigration of family members, predominately male, as well as the support of family members from overseas remittances, was already the most important survival strategy within the archipelago by the early eighteenth century (Meintel 1984). After centuries of Cape Verdean migration, the diaspora population now outnumbers the approximately 550,000 inhabitants of the islands (Halter 1993; Carling and Batalha 2008), and transnationalism has become the dominant way of living.

Brava and Fogo, the two islands included in my research, lie in the south-western part of the archipelago, the former having a population of slightly more than 5000 inhabitants, the latter approximately 40,000. Both have mountainous landscapes and a relatively humid climate in comparison to the other islands. On both islands most inhabitants have access to fishing and cultivate corn, legumes and vegetables and also occasionally raise goats, pigs and rarely, cows. The most important means for making a good living, however, is to combine local economic activities, such as the wage labour of some family members, with remittances sent by relatives living abroad. The majority of households on these two islands maintain social linkages to relatives or friends living in the USA or Portugal.[2] Their monetary transactions, telephone calls and *bidons*—oil drums filled with textiles, food, personal gifts and other kinds of consumer items that reach the islands several times a year—as well as regular visits from those living overseas, all constitute important elements in a complex field of social encounters and negotiations (Drotbohm 2009).

The deportation of Cape Verdean migrants from the USA and Europe back to their country of origin has been an important issue since the early 1990s. In the aftermath of the events of 11 September 2001, the rates of forced return have increased annually. Recent statistics put out by the Cape Verdean Government show that almost every month since 9/11 migrants have been returned to Cape Verde against their will.[3] Given the history of migration and the different destination countries of each Cape Verdean island, the ratio of repatriation differs. Brava is the only Cape Verdean island with almost exclusive linkages to the USA; consequently, the vast majority of deportees returning to Brava return from the USA, while Fogo receives deportees from the USA as well as Portugal and sometimes France.

My account is based on 12 months of ethnographic fieldwork conducted between 2006 and 2008 on Brava and Fogo, where I examined the impact of the legal regulation of transnational mobility on family lives and practices. I lived with my own family among the residents of these small island towns, engaging with them in all the daily routines of normal family life. I concentrated on exemplary transnational households (Drotbohm 2009) and carried out interviews with selected family members. Furthermore, I later visited family members still living in Portugal and the USA (Boston and Brockton) in order to incorporate their perspectives as well. While deportation was not initially at the centre of my research project, its impact on transnational livelihoods was undeniable, and the precarious social position of deportees on the island reflected the crucial significance of mobility and return for understanding the inner moral logics of transnational social fields. The following account relies on the situation and reflections of 27 deportees. Given the uneven ratio of deportees, I ended up interviewing far more men than women (24 male, 3 female). Thus, while my sample of female deportees is too small to make any generalisations, I believe the female interviewees help complete the picture and provide an important contrast to the men's statements.

The majority of these deportees (22) had been returned from the USA, with only four from Portugal and one from France. The semi-structured interviews, most of them carried out in English, traced their deportation experience, beginning with their living conditions abroad, then moving on to the moment of arrest and detention and the procedure of return, then to their experience of social reintegration and finishing with a final reflection on their social condition in Cape Verde. While these cases cannot be understood as representative in any statistical sense, they do illustrate the complex relationship between deportation and family life most vividly.

Moral Economies of Support after an 'Irregular' Return

For several reasons, the 'regular' (i.e. voluntary) return of a migrant, be it temporary or permanent, is generally greeted with great appreciation in the context of transnational livelihoods. It is understood as a kind of 'homecoming', affirming the migrant's continuing connection to the country of birth, which includes his or her home community. This affirmation is not taken for granted, as migrants need the necessary financial and temporal means to travel, as well as the required legal status. Hence, voluntary returns not only confirm the migrants' status and successes abroad but also their willingness to foster ties with their country of origin. Additionally, receiving a returning migrant improves the social position of his hosts, often relatives or friends, who may expect gifts or financial compensation, but also greater respect within their local communities. Due to the social significance of return, many migrants only return under appropriate conditions, when they are able to afford a certain 'style of return', which would in many parts of the world imply the distribution of money and gifts and the invitation of friends and family to drinks and food (Baldassar 2001; Drotbohm 2012).

It should come as no surprise, then, that an involuntary return, initiated by state force, cannot meet these expectations, and therefore gives rise to a negative reception. In Cape Verde, deportees are deprecatingly referred to as *deportados* or 'DPs' and are seen as failed immigrants and a disappointment to everybody related to them. This attitude needs to be understood in light of the economic foundations of the transnational family life. As will become clear in the following, a migrant returning empty-handed to his country of origin usually causes financial difficulties in the country of destination as well as in the country of origin to which he or she returns.

In the first case, when a father or a mother is deported from a country in the global North, single-parent households left behind in the country of destination have to compensate for the loss of the deportee's income. For a deported migrant, the intention to support his or her family living in the global North proves unrealistic, especially during the first phase after his or her return. Dreby found a similar situation in the case of Mexicans living in the USA, where deportees are usually male, households lose an important, and often the principal, breadwinner, and their female partners remaining behind have to bear the financial burden (2012, 837). Sometimes even the children who remain in the North have to provide support for their deported parents (Kanstroom 2012, 140).

In Cape Verde, these economic challenges reach far beyond the rearrangement of financial matters and need to be viewed in light of a 'moral economy' of transnational family lives. In an earlier article, I concentrated on the fact that economic support in transnational settings serves as a 'social glue', affirming and strengthening kinship ties. When calling on the telephone and sending letters, money or gifts become key social acts for expressing love, commitment and the continuity of relationships (Drotbohm 2009), a tapering off or, worse yet, complete cessation of these acts may be interpreted as the end of a relationship.

At the same time, the symbolic implications of transnational support are highly gendered. Research on gendered expectations has shown that the sending of remittances and hence the adequate material provision for those left behind constitutes an important means of demonstrating masculinity and 'doing fatherhood' across national borders (Pribilsky 2007). When male deportees have difficulties finding employment and supporting their relatives back in the destination country, they often struggle with their key role (Hagan, Eschbach, and Rodriguez 2008). As Dreby (2012, 838) puts it, 'Men who are deported are emasculated; they cannot provide for their families economically anymore and have become an economic burden'.

These constraints also affect the position of deportees back in their countries of origin, where they are returned to households that need economic assistance from abroad. Unlike voluntary returnees who embody the successful cosmopolitan and will provide assistance to those who come in contact with them, deportees actually absorb support capacities that would, under different circumstances, reach those who now have to provide for the deportees in their houses. Depending on the amount of time deportees have spent abroad, they may have virtually forgotten the local language, may not have the relevant skills to enter the local labour market and can be uninformed about the local lifestyle and relevant networks (Drotbohm 2011a).

These difficulties are not limited to the period immediately following the return. Even after months or years, deportees still face the pressure of migration-related expectations articulated within their social environment and the stigma of having failed to fulfil them. Claude, who was 35 years old at the time of our encounter, had been returned to Cape Verde only two years prior to our meeting and lived at his mother's brother's place. He spoke at length about his ambiguous position in a household where the role of *emigrante* continued to be ascribed to him:

> The first problem was that nobody was interested in my skills. I was not able to find any normal job; I mean, I went to the garage, they hardly have any good cars here; I wanted to open an Internet café, but nothing worked. In the end I have to do what they do and receive some help from abroad. In my uncle's house they started to complain. They called me either *vagabundo* or *merikanu*. They think I have access to an American bank account and that's why [they think] they can always scrounge up some money [from me]. I mean, they know that I cannot travel anymore, that I am just living the way they do. But they always try.

What becomes clear from Claude's words is that deportees continue to be perceived as migrants despite the fact that they have lost the ability to migrate (at least to the place from which they have been returned). Not being migrants anymore and, hence, being rendered unable to fulfil the financial responsibilities necessary to maintain their social position reduces their potential for social interaction at both ends of the deportation corridor.

'I'm Not That Kind of Woman': Gender and the Re-creation of Affective Ties

The process of social reintegration of deportees also varies according to gendered norms and expectations. Ratia and Notermans, who have produced one of the very few articles on the situation of female deportees, write, 'Not only is gender significant in the way in which migration is seen in the context of the deportees' origin; it also structures the experiences of deportation and post-deportation life' (2012, 160).

Cynthia, one of the few female deportees I met on the two islands, was 39 years old at the time of our encounter. During my fieldwork she invited me several times into her sparsely furnished little house on the island of Brava, where we talked for hours about the bumpy life trajectory that had brought her there, the experience of growing up in a 'good, white' neighbourhood in Brockton, Massachusetts, her girls' gang, her memories of being convicted of drug dealing, the two years in jail, her 'attended', handcuffed flight back to Cape Verde, and the first months on the island when she needed to talk to her mum every day on the phone.

In her biographical narrative she reflected intensively on her experience of being socially excluded after her involuntary return, which she immediately associated with the negative reputation of female deportees. Generally, the island population spreads the news about the legal reasons for a person's deportation, whether it has simply been a visa violation, an undocumented residency, a missing driving licence or a more serious crime. In the case of female deportees, however, I was struck by the fact that they, in comparison to males, had to struggle with a particularly bad reputation as a result of their deportation. While the actions of male deportees were often excused on the grounds of 'dysfunctional' parents, 'bad' neighbourhoods or cruel urban gang wars, female deportees were judged in a much harsher tone.

Perhaps it is simply the uncommonness of female deportees that contributes to the fact that they are judged so unforgivingly. I overheard one Cape Verdean give the following explanation: 'If only so few women are deported, this is because they belong to their children. They [the state] do not deport mothers, because their children need them. Those very few who are returned are the very, very bad ones.' This widespread hostility towards female deportees needs to be understood in light of the contrasting Cape Verdean gender roles in transnational contexts. Many inhabitants of Nova Sintra, Brava's main town, knew that Cynthia had been deported for being in possession of a certain amount of marijuana. The image of a childless woman who takes drugs and gets into trouble with the police violates common expectations people have of migrating women and mothers, who are expected to live morally impeccable lives and dedicate themselves to earning money to send back to the families they left behind.

In contrast to female deportees, who are already 'marked' as 'bad women' by the mere fact of deportation, Cape Verdean men can even draw positively on their criminal experiences and their reputations as *criminosos*. In an earlier article (Drotbohm 2012), I have elaborated on the fact that male deportees sometimes play the 'gangster card' and try to show off by exaggerating the brutality of crimes they committed. Their experiences in the criminal sphere, as well as their urban fashion, gestures and movements, confirm their masculinity, produce envy among their local peers and even make them attractive on the local romance scene.

Cynthia, however, experienced just the opposite:

> See how they look at me? The kids call me *li bem ditras, li bem ditras* [creole for 'she was returned'] and they sometimes even throw stones at me. I like wearing pants, of course—I grew up in the States. American girls don't wear neat dresses and sexy skirts. This [points to her oversized T-shirt] is who I am, how I feel comfortable. I need my sneakers and all this. I want to smoke, I drink, yes. Of course I do! I am not that type of woman!

In this final statement in particular, Cynthia consciously distances herself from the local stereotype of the 'good' Cape Verdean woman, who dresses and behaves according to societal expectations. Generally, female deportees suffer much more from the experience of social exclusion than do male deportees. With regard to her affective life, Cynthia has to rely on other deportees, with whom she shares a similar biographical background. Her situation is comparable to other contexts in which the mutual experience of deportation may unite deportees, compensate for the experience of social exclusion and even substitute for family bonds. Writing about the situation in El Salvador, where gang violence is extremely widespread, Kanstroom (2012, 149) notes, 'Most tragically, the gangs are often the only social group available to deportees'. At the same time, however, these 'alternative families' often provide neither the emotional reliability nor the necessary introduction into local networks of support. While Cynthia may be accepted among male deportees as a kind of 'drinking buddy', these friends apparently still continue to search for stable relationships with local women who conform to the ideal of 'creole femininity' and support the men's reintegration into the local community. Over the course of a number of years, Cynthia experienced physical violence and mental abuse at the hands of male deportees with whom she lived and finally decided to live on her own.

Due to her difficulties in forming stable relationships, Cynthia relies on her family living in the USA, not only in an emotional but also in a material sense. Since the monthly remittances she receives from her parents constitute her only regular 'income', she feels highly dependent and forced to behave according to their expectations. 'You can't imagine how fast information can travel from Brava to Boston', she said 'When I drink or smoke weed I can be sure that somebody will tell them immediately. I have to be the "nice daughter", a "good family's" daughter. If I fail, if I am just who I am, they do not support me anymore'.

Cynthia's extremely difficult situation was typical of the few female deportees I encountered and reveals the moral subtleties of social reintegration after an involuntary return. Gender plays an important role in how a deportee's status as a *criminoso* shapes his or her position on the islands, where they have to reorient themselves vis-à-vis fellow deportees, the receiving communities and their cross-border support networks.

'And Then You're Out!': 'Mixed-Status Families' and Parental Ties

José was 47 years old when I met him on Brava's neighbouring island, Fogo. After being convicted on charges of domestic violence several times, José left New Bedford, Massachusetts, and returned 'voluntarily' to his family's 'home island' eight years ago, where he had not been since he was a child. Sometimes, foreign nationals whose legal procedures in a foreign country are pending and who have not yet been arrested take this option.[4] In the USA, José left behind his wife and two daughters, who were about 15 years old at the time he left, as well as other close relatives, including his parents and three siblings. The years leading up to his departure, he told me, had been full of conflicts. In the end, frequent family fights that erupted in violence combined with his alcoholism and ultimately forced him to return to Cape Verde. During our interview José was slightly drunk; his speech was agitated, even outraged, and he gestured wildly:

> My eldest called the cops! I mean, hey man! She knew that I could get into trouble. She knew this. She knew exactly what she was doing. Always, she had, like, she even threatened me, she was like saying, 'If you do this or that, I'll call the police and then that's it. And then you're out.' I mean, she's a girl! Children's rights are so powerful in the States, it's crazy. As a father, you have nothing to say. Children learn this at school. So, when you want to educate them, you want to tell them what's right and wrong, I mean, she's a teenager, no? She needs some advice, no? But this can bring you into big shit. It's crazy, man!

After the bitter experience of having to leave 'his country' due to what he called the 'betrayal' by his eldest daughter, José received a letter informing him that he had lost custody of his two children. Since his return, José had completely severed contact with his family in the USA.

José's situation may be extreme, but it says a lot about the complicated situation within so-called mixed-status families, which often come into existence in the context of migration. In the USA, where access to citizenship is provided via *jus soli*, US-born children of foreign-born residents are American citizens by birth and have all the rights and privileges this entails, while their parents, if they are undocumented migrants, have almost no chance to change their citizenship status (Brabeck and Xu 2010). In addition to this legal constellation, if one member of a migrant family marries a citizen, he or she may obtain citizenship more easily than his or her relatives. Because of the principle of *jus soli*, it is not uncommon to find not only parents with a different citizenship status from their children, but even siblings with different citizenship statuses in those cases where younger children were born in the USA while their older siblings were born in the country of origin. According to Thronson (2008), one of every 10 children living in the USA is part of a mixed-status family. This difference, which directly correlates with the individuals' different legal positionings, different educational opportunities and differential access to health and social services, causes psychological stress and conflicts among many migrant families (Menjívar 2012, 314). These general difficulties increase when deportation comes into play. The deportability of certain family members causes anxiety among their children, who either fear the arrest of their parents or the risk of also being deported themselves (Brabeck and Xu 2010, 344). Evidently, the threat of deportation weakens a migrant's social position, which can also have an impact on his or her intimate ties within the family. In the particular case described above, José's teenage daughters, who were US citizens by birth, were aware of their father's vulnerability and made use of their legal upper hand in moments of a violent family dispute.

Interestingly, José is one of those deportees whose social reintegration in Cape Verde can be considered a success. He remains in touch with some friends in the USA, and with their support he established a small but quite successful import business. He also found and married a new wife and became the father of twins. Being accepted by a local woman complements his economic integration and constitutes an important means of demonstrating his moral integrity within the island community. According to him, his former deportation no longer defines who he is: 'I was out, and I had to reinvent myself', he said matter-of-factly.

Unlike José, other deported fathers and mothers struggle with the involuntariness of their separation and with limited access to their children's lives. Roberto, a man at the end of his forties when we met, who had been returned to Cape Verde more than a decade ago, complained about how difficult it was to follow his child's developments. Since his son's mother had died some years before his deportation, he had to leave his son with his own parents in the USA, who were already over the age of 70 when he left. When I tried to get into the details of the decision to leave his son behind, he only said that nobody would take a child to 'Alcatraz'. Over the course of time, his child grew older and the emotional distance grew greater. One of the most difficult moments after his forced return to Cape Verde was when his son was placed with a foster family because his parents were no longer able to care for him properly. Unable to influence this decision, he was at the mercy of administrative procedures.

Despite the fact that many parents deported from the USA fear that they might lose custody of their children (Dreby 2012, 835), very few opt for taking their children or their entire families with them. It is generally considered important to preserve what has been gained by cross-border mobility: the access to labour, education, health and a more secure future in general. The burden of taking a family back, which has been termed 'co-deportation', has mainly been studied in the context of US-born children who are American citizens and who are taken by their deported parents to countries they hardly know (Thronson 2008, 415; Kanstroom 2012, 141). In those few cases I came across in Cape Verde, the children had to be integrated into a more or less unfamiliar cultural context, where they were stigmatised as members of a 'DP's family'. Again, the legal status within these families is 'mixed', as usually only one family member is forced to stay in the country of origin, while his or her partner as well as their children are usually still eligible to travel internationally. Understandably, conflicts surface, especially in the heat of family disputes, over the reasons for their stay on the islands, their limitations and their opportunities to travel.

'We Focus on More Promising Actions': Moral Reorientations among Those Who Stay

Cynthia's family was not the only one I visited in the diaspora. In contrast to her parents, who received me in a particularly welcoming manner, most families of deportees first reacted with reticence when I contacted them. While deported migrants are often perceived as criminals and immoral and failed individuals (Zilberg 2004; Drotbohm 2011a; Schuster and Majidi 2014), the mistrust of persons related to deportees shows that the deportation-related stigma is not limited to the deported individual; it can 'infect' entire social networks.

In an earlier article that addresses the perception of deportation among Haitian migrants in Canada (Drotbohm 2011b), I have argued that migrants of the so-called first migrant generation, who have successfully 'made their lives' abroad, are particularly susceptible to perceiving the expulsion of their fellow countrymen as an attack on their own reputations, as it might reinforce cultural stereotypes and xenophobic attitudes against their particular ethnic group.

In my interviews, it became obvious that this stigma, as it is felt among those living in the North, also weighs heavily on migrants' relationships with their deported kin. Relatives of deported migrants who remain in the country of destination try to protect their social integrity and usually they plan for their own future in the diaspora. In many cases, it was only a matter of time before they distanced themselves from their deported relatives. Cynthia's parents, for instance, went to great lengths to justify why they only remitted $150–200 per month to their daughter. In the course of our conversation it became clear that it was not only their financial obligations to their other children still living in the USA (particularly to their educations) that caused them to limit their financial commitment to Cynthia but also their ambivalent attitude towards their 'disappointing' daughter, whom they had 'lost' due to her 'risky' behaviour, as her father put it. Both parents lamented Cynthia's drug addiction, which had been reported to them by some friends living on the islands, and expressed their unwillingness to support this behaviour—an attitude I interpreted as their creeping dissociation from their daughter and their gradual renunciation of their commitment.

Some migrants try to deal with their sense of not being able to care adequately for their deported family members by reorienting their activities towards local forms of political activism. A mother of one deportee told me that she 'tried to remain active' and referred to a civil rights group they had joined to fight against the ordeal of deportation. 'We feel helpless', the father of another young deported migrant told me in an interview. 'We can't change the situation. We have to focus on more promising actions'.

The members of one activist group in Boston that was functioning during my fieldwork in 2008 focused on the tension between immigration law and the fundamental human right to a family life. To raise awareness about this legal contradiction, they initiated a street demonstration against the deportation-related separation of migrants and their families. These activists invoked humanitarian values in defence of families that were well-integrated and 'deserved' at least a moratorium on deportation. Particularly in cases of migrants who had been charged with relatively minor crimes, they argued that the punishment of deportation was disproportionate to the crimes committed, and they tried to attract media attention to such cases. In this context, a distinction was drawn between the 'good' migrant citizen who had always cared well for his or her family and community but simply committed a 'minor error', and migrants who were convicted of more serious offences and therefore allegedly deserved to be deported (see also Hasselberg 2014). This calls to mind Susan Coutin's observations about deportation hearings in juridical contexts, where family ties served as a crucial marker of exception, framing the individual's 'deservingness' for calling upon the authority's compassion (2003, 62). In these moments of judgement, individual migrants are placed off against those who are able to rely on their family ties for proving their moral integrity.

When I discussed these issues with the representative of a legal advisory organisation for undocumented immigrants, he said:

> This is a crazy situation. This government supports the right to family life. I mean, migrants' family members are brought here. This is fundamental for living a peaceful, dignified life. This has been accepted and people can rely on this as long as they can rightly prove that they are related. Related in some certain senses, of course—spouses, underage children, and the like. But then, if people are undocumented, they don't have any kinds of rights and are deported—although their family members may be citizens and live here. This is not logical. Family or not—this does not matter anymore, from one moment to the next. Some years later the same child may file a petition for his father, and the father eventually, if they are lucky, may join his son. But when the son is still a minor, his father is deported. And then the government invests millions of dollars into child protective services, programmes for immigrant children with psychological difficulties, and all this. I mean, justice is something else, you know what I mean?

This quote highlights two main aspects of deportation from the perspective of rights' activists: First, the arbitrariness of deportation, which causes suffering not only for deportees but also for their relatives, is perceived as an 'unjust' state action, as it punishes a larger group of people who did not commit a crime. This happens also in other cases, such as prison sentence, but the spatial separation of family members takes place on a much more radical level in the context of deportation. In many cases, not only the economic but also the human and psychological costs of this suffering will need to be compensated by the deporting state (Hagan, Rodriguez, and Castro 2011). Second, when the moral standards regarding the question, who might deserve compassion and mercy, are contested, not only the seriousness of offence but also social aspects such as active kin relations are taken into account. Migrants have to prove the reliability of their kin relations in order to be eligible to a delay or a suspension of their deportation. The fact that the respective juridical or administrative decisions underlie discretionary powers once more proves the selectiveness and incoherence of detention and removal (see also Coutin 2014).

Conclusion: The 'Reversal' of Migratory Family Lives

Many transnational studies around the globe have shown that being a family does not have to mean living in the same place; relatives often manage successfully to adapt their habits of support, communication and intimacy to the conditions of spatial separation. However, as I demonstrated in this article, the prerequisites of transnational family lives are based on certain assumptions concerning kinship, support and a moral perception of the 'good' relative. In the context of deportation, the common vectors of transnational mobilities are reversed: when country of origin and country of destination switch their positions, when migrants become immobile in their countries of origin and have to receive remittances sent from their children who 'remain behind' in the diaspora, established norms and hierarchies as well as common expectations are turned upside down.

Against this background, it becomes clear that deportation contains an imponderable element with regard to the maintenance of intimate relations and can be understood as a 'reverse migration', not only because the direction of migration is reversed but also because former achievements of transnational mobility and support capacities are negated. Migrant deportation not only 'reverses' the position of migrants in a given territory, these processes of 'reversal' also extend to the mode of return, the mode of transnational contact and support and even to the question of who belongs to whom.

In all cases, the maintenance of family ties under these conditions remains a challenge. When migrants are returned empty-handed and are unable to fulfil their role, especially with regard to support expectations, they are 'unabled' to act according to social expectations and risk falling out of their social networks. In the ranking of 'deservingness' based on family ties, single, childless women find themselves at a particular disadvantage. In the end, deportation is nearly always a highly individualising, or even atomizing, experience, and deportees have to 'reinvent themselves' by relying on alternative kinds of support networks such as friends, fellow deportees, local churches or 'new' families.

Besides highlighting the incoherence and injustice of these processes, this article furthermore highlights the contradictory dynamics between migration policies and family policies. When state officials have control over the spatial movement of populations, they can foster the continuity of some kin relations, as family reunification programmes are supposedly intended to do. At the same time, however, the notion of the family is a highly contested field and the question, who belongs to a family, is answered differently in many world areas. Furthermore, a 'family' requires a certain kind of social stability in order to be protected by state law. An 'irregular' status, for instance, can question the legitimacy of 'proper' parenthood, and migrants can lose custody of and access to their offspring after a state-initiated return. After all, state officials' control over family relationships increases when migration policies are brought into the equation. This intersection of morality, legal framings of 'the family'

DEPORTATION, ANXIETY, JUSTICE

and practices of eligibility, especially in the context of the regulation of transnational mobility, will be a direction for more deportation studies.

Acknowledgements

This essay is based on anthropological fieldwork in Cape Verde, which was divided into two parts (October 2006–July 2007 and March–April 2008) and was financed by the German Academic Exchange Service (DAAD) in the form of a postdoctoral scholarship. My attendance at the meeting of the European Association of Social Anthropologists in 2012 was financed by the International Research Institute 'Work and the Life-Cycle in Global History' (Re:work) at Humboldt University in Berlin. I owe a special note of appreciation especially to Ines Hasselberg, my co-editing colleague, and also to Christin Achermann, Susan Coutin, Brian Donahoe, Barak Kalir and an anonymous reviewer for their thoughtful comments on an earlier version of this paper. Furthermore, I wish to express my gratitude to the Cape Verdean *Instituto das Comunidades*, the *Ministério dos Negócios Estrangeiros* and the Cape Verdean consulate in Boston for providing valuable background information and statistics and to those individuals I met in the field who shared their time and gave insights into their perceptions of life.

Notes

[1]   Due to the increasing application of deportation measures, the deportation of more than one member of the same family occurs more and more frequently. For ease of reading, I will use the singular in reference to deported family members, and only indicate plural deportees where relevant.

[2]   Each of the nine Cape Verdean islands has a tendency to certain migration destinations, which is the result of historical migration patterns. For instance, the two eastern islands, Sal and Boavista, have huge diaspora populations in Italy, while Sao Vicente, one of the northern islands, has a strong migrant presence in England and the Netherlands (Carling 2001, 9). In the USA, larger Cape Verdean migrant communities can be found in the Greater Boston metropolitan area (Halter 1993).

[3]   According to a statistical overview provided by the *Instituto das Comunidades* (part of the *Ministério dos Negócios Estrangeiros, Cooperação e Comunidades de Cabo Verde*), the number of deportations has increased annually. As of 2002, there were only a total of 460 deportees in the entire country, 449 male and 11 female (2%). Between 2002 and 2011, 857 Cape Verdean nationals were deported, 759 male, 98 female (11%). Until 2002, Portugal was the country sending back the largest contingent, but since 2002 the majority have been sent back from the USA. The majority of those sent back from the USA had been convicted of aggression (29%), possession and dealing of narcotics (82%), robbery (16%) and being undocumented (15%; Neves 2012). It is important to note that only a minority of deportees get registered at the moment of their entry into Cape Verde. Therefore, estimates of the actual number of deportees should be considerably higher.

[4]   Government officials, especially in the USA, sometimes offer this option. Those who 'self-deport', an expression often used in Cape Verde, avoid getting a black mark on their immigration record and retain greater freedom of travel, albeit not to the country that was planning to deport them. For the case of the USA, see Walsh (2005).

References

Baldassar, L. 2001. *Visits Home: Migration Experiences between Italy and Australia*. Melbourne: Melbourne University Press.

Baldassar, L. 2007. *Families Caring across Borders. Migration, Ageing and Transnational Caregiving.* London, NY: Routledge.

Benhabib, S. 2004. *The Rights of Others. Aliens, Residents and Citizens.* Cambridge: Cambridge University Press.

Brabeck, K., and Qingwen Xu. 2010. "The Impact of Detention and Deportation on Latino Immigrant Children and Families: A Quantitative Exploration." *Hispanic Journal of Behavioral Sciences* 32 (3): 341–361. doi:10.1177/0739986310374053.

Carling, J. 2001. *Aspiration and Ability in International Migration. Cape Verdean Experiences of Mobility and Immobility.* Oslo: University of Oslo, Centre for Development and the Environment.

Carling, J., and L. Batalha. 2008. "Cape Verdean Migration and Diaspora." In *Transnational Archipelago. Perspectives on Cape Verdean Migration and Diaspora*, edited by L. Batalha and J. Carling, 13–32. Amsterdam: Amsterdam University Press.

Carling, J., C. Menjivar, and L. Schmalzbauer. 2012. "Central Themes in the Study of Transnational Parenthood." *Journal of Ethnic and Migration Studies* 38 (2): 191–217. doi:10.1080/136918 3X.2012.646417.

Carsten, J. 2000. *Cultures of Relatedness. New Approaches to the Study of Kinship.* Cambridge: Cambridge University Press.

Coutin, S. 2003. "Suspension of Deportation Hearings and Measures of 'Americanness.'" *Journal of Latin American Anthropology* 8 (2): 58–95. doi:10.1525/jlca.2003.8.2.58.

Coutin, S. 2007. *Nations of Emigrants. Shifting Boundaries of Citizenship in El Salvador and the United States.* Ithaca, NY: Cornell University Press.

Coutin, S. B. 2014. "Deportation Studies: Origins, Themes, and Directions." *Journal of Ethnic and Migration Studies* 41 (4): 671–681. doi:10.1080/1369183X.2014.957175.

De Genova, N. 2002. "Migrant 'Illegality' and Deportability in Everyday Life." *Annual Review of Anthropology* 31: 419–447. doi:10.1146/annurev.anthro.31.040402.085432.

De Genova, N. 2007. "The Production of Culprits: From Deportability to Detainability in the Aftermath of 'Homeland Security.'" *Citizenship Studies* 11 (5): 421–448. doi:10.1080/ 13621020701605735.

Dreby, J. 2010. *Divided by Borders. Mexican Migrants and Their Children.* Berkeley, CA: University of California Press.

Dreby, J. 2012. "The Burden of Deportation on Children in Mexican Immigrant Families." *Journal of Marriage and Family* 74 (4): 829–845. doi:10.1111/j.1741-3737.2012.00989.x.

Drotbohm, H. 2009. "Horizons of Long-distance Intimacies. Reciprocity, Contribution and Disjuncture in Cape Verde." *History of the Family* 14 (2): 132–149. doi:10.1016/j.hisfam. 2009.02.002.

Drotbohm, H. 2011a. "On the Durability and the Decomposition of Citizenship: The Social Logics of Forced Return Migration in Cape Verde." *Citizenship Studies* 15 (3/4): 381–396. doi:10. 1080/13621025.2011.564790.

Drotbohm, H. 2011b. "Deporting Diaspora's Future? Forced Return Migration as an Ethnographic Lens on Generational Differences among Haitian Migrants in Montréal." In *Geographies of the Haitian Diaspora*, edited by R. Jackson, 185–204. Oxford: Routledge.

Drotbohm, H. 2012. "'It's Like Belonging to a Place That Has Never Been Yours.' Deportees Negotiating Involuntary Immobility and Conditions of Return in Cape Verde." In *Migrations: Interdisciplinary Perspectives*, edited by R. Schröder and R. Wodak, 129–140. Wien, NY: Springer.

Drotbohm, H., and I. Hasselberg. 2014. "Editorial Introduction to Deportation, Anxiety, Justice: New Ethnographic Perspectives." *Journal of Ethnic and Migration Studies* 41 (4): 551–562. doi:10.1080/1369183X.2014.957171.

Grillo, R. 2008. *The Family in Question. Immigrant and Ethnic Minorities in Multicultural Europe. IMISCOE Research Series.* Amsterdam: Amsterdam University Press.

Hagan, J., K. Eschbach, and N. Rodriguez. 2008. "U.S. Deportation Policy, Family Separation, and Circular Migration." *International Migration Review* 42 (1): 64–88. doi:10.1111/j.1747-7379.2007.00114.x.

Hagan, J. M., N. Rodriguez, and B. Castro. 2011. "Social Effects of Mass Deportations by the Unites States Government, 2000–10." *Ethnic and Racial Studies* 34 (8): 1374–1391. doi:10.1080/01419870.2011.575233.

Halter, M. 1993. *Between Race and Ethnicity: Cape Verdean American Immigrants, 1860–1965.* Chicago: University of Illinois Press.

Hasselberg, I. 2014. "Balancing Legitimacy, Exceptionality and Accountability: On Foreign-national Offenders' Reluctance to Engage in Anti-deportation Campaigns in the UK." *Journal of Ethnic and Migration Studies* 41 (4): 563–579. doi:10.1080/1369183X.2014.957173.

Kanstroom, D. 2007. *Deportation Nation: Outsiders in American History.* Cambridge, MA: Harvard University Press.

Kanstroom, D. 2012. *Aftermath. Deportation Law and the New American Diaspora.* Oxford: Oxford University Press.

Kofman, E., A. Kraler, M. Kohli, and C. Schmoll. 2011. "Introduction. Issues and Debates on Family-related Migration and the Migrant Family. A European Perspective." In *Gender, Generations and the Family in International Migration*, edited by A. Kraler, E. Kofman, M. Kohli, and C. Schmoll, 13–54. Amsterdam: Amsterdam University Press.

Meintel, Deirdre. 1984. *Race, Culture, and Portuguese Colonialism in Cabo Verde.* New York: Maxwell School of Citizenship and Public Affairs, Syracuse University.

Menjívar, C. 2012. "Transnational Parenting and Immigration Law: Central Americans in the United States." *Journal of Ethnic and Migration Studies* 38 (2): 301–322. doi:10.1080/1369183X.2011.646423.

Morris, L. 2002. *Managing Migration: Civic Stratification and Migrants' Rights.* London: Routledge.

Neves, S. R. 2012. *Critical Analysis of the Deportee Integration Project of Cape Verde.* Unpublished report. Praia: Instituto das Comunidades.

Parreñas, R. S. 2005. *Children of Global Migration. Transnational Migration and Gendered Woes.* Stanford, CA: Stanford University Press.

Pribilsky, J. 2007. *La Chulla Vida. Gender, Migration, and the Family in Andean Ecuador and New York City.* Syracuse, NY: Syracuse University Press.

Ratia, E., and Catrien Notermans. 2012. "' I Was Crying, I Did Not Come Back with Anything': Women's Experiences of Deportation from Europe to Nigeria." *African Diaspora* 5: 143–164. doi:10.1163/18725457-12341235.

Schuster, L., and Nassim Majidi. 2014. "Deportation Stigma and Re-migration." *Journal of Ethnic and Migration Studies* 41 (4): 635–652. doi:10.1080/1369183X.2014.957174.

Strasser, E., A. Kraler, S. Bonjour, and V. Bilger. 2009. "Doing Family. Responses to the Constructions of 'the Migrant Family' across Europe.'" *History of the Family* 14 (2): 165–176.

Thronson, D. B. 2008. "Creating Crisis: Immigration Raids and the Destabilization of Immigrant Families." *Wake Forest Law Review* 43: 391–418.

Walsh, C. 2005. "Voluntary Departure: Stopping the Clock for Judicial Review." *Fordham Law Review* 73 (6): 2857–2895.

Willen, S. 2007. "Toward a Critical Phenomenology of 'Illegality': State Power, Criminalization, and Objectivity among Undocumented Migrant Workers in Tel Aviv, Israel." *International Migration* 45 (3): 8–38. doi:10.1111/j.1468-2435.2007.00409.x.

Zilberg, E. 2004. "Fools Banished from the Kingdom: Remapping Geographies of Gang Violence between the Americas (Los Angeles and San Salvador)." *American Quarterly* 56 (3): 759–779. doi:10.1353/aq.2004.0048.

Deportation Studies: Origins, Themes and Directions

Susan Bibler Coutin

The new field of deportation studies emerged at the intersection of immigration and security studies in the early 2000s. Focusing on deportation raises new questions about migration and enforcement tactics, but reproduces assumptions about the nature of movement and the centrality of the state in enforcement efforts. Through ethnographic work on deportation in various regions of the world, this volume questions these assumptions and emphasises important themes, including the role of emotions, the agency of migrants, the technicality of law and the variability of law. These themes also suggest several new and not-so-new directions for further research.

The new field of deportation studies emerged at the intersection of immigration and security studies in the early 2000s, as immigration enforcement escalated in size, scope and technological sophistication. By the early 1990s, immigrant-receiving countries in various parts of the world ratcheted up their enforcement tactics (Cornelius, Martin, and Hollifield 1994; Walters 2002), restricting irregular migrants' access to employment and services (Perea 1997), militarising border crossings (Nevins 2002), imposing harsher sanctions on those who defied restrictions (Welch 2002) and expanding surveillance (Fassin 2011). Due to contradictory enforcement and humanitarian mandates, seeming humanitarian exceptions (Ticktin 2011) or opportunities for legalisation (Calavita 2005) have not always provided migrants with legal relief. In this context, scholars' attention was drawn to the intensified policing dedicated to detecting unauthorised migrants, the new detention-centre complexes constructed to hold those apprehended, the massive numbers of individuals displaced through deportation, the legal changes that propelled and accommodated these practices, the communities in sending and receiving societies that were impacted by deportations and, for all of its escalation, the inadequacy of deportation as a means of removing unauthorised immigrant populations that were vast in size (De Genova

---

Susan Bibler Coutin, Professor, Departments of Criminology, Law and Society and Anthropology, University of California, Irvine, CA, USA.

2002; Ellermann 2009; Peutz 2006; Willen 2007). Confronted with these phenomena, scholars began to ask why this intensified enforcement regime had been created, and with what impacts. With these questions, the field of deportation studies was born.

The focus of deportation studies is somewhat different from that of its cousin, immigration studies. Immigration scholars have examined why individuals immigrate, how well they become assimilated into the societies they join, the relationships that they maintain with their countries of origin, the ways that migration impacts both sending and receiving countries, the impacts of enforcement practices on immigrant communities, nativism and the racialisation of immigration and the increasingly transnational nature of immigrant families (see, e.g., Bach 1978; Basch, Schiller, and Szanton-Blanc 1994; Bean, Vernez, and Keely 1989; Bosniak 2000; Chavez 2008; Higham 1963; Inda 2008; Kearney 1986; Menjívar et al. 1998; Portes and Rumbaut 1990; Portes and Zhou 1993). At the risk of oversimplifying, early immigration literature started from the assumptions that immigration most often entailed leaving one country (usually in the Global South) and moving to another one (most often, in the Global North), that this was an act of volition on the part of the migrant and that movement was accompanied by a transfer (to at least some degree) of allegiance, family relationships and cultural practices. Migrants, it was also assumed, were conduits for new ideas that could transform their communities of origin. These assumptions were questioned by more recent research, which stressed that migration was multidirectional (Rouse 1991) and that choice was very much shaped by structural conditions and especially the labour market; whether immigration entailed a transfer of allegiance or the formation of a transnational social sphere was very much an open question. As a social practice, deportation further calls migration studies' originary assumptions into question (see Galvin 2014 and Drotbohm 2014). Deportation is forcible rather than voluntary, the decision to deport is in the hands of the state rather than that of individual migrants, the direction of movement is from so-called 'receiving' country to 'sending' country and definitions of 'origin' and 'membership' are disrupted by the act of removal. Indeed, even to refer to deportation as a form of migration challenges common understandings of this term. This contrast is even more striking given that some of the same questions raised in the field of migration studies—Who moves? With what effects? And will they become assimilated?—arise in the context of deportation.

Likewise, deportation studies raises new questions for security studies scholars. Security studies became consolidated during the cold war as an international relations subfield that focused centrally on the ways that states defended their core values from military threats posed by other nations (Krause and Williams 1996). In the post-cold war era, as threats became more diffuse in nature, took non-military as well as military forms and targeted subnational groups, the field of security studies both broadened and deepened, to examine a wider range of behaviours, tactics and entities, of both sub- and supranational varieties (Buzan and Hansen 2009). In the post-9/11 era, the focus shifted further from security to securitisation, that is, to studying the social process through which 'issues become "securitized," treated as security issues, through these speech-acts which do not simply describe an existing security situation, but bring it into being as a security situation by successfully representing it as such' (Williams 2003, 513).[1] Securitisation is pervasive throughout society as numerous processes—e.g., financial transactions, immigration procedures, education—are deemed vulnerable to threats (theft, fraud, violence) and therefore incorporate measures designed to fight such threats. These measures include surveillance, identification technologies, policing tactics and the reconfiguration of physical space in ways that guide or prevent movement. Studying such developments makes it possible to examine shifts in security apparatuses, forms of governmentality, militarisation, spatialised enforcement tactics and new forms of subjectivity associated with these enforcement regimes (Amoore and de Goede 2008; Bigo 2002; Cole 2002; Dean 1999; Dow 2004; Hernandez-Lopez 2010; Mountz 2010). The rise in deportation and immigrant detention (Simon 1998) has drawn the attention of security scholars both because it is a component of the broader phenomena of infusing security issues into a variety of domains (Doty 1998) and because the security 'threat' posed by unauthorised migrants is generally low level or non-existent and therefore quite disproportionate to the security measures that have been adopted (Chavez 2008).

Scholars who study deportation have sought to explain the recent rise in immigration enforcement, attributing it to heightened fears associated with the war on terror, the prison-industrial-detention-centre complex's need to justify its existence, racialisation, scapegoating, and the needs of capitalism in the neoliberal era (De Genova 2002; De Genova and Peutz 2010; Inda 2008; Welch 2002, 2006). De Genova (2002), for example, argued that because, in the USA, it was almost impossible both physically and politically to remove the some 12 million unauthorised immigrants living in the country, deportation policies could not be attributed to this goal. Rather, De Genova contends, deportation produces deportability, that is, unauthorised migrants' awareness that they could be deported, an awareness that reduces unauthorised workers' capacity to challenge exploitative labour conditions. Scholars have also attended to the life conditions of those who undergo deportation, as well as the relatives of such individuals. Joanna Dreby (2012, 2013) found that children in Mexican immigrant families experienced a pervasive fear that their relatives would be deported, and therefore faced the future with uncertainty. Calling for an anthropology of removal, Nathalie Peutz (2006) discussed ways that Somalis' post-9/11 deportations underscored the suspicion at the root of deportation policies—US authorities deemed Somali remittances to family members to be potential contributions to terrorists. Elana Zilberg (2011) has examined the ways that deportations from the USA to El Salvador dispersed gang members, giving rise to transnational security scapes. Daniel Kanstroom (2012) has highlighted both the way that law fails to provide a remedy for individuals erroneously deported and the de facto deportation of US citizen children who, while not forbidden to remain in the USA, accompany their deported parents.

Through this and other research, deportation scholars have analysed the macro-level structures that shape enforcement regimes, the human experience of deportation and societal impacts of removal, but have also imported some assumptions derived from both immigration and security studies. Analyses of deportation that draw on insights from immigration research have tended to treat deportation as a *move*, albeit one that occurs by force. This understanding of deportation-as-move implies that deportation is a discrete event, directs attention towards the deportee as the person who moves and highlights the significance of national borders in shaping subjectivity and mobility. In contrast, analyses that are grounded in the security literature treat deportation as an *enforcement event*. Such approaches emphasise the centrality of the state as the enforcement agent, and often draw heavily on Giorgio Agamben's (1998) notion of the state of exception, that is, the suspension of law in order to further the ends of law, as when civil liberties are suspended during a national emergency, a suspension that, according to Agamben, reinforces law itself and has become the norm, instead of an exception.[2] This idea resonates for deportation studies scholars given that deportees' legal rights are often limited (in the USA, for example, removal hearings are administrative proceedings that involve fewer constitutional protections than do criminal proceedings; see Eagly 2010), even as the need to restore law is often given as a justification for deportation. As well, analyses of securitisation tend to emphasise global inequalities, which in turn directs attention to removals from the Global North to the Global South. Though valuable in many ways, these influences could potentially lead deportation scholars to underestimate the roles of non-state actors, overemphasise deportees' powerlessness and disconnect deportation from the events and histories within which it is embedded.

By using ethnographic research to interrogate the understandings of deportation that have shaped deportation studies to date, the articles in this issue of the *Journal of Ethnic and Migration Studies* challenge these assumptions and thus break new theoretical ground. Most importantly, through research that accesses the lived experiences of deportation as well as the multiple actors and institutions involved, this issue broadens scholars' understandings of what deportation entails. Temporally, the work in this special issue emphasises that deportation is not a discrete event; rather, it begins long before an individual is apprehended, through the myriad practices that make someone vulnerable to deportation in the first place. As well, deportation continues long after an individual is returned, through the difficult process of readjustment, the ripple effects on family members and the continued prohibition on reentry. Tellingly, one deportee interviewed by Drotbohm (2014) referred to Cape Verde as 'Alcatraz', implying that returning 'home' was a continuation of an earlier period of incarceration (see also Coutin 2010). Deportations are also connected to earlier historical moments, such as political developments that lead individuals to migrate or that deny them legal access to territories of other nations (Coutin 2011), and to later ones, as when migrants' children's births cannot be registered, thus leading to yet another generation of 'documentless' individuals (Galvin 2014). Indeed, according to Galvin, Zimbabweans living in Botswana experience daily life as an effort to ward off deportation; thus, they continually anticipate, even as they try to avoid, this event. Such broadening also redirects attention from the act of removal itself to other phases, such as the period between apprehension and removal (Hasselberg 2014).

Likewise, spatially, the notion of a 'deportation corridor' expands understandings of where and through which institutions deportation occurs (Drotbohm and Hasselberg 2014). This concept suggests that deportations involve and generate movements in multiple directions, not only to a deportee's country of origin via forcible return but also, perhaps, back to a former country of residence. Such multidirectionality of movement raises questions about what origin means—Can migrants be said to have 'originated' in their countries of birth, or do they originate in the countries to which they migrated, or do they have multiple origins (Galvin 2014; see also Yngvesson 2010)? Furthermore, deportation involves not only the state but also a host of other individuals and institutions, including employers who might report their workers, family members who accompany or are left behind, other relatives who receive or reject deportees, non-governmental organisations (NGOs) that offer assistance or launch anti-deportation campaigns and more. Importantly, the papers investigate movements within the Global South as well as those between North and South.

Temporal and spatial broadening is linked to three other themes central to this special issue. The first is the role that emotions play within the process of deportation. A range of emotions and emotion-laden processes are considered, including adaptation, normalisation, stigma and anxiety. Migrants, authors demonstrate, experience uncertainty, given that they may not know whether they will be apprehended, what has happened to relatives taken into custody and what their future will hold if they are removed. Importantly, though, authors assess not only the emotional experiences of migrants, but also those of other groups, including sending communities, receiving communities, state actors and NGOs. The emotions that these groups experience are closely connected, in these analyses, to the fantasies that they seek to maintain. Thus, if individuals in immigrant-producing societies want to maintain their fantasies that migration is a pathway to progress, then they are more likely to stigmatise deportees as failures than to attribute deportation to conditions in the country from which deportees were removed (Schuster and Majidi 2014). Individuals who are subject to deportation sometimes distinguish themselves from other, more dangerous, individuals who are the ones who, they say, really deserve to be deported, and first-generation migrants sometimes regard the deportation of more recent arrivals as a slight against their own ethnic or racial group (Drotbohm 2014). Deportation policies may reveal anxieties that are common in the deporting nation. For example, Kalir (2014) analyses the ways that officials' denunciations of migrants as existential threats to the nation of Israel help to reproduce Israel's status as a Jewish state. Kalir argues that stigmatisations of migrants are thus linked to anxiety about anti-Semitic persecution, and that such critical rhetoric depoliticises the structural violence experienced by migrants. Even intermediaries, such as NGO representatives or care workers who provide services to detainees, perform 'emotion work' as they carry out their institutional responsibilities while contending with the traumas recounted or performed by migrants (Fischer 2014).

A second theme is the agency of migrants and their advocates. Agency takes many forms, including organising one's life to minimise chances of being deported, creating support networks, sharing information about raids, launching anti-deportation campaigns, appealing an order of removal and returning following a deportation. These actions arise despite a number of double binds that constrain advocates' and migrants' activities. For instance, according to Kalir (2014), Israeli NGOs that appeal to Jewish history in order to generate compassion for migrants reproduce the very trauma that shapes officials' anti-immigrant rhetoric. Similarly, French care workers who work in deportation centres where some detainees resort to self-mutilations must navigate potential complicity with guards, who attempt to control detainees' behaviour, and adherence to humanitarian goals of respecting detainees' autonomy (Fischer 2014). And, in the UK, anti-deportation campaign organisers fail to acknowledge foreign-national offenders' senses that they may be partially to blame for their own legal predicaments (Hasselberg 2014). The pervasiveness of such double binds suggests that they may stem from overarching contradictions intrinsic to deportation, such as that between individuals' rights to have families and states' rights to control entry (Drotbohm 2014; see also Bosniak 1991), or that between humanitarianism and enforcement (Ticktin 2011). The questions posed by Maria, a foreign-national offender facing deportation from the UK and quoted by Hasselberg (2014), strike me as profound: 'When does a person stop being an ex-offender? I mean, please, somebody let me know. How many good deeds do I have to do to make up for my one bad deed?' Maria's questions capture the temporal contradiction inherent in having a criminal record: the very term 'ex-offender', which places an offence squarely in the past, simultaneously marks the designated person as 'offender' in the present and future (see also Stumpf 2006).

The third theme is that of legal technicalities. The articles in this special issue are replete with discussions of permits, policies and procedures that shape the emotions and agency described above. Galvin describes the 90-day entry permits that Zimbabwean migrants to Botswana can obtain. These permits shape Zimbabweans' experiences of legality and illegality, creating a spectrum of actual and potential statuses. The ways that Zimbabweans describe these permits, for instance, in the words of one interviewee, 'My days are finished', strike me as suggestive of life and death. In contrast, Israel granted Eritrean and Sudanese migrants group protection as temporary migrants, rather asylum, even though the former status is only supposed to be used in the case of sudden large-scale movements, which these were not (Kalir 2014). As a result, their status was unclear to employers, making it difficult for the migrants to obtain jobs. According to Kalir, the claim that Israel lacks refugees is a 'manufactured reality' that results precisely from institutional processes that fail to grant refugee status or asylum to individuals even when they are fleeing political violence. Attending to legal technicalities, as do these authors, denaturalises immigration categories, making it clear that rather than being intrinsically unauthorised, irregular, undocumented or illegal, people are constituted as such through a process of illegalisation (see also De Genova and Peutz 2010).

This special issue's focus on broadening understandings of deportation and its discussion of emotions, agency and legal technicalities suggest several new and not-so-new directions for further research. First, this work suggests the importance of studying normalisation. If, by demarcating the exceptional and the prohibited, deportation simultaneously produces the normal, then examining the boundaries that deportation establishes sheds light on the contours of the citizenry. In this sense, deportation scholarship can partake of a longer theoretical tradition of studying aberrant cases or instances of trouble in order to discern the norms against which they are measured (Llewellyn and Hoebel 1941; Merry 1984; Yngvesson 1993). Such a focus is made all the more compelling by some of the data presented in this special issue. For instance, in Galvin's material (2014), there is a jarring juxtaposition of daily routines (sleeping, nursing a baby) and a sudden abduction and deportation. Likewise, Hasselberg (2014) quotes an interviewee who insisted, 'So yes, they should deport people, but dangerous people, people that already have records of being criminal'. When and how did it become normal for deportation to appear to be an appropriate response to crime, given that exile and transportation are no longer acceptable criminal penalties (Bleichmar 1999; Kanstroom 2000)? What assumptions about borders, membership, territory and alienage are implicated in this statement? And how does law become the basis for consequences (banishment) that have been deemed archaic?

A second and not-so-new question inspired by the work in this special issue is, Why are deportations escalating? Again, material presented by these authors repeatedly emphasises the irrationality of deportation. Drotbohm's contribution is a case in point. One of the legal advocates she interviewed stated:

> This is a crazy situation. This government supports the right to family life.... But then, if people are undocumented, they don't have any kinds of rights and are deported— although their family members may be citizens. This is not logical.... Some years later the same child may file a petition for his father, and the father eventually may join his son. But when the son is still a minor, his father is deported. And then the government invests millions of dollars into child protective services, programs for immigrant children with psychological difficulties, and all this. I mean, justice is something else, you know what I mean?

While this speaker concludes by emphasising the injustice of the circumstances described, his initial statement, 'This is a crazy situation', may be more telling. Why, if deportation is so counterproductive, does it occur, and on a massive scale? Explanations such as capitalism's need to produce deportability in order to render migrants exploitable (De Genova 2002), though persuasive, seem insufficient to account for the dynamics described by this legal advocate. Instead, if deportation is irrational, then perhaps explanations need to examine the fantasies that are made possible through deportation. What investments, whether material or psychological, require stigmatised others in order to persist? How do non-migrants' senses of self depend on the foil of the criminalised alien? How do deportations reinvigorate such irrationalities over time?

Finally, and this is also not a new question, reflecting on the work that is presented here leads me to wonder how the field of deportation studies is enabled by the very alienation and dislocation that scholars analyse and critique. This is, of course, a broad question, encountered in a range of scholarly work that attempts to accurately depict violence and suffering without sensationalising violence or engaging in intellectual voyeurism (see, e.g., Bourgois 1996, 2003, for a discussion of these issues). The contributors to this issue ably present the lives of migrants, deportees and others without falling into either of these traps. Yet, a question that could be explored further in future ethnographic work on deportation is whether, despite presumably vast differences in ethnographers' and deportees' social positions, affinities associated with 'foreignness' facilitate these ethnographic encounters. If so, what are the fieldwork moments when those affinities become irreconcilable incompatibilities (as, e.g., when an ethnographer is able to travel where an interlocutor cannot)? And how do ethnographies of deportation speak to the multiple audiences that move into and out of the corridor of deportation?

Examining such questions will help to expand deportation studies to include a focus on the production of the society that deports, the fantasies implicated in deportation and the (re)encounters that ethnography makes possible. By directing scholars' attention to deportation, anxiety, and justice, and to the value of ethnography as a means of explicating these interrelated phenomena, the contributors to this special issue have advanced not only deportation studies, but also the fields from which it derives.

Acknowledgements

I thank Heike Drotbohm and Ines Hasselberg for inviting me to write this comment, Cecelia Lynch for commenting on an earlier draft and Véronique Fortin for assistance with references.

Notes

[1]   As well, Doty (1998) defines 'securitisation' as:

> a process through which the definition and understanding of a particular phenom-
> enon, its consequences, and the policies/courses of action deemed appropriate to
> address the issue are subjected to a particular logic. The kind of logic that drives
> securitization of an issue leads to certain kinds of politics which are associated with
> particular realms of policy options.... The issues of immigration, especially undocu-
> mented immigration, and refugee movements are prominent among those being
> securitized today. (71–72)

[2]   As Agamben explains, the state of exception not only distinguishes what within the juridico-
political order from that which is outside but also 'traces a threshold (the state of exception)
between the two, on the basis of which inside and outside, the normal situation and chaos,

enter into those complex topological relations that make the validity of the juridical order possible' (1998, 19).

References

Agamben, Giorgio. 1998. *Homo Sacer. Sovereign Power and Bare Life.* Translated by Daniel Heller-Roazen. Stanford: Stanford University Press.

Amoore, Louise, and Marieke de Goede, eds. 2008. *Risk and the War on Terror.* Abingdon: Routledge.

Bach, Robert L. 1978. "Mexican Immigration and the American State." *International Migration Review* 12 (4): 536–558. doi:10.2307/2545450.

Basch, Linda, Nina Glick Schiller, and Christina Szanton Blanc. 1994. *Nations Unbound: Transnational Projects, Postcolonial Predicaments, and Deterritorialized Nation-States.* Langhorne, PA: Gordon and Breach Publishers.

Bean, Frank D., Georges Vernez, and Charles B. Keely. 1989. *Opening and Closing the Doors: Evaluating Immigration Reform and Control* (Vol. 1). Washington, DC: The Urban Institute.

Bigo, Didier. 2002. "Security and Immigration: Toward a Critique of the Governmentality of Unease." *Alternatives: Global, Local, Political* 27 (Suppl. 1): 63–92.

Bleichmar, Javier. 1999. "Deportation as Punishment: A Historical Analysis of the British Practice of Banishment and Its Impact on Modern Constitutional Law." *Georgetown Immigration Law Journal* 14: 115.

Bosniak, Linda S. 1991. "Human Rights, State Sovereignty and the Protection of Undocumented Migrants under the International Migrant Workers Convention." *International Migration Review* 25 (4): 737–770. doi:10.2307/2546843.

Bosniak, Linda S. 2000. "Citizenship Denationalized." *Indiana Journal of Global Law Studies* 7: 447.

Bourgois, Philippe. 1996. "Confronting Anthropology, Education, and Inner-City Apartheid." *American Anthropologist* 98 (2): 249–258. doi:10.1525/aa.1996.98.2.02a00020.

Bourgois, Philippe. 2003. *In Search of Respect: Selling Crack in El Barrio.* Cambridge: Cambridge University Press.

Buzan, Barry, and Lene Hansen. 2009. *The Evolution of International Security Studies.* Cambridge: Cambridge University Press.

Calavita, Kitty. 2005. *Immigrants at the Margins: Law, Race, and Exclusion in Southern Europe.* Cambridge: Cambridge University Press.

Chavez, Leo R. 2008. *The Latino Threat: Constructing Immigrants, Citizens, and the Nation.* Stanford: Stanford University Press.

Cole, David. 2002. "Enemy Aliens." *Stanford Law Review* 54 (5): 953–1004. doi:10.2307/1229690.

Cornelius, Wayne A., Philip L. Martin, and James F. Hollifield, eds. 1994. *Controlling Immigration: A Global Perspective.* Stanford: Stanford University Press.

Coutin, Susan B. 2010. "Confined within: National Territories as Zones of Confinement." *Political Geography* 29 (4): 200–208. doi:10.1016/j.polgeo.2010.03.005.

Coutin, Susan B. 2011. "Falling Outside: Excavating the History of Central American Asylum Seekers." *Law & Social Inquiry* 36 (3): 569–596. doi:10.1111/j.1747-4469.2011.01243.x.

Dean, Mitchell. 1999. *Governmentality: Power and Rule in Modern Society.* London: Sage.

De Genova, Nicholas. 2002. "Migrant 'Illegality' and Deportability in Everyday Life." *Annual Review of Anthropology* 31 (1): 419–447. doi:10.1146/annurev.anthro.31.040402.085432.

De Genova, Nicholas, and Nathalie Peutz. 2010. *The Deportation Regime.* Durham: Duke University Press.

Doty, Roxanne Lynn. 1998. "Immigration and the Politics of Security." *Security Studies* 8 (2–3): 71–93. doi:10.1080/09636419808429375.

Dow, Mark. 2004. *American Gulag: Inside US immigration prisons.* Berkeley and Los Angeles: University of California Press.

Dreby, Joanna. 2012. "The Burden of Deportation on Children in Mexican Immigrant Families." *Journal of Marriage and Family* 74 (4): 829–845. doi:10.1111/j.1741-3737.2012.00989.x.

Dreby, Joanna. 2013. "The Modern Deportation Regime and Mexican Families." In *Constructing Immigrant "Illegality": Critiques, Experiences, and Responses*, edited by Cecilia Menjívar and Daniel Kanstroom, 181–202. Cambridge: Cambridge University Press.

Drotbohm, H. 2014. "The Reversal of Migratory Family Lives: A Cape Verdean Perspective on Gender and Sociality pre- and post-deportation." *Journal of Ethnic and Migration Studies* 41 (4): 653–670. doi:10.1080/1369183X.2014.961905.

Drotbohm, H., and I. Hasselberg. 2014. "Editorial Introduction to Deportation, Anxiety, Justice: New Ethnographic Perspectives." *Journal of Ethnic and Migration Studies* 41 (4): 551–562. doi:10.1080/1369183X.2014.957171.

Eagly, Ingrid V. 2010. "Prosecuting Immigration." *Northwestern University Law Review* 104: 1281–1360.

Ellermann, Antje. 2009. *States against Migrants: Deportation in Germany and the United States.* Cambridge: Cambridge University Press.

Fassin, Didier. 2011. "Policing Borders, Producing Boundaries. The Governmentality of Immigration in Dark Times." *Annual Review of Anthropology* 40 (1): 213–226. doi:10.1146/annurev-anthro-081309-145847.

Fischer, Nicolas. 2014. "The Management of Anxiety. An Ethnographical Outlook on Self-mutilations in a French Immigration Detention Centre." *Journal of Ethnic and Migration Studies* 41 (4): 599–616. doi:10.1080/1369183X.2014.960820.

Galvin, T.M. 2014. "'We Deport Them but They Keep Coming Back': The Normalcy of Deportation in the Daily Life of 'Undocumented' Zimbabwean Migrant Workers in Botswana." *Journal of Ethnic and Migration Studies* 41 (4): 617–634. doi:10.1080/1369183X.2014.957172.

Hasselberg, I. 2014. "Balancing Legitimacy, Exceptionality and Accountability: On Foreign-national Offenders' Reluctance to Engage in Anti-deportation Campaigns in the UK." *Journal of Ethnic and Migration Studies* 41 (4): 563–579. doi:10.1080/1369183X.2014.957173.

Hernandez-Lopez, Ernesto. 2010. "Guantanamo as a 'Legal Black Hole': A Base for Expanding Space, Markets, and Culture." *University of San Francisco Law Review* 45: 141–214.

Higham, John. 1963. *Strangers in the Land: Patterns of American Nativism, 1860–1925.* New York: Atheneum.

Inda, Jonathan Xavier. 2008. *Targeting Immigrants: Government, Technology, and Ethics.* Oxford: Blackwell Publishing.

Kalir, Barak. 2014. "The Jewish State of Anxiety. Between Moral Obligation and Fearism in the Treatment of African Asylum Seekers in Israel." *Journal of Ethnic and Migration Studies* 41 (4): 580–598. doi:10.1080/1369183X.2014.960819.

Kanstroom, Daniel. 2000. "Deportation, Social Control, and Punishment: Some Thoughts about Why Hard Laws Make Bad Cases." *Harvard Law Review* 113 (8): 1890–1935. doi:10.2307/1342313.

Kanstroom, Daniel. 2012. *Aftermath: Deportation Law and the New American Diaspora.* Oxford: Oxford University Press.

Kearney, Michael. 1986. "From the Invisible Hand to Visible Feet: Anthropological Studies of Migration and Development." *Annual Review of Anthropology* 15 (1): 331–361. doi:10.1146/annurev.an.15.100186.001555.

Krause, Keith, and Michael C. Williams. 1996. "Broadening the Agenda of Security Studies: Politics and Methods." *Mershon International Studies Review* 40 (2): 229–254. doi:10.2307/222776.

Llewellyn, Karl N., and Adamson E. Hoebel. 1941. *The Cheyenne Way.* Norman: University of Oklahoma Press.

Menjívar, Cecilia, Julie DaVanzo, Lisa Greenwell, and R. Burciaga Valdez. 1998. "Remittance Behavior among Salvadoran and Filipino Immigrants in Los Angeles." *International Migration Review* 32 (1): 97–126. doi:10.2307/2547562.

Merry, Sally Engle. 1984. "Anthropology and the Study of Alternative Dispute Resolution." *Journal of Legal Education* 34: 277–284.

Mountz, Alison. 2010. *Seeking Asylum: Human Smuggling and Bureaucracy at the Border*. Minneapolis: University of Minnesota Press.

Nevins, Joseph. 2002. *Operation Gatekeeper: The Rise of the "Illegal Alien" and the Making of the US-Mexico Boundary*. New York: Routledge.

Perea, Juan F., ed. 1997. *Immigrants Out!: The New Nativism and the Anti-Immigrant Impulse in the United States*. New York: New York University Press.

Peutz, Nathalie. 2006. "Embarking on an Anthropology of Removal." *Current Anthropology* 47 (2): 217–241. doi:10.1086/498949.

Portes, Alejandro, and Min Zhou. 1993. "The New Second Generation: Segmented Assimilation and Its Variants." *The Annals of the American Academy of Political and Social Science* 530 (1): 74–96. doi:10.1177/0002716293530001006.

Portes, Alejandro, and Rubén G. Rumbaut. 1990. *Immigrant America: A Portrait*. Berkeley: University of California Press.

Rouse, Roger. 1991. "Mexican Migration and the Social Space of Postmodernism." *Diaspora: A Journal of Transnational Studies* 1 (1): 8–23. doi:10.1353/dsp.1991.0011.

Schuster, L., and Nassim Majidi. 2014. "Deportation Stigma and Re-migration." *Journal of Ethnic and Migration Studies* 41 (4): 635–652. doi:10.1080/1369183X.2014.957174.

Simon, Jonathan. 1998. "Refugees in a Carceral Age: The Rebirth of Immigration Prisons in the United States." *Public Culture* 10 (3): 577–607. doi:10.1215/08992363-10-3-577.

Stumpf, Juliet P. 2006. The Crimmigration Crisis: Immigrants, Crime, and Sovereign Power. American University Law Review 56 (2): 367–419.

Ticktin, Miriam I. 2011. *Casualties of Care: Immigration and the Politics of Humanitarianism in France*. Berkeley and Los Angeles: University of California Press.

Walters, William. 2002. "Deportation, Expulsion, and the International Police of Aliens." *Citizenship Studies* 6 (3): 265–292. doi:10.1080/1362102022000011612.

Welch, Michael. 2002. *Detained: Immigration Laws and the Expanding INS Jail Complex*. Philadelphia: Temple University Press.

Welch, Michael. 2006. *Scapegoats of September 11th: Hate Crimes & State Crimes in the War on Terror*. Piscataway: Rutgers University Press.

Willen, Sarah S. 2007. "Toward a Critical Phenomenology of 'Illegality': State Power, Criminalization, and Abjectivity among Undocumented Migrant Workers in Tel Aviv, Israel." *International Migration* 45 (3): 8–38. doi:10.1111/j.1468-2435.2007.00409.x.

Williams, Michael C. 2003. "Words, Images, Enemies: Securitization and International Politics." *International Studies Quarterly* 47 (4): 511–531. doi:10.1046/j.0020-8833.2003.00277.x.

Yngvesson, Barbara. 1993. *Virtuous Citizens, Disruptive Subjects: Order and Complaint in a New England Court*. New York: Routledge.

Yngvesson, B. 2010. *Belonging in an Adopted World: Race, Identity, and Transnational Adoption*. Chicago: University of Chicago Press.

Zilberg, Elana. 2011. *Space of Detention: The Making of a Transnational Gang Crisis between Los Angeles and San Salvador*. Durham: Duke University Press.

Index

activism, political 13-14, 18-19, 25-6, 115-16
administrative removal 16
advocacy work 24
Afghanistan 4-5, 82, 85, 88-97
African Refugee Development Centre, Israel 43
Agamben, G. 18, 34, 50-3, 63
Alpes, M.J. 5, 93
Amnesty International 36
Anderson, B. 14, 24-5
Anderson, L. 93
anthropology 103
anti-deportation campaigns (ADCs) 13-15, 19-27
appeals against immigration decisions 6, 16-17
asylum seekers 4-8; in Israel 30-45; in the UK 18-21, 25
Australia 32, 90, 97

bail, granting of 16, 19
'bare life' 51, 63
Barrios, L. 87
Bauman, Z. 35
Ben Ari, Michael 41
Bhattacharyya, G. 19, 22
bio-legitimacy 51, 63
biopower and biopolicies 51
Bloch, A. 76
Bosworth, M. 15
Botswana 4-7, 67-82
Brava 107-8
bribery 71, 77
Brotherton, D. 87

Cameroon 5
campaigning 18-21, 24-6
Cape Verde 4, 71, 95, 103-14
Carling, J. 92
case studies 3
Castro, B. 106
children's experience 7, 106, 109

Cimade organisation 54-64
citizenship 7, 14, 38, 69, 113; global regime of 34
civil rights groups 18
co-deportation 114
Convention on the Rights of the Child 104
coping strategies of migrants 92-4; see also survival strategies
corridors 3
corruption 92-3; see also bribery
Coutin, Susan Bibler 2, 8-9, 26, 45, 116
criminality 111-12
Csordas, Thomas 105

daily life, impact of deportability on 69-74, 79-82, 105-6
De Genova, Nicholas 105
deportability, sense of 72-3, 106, 114
deportados (DPs) 109, 114
deportation 1-2, 90-8, 103-4, 108, 110, 114-17; arbitrariness of 116; as a constant threat rather than a single event 67, 69, 82; effects of 9; failure to deter migration 98; 'fantasies' relating to 9; inability of states to implement 16; normal-isation of 95-7; process of 74-7, 103-4; used by migrants to their own advantage 80-1; see also social outcomes of deportation
'deportation corridor' concept 3-5, 8-9, 105, 107, 110
deportation orders 107
deportation studies 2-5, 8, 118
'deportation turn' 2
'deservingness' of potential deportees 116-17
detention centres 2, 31, 36-7, 74, 88, 97; in France 49-64
Dreby, Joana 106, 109-10
Drotbohm, Heike 4-8, 71, 77, 79, 87, 95

earnings of migrant workers 73
economic migrants 32, 36-7, 41

INDEX

Egypt 31, 41
El Salvador 112
Ellermann, A. 24
emotional issues 53-4, 58-64, 106-7
emotions, sociology of 53, 64
employment opportunities 80
enforcement regimes 52
Eritrea 30-1, 35-40
ethnic groups 78
ethnographic research 8-9, 70, 82, 107-8
European Association of Social Anthropologists 3
exceptional cases 23-6
expectations of and about migrants 90, 92, 117
exploitation of migrants 73, 105

family relationships and obligations 6-8, 71-4, 103-9, 113-17
Fassin, Didier 51, 63-4
'fearism' 6, 30, 35, 43-5
female migrants 73, 78, 108, 111-12
fencing of borders 31, 41
Fischer, Nicholas 4-9
Fisher, R.M. 35
Fogo 107-8
Foucault, Michel 51
France 4, 6, 49-64, 108
Francistown centre for illegal immigrants 74-9
Fussell, E. 73

Gaborone prison 75-6
Gabriel, J. 19, 22
Galvin, T. 4-7, 95
gangs 112
Ganot, Yaakov 37
gendered status 112
Germany 90
Gibney, M.J. 14-15, 24-5
Goffman, E. 61, 85-7, 91-2
Graham, Mark 53
'group protection' visa 36

Hagan, J.M. 106
Hall, A. 5
Hanin, Dov 43
Hasselberg, Ines 4, 8
health concerns 69, 76, 78
Hernandez-Carratero, M. 92
HIV status 86
Holocaust, the 32-5, 43
Hotline for Migrant Workers, Israel 42-3
human rights 15-18, 32-4, 42-5, 55, 115; global regime of 38
humanitarianism 34, 51-4, 57-61, 64, 116
hunger strikes 51, 53, 59, 62

identity cards 79
'illegal immigrants', use of the term 70-6
'illegalisation' 105
'immigration consultants' 78
immigration removal centres 16, 18
immigration status, experience of 71-2, 80-1
Immigration Tribunal, United Kingdom 16-17, 25
'infiltrators' 37, 40-2, 45
injustice, sense of 68
'intermediary position' between 'helping' and 'controlling' detainees 61
international law 8, 104
International Organisation for Migration (IOM) 74-5
investment in migration 96-8
Iran 82, 88-90, 95-8
Israel, State of 4-8, 30-45; existential threat to 32-3, 41-4
Italy 106-7

Jacobsen, C.M. 89
Jewish history of persecution and victimhood 31-3, 42-5
jus soli principle 113
justice, perceptions of 7-8; *see also* injustice, sense of

Kalir, Barak 4-9
Kanstroom, D. 7, 107, 112
Kapur, R. 32
Khosravi, S. 91
kristallnacht (1938) 41

'labelling' of migrants 72, 76, 87, 92-3
Lapid, Yair 43
Laubenthal, B. 17-18
leave to remain 16, 26
legal protection for migrants 55
Link, B.G. 86-8
lobbying 13, 21-4
Lybia 64

Majidi, Nassim 4-6, 81-2, 85, 88, 95-6
marginalisation 73-4
marriage 92, 104
Mexico 106, 109
migration: as a livelihood strategy 69-73, 79-82; in reverse 117
mixed-status families 105, 113-14
mobile phones, use of 79

nation-state system 34
national security 2, 5-9; Israeli 31-7, 41, 44
Ne'eman, Yackov 41
Netanyahu, Benjamin 31, 37, 40-1

INDEX

No One Is Illegal (NOII) organisation 18, 20, 22
non-governmental organisations (NGOs) in Israel 42-4
Notermans, C. 77, 106-7, 111
Nyers, Peter 62

O'Connell-Davidson, J. 89
offenders facing deportation 14-27, 116
Oppenheimer, Yariv 41
'Othering' 32-5, 38, 44-5

Pakistan 90, 95-8
Paoletti, E. 14, 16, 24-5
parenting 105
participation in society 16
Paz, J. 43
petitions 25
Peutz, Nathalie 3, 91, 94
Phelan, J.C. 86-8
Physicians for Human Rights -Israel 36
Plumtree border post 74, 76
policing 50-1, 57-63, 73-7, 106
political action to resist deportation 13-14, 18-19, 25-6, 115-16
Portugal 108
power relations 51, 103
prison staff 53, 61
'prohibited' immigrants 69
protection of detainees combined with repression 51-5, 58-64
protest action 18-26
public opinion 21, 33

racism 40-4
Ratia, E. 77, 106-7, 111
refugee status 30-1, 36-7, 41
Regev, Miri 41, 43
re-migration 85-6, 90-8; reasons for 85, 97-8
remittances 71, 73, 78, 80, 96, 107-12, 117
repatriation 105, 108; *see also* deportation
reporting centres 16
residence permits 51
resistance to deportation 18-19
return migration 70, 81, 90-4, 104-10; *voluntary and invol- untary* 109
reverse migration 79
Right Now (NGO, Israel) 43
Rodriguez, N. 106
Rubinstein, Amnon 31

Sang Sefid detention centre 97
Schlagman, Nic 43
Schuster, Liza 4-6, 76, 81-2, 85, 88-9, 96
self-mutilation by detainees 8, 49-55, 58-64
Senegal 92

September 11th 2001 attacks 108
sex work 86
Shamalov-Berkovitch, Yulia 44
Siméant, Johanna 51
Skilbrei, M.L. 89
Snow, D. 93
social exclusion 72-3, 81, 111-12
social networks 79-80, 115, 117
social outcomes of deportation 6, 105-7
Somalia 91, 94
South Africa 5, 68-9
South Sudan 38
Southern African Development Community (SADC) 68
sovereignty, state-centric model of 3
Spire, A. 5
stereotypes 92
stigma: of contamination 94-5; definition of 86
stigmatisation of migrants 5-6, 72, 77, 85-93, 96-8, 110, 115; elements in the process of 87; reversal of 92-3
Stumpf, Juliet P. 17
Sudan 30-1, 35-40
support networks 117
surveillance procedures 17, 21, 73, 81, 105-6
survival strategies 107; *see also* coping strategies

'temporary protection' 36-7
temporary travel documents (TTDs) 79
Thronson, D.B. 106, 113
Ticktin, Miriam 34, 51, 63
trade unions 18
Tylor, I. 24

undocumented migrants 17-20, 32-6, 67-73, 76-82, 87-91, 105-6
United Kingdom 4-5, 13-27
United Nations: Conventions and Declarations 32, 104; High Commission for Refugees (UNHCR) 37
United States 32, 105-9, 113
Universal Declaration of Human Rights 104
'unsafe' countries 25

Vigneswaran, D.V. 5

Walters, W. 78
Webber, F. 24
Willen, Sarah 105-6
Wurgaft, Nurit 31

Yishai, Eli 41-2

Zembylas, M. 35
Zimbabwe 4-7, 67-82
Zionism 32-5, 44